A Companion
to Petronius

EDWARD COURTNEY

OXFORD
UNIVERSITY PRESS

OXFORD
UNIVERSITY PRESS

Great Clarendon Street, Oxford OX2 6DP

Oxford University Press is a department of the University of Oxford.
It furthers the University's objective of excellence in research, scholarship,
and education by publishing worldwide in

Oxford New York

Athens Auckland Bangkok Bogotá Buenos Aires Cape Town
Chennai Dar es Salaam Delhi Florence Hong Kong Istanbul Karachi
Kolkata Kuala Lumpur Madrid Melbourne Mexico City Mumbai Nairobi
Paris São Paulo Shanghai Singapore Taipei Tokyo Toronto Warsaw

with associated companies in Berlin Ibadan

Oxford is a registered trade mark of Oxford University Press
in the UK and in certain other countries

Published in the United States
by Oxford University Press Inc., New York

British Library Cataloguing in Publication Data

Data available

Library of Congress Cataloging in Publication Data

Data applied for

ISBN 0-19-924552-5
0-19-924594-0 pbk

1 3 5 7 9 10 8 6 4 2

Typeset in Imprint
by Joshua Associates Ltd., Oxford
Printed in Great Britain
on acid-free paper by
T.J. International Ltd., Padstow, Cornwall

Preface

WHEN I took up my first tenure-track appointment at King's College, London in 1959, I was told that my first task would be to give a series of lectures on Petronius. The outcome of this was an article which appeared in *Philologus* 106 (1962), 86, and which is still sometimes referred to as a standard source (not always in support of positions with which I would agree). I should be sorry if I now regarded that article as totally misguided, but equally sorry if I felt that after almost forty years I had learned nothing to add to or adjust in the views then taken. My long engagement with this author has had one unfortunate consequence, namely that happy phrases coined by others have stuck in my mind; in two cases I know and in my text identify the sources, but I cannot now trace others, and am probably not even aware of some. I therefore have to request indulgence for such unintentional *furta*.

One personal debt requires warm acknowledgement here. At a time when his own commentary on Petronius was approaching completion, Gareth Schmeling was willing to divert effort to reading my typescript and to note an array of helpful comments and suggestions from which I have derived great benefit (and probably should have derived even more). Not just I, but all *viri Petroniani* are indebted to him for the foundation and survival of the *Petronian Society Newsletter*. Parts of the book were also read by John Dillery and Sara Myers; they too have earned my gratitude, as has an anonymous reader for the Press.

E. Courtney

University of Virginia
September 2000

Contents

Contents

Bibliography

(Works referred to only once in the text, or only in one context, are not listed here)

Texts

F. Bücheler, edn. maior, Berlin 1862; repr. (edn. 7) with additions 1958.
K. Müller, Munich 1961, 1983 (3rd edn., Tusculum series, with translation by W. Ehlers), Stuttgart and Leipzig 1995 (Teubner).

Commentaries on Cena Trimalchionis

L. Friedlander, edn. 2, Leipzig 1906.
A. Maiuri, Naples 1945.
W. B. Sedgwick, corrected edn. 2, Oxford 1959.
E. V. Marmorale, edn. 2, Florence 1961.
M. S. Smith, Oxford 1975.

Commentary on other parts of the Satyrica

E. Courtney, *The Poems of Petronius* (Atlanta 1991).

Concordances

J. Segebade and E. Lommatzsch (Leipzig 1898).
M. Korn and S. Reitzer (Hildesheim 1986).

Translations

J. P. Sullivan, Harmondsworth 1956 (Penguin Books).
R. Bracht Branham and D. Kinney, Berkeley and Los Angeles 1996.
P. G. Walsh, Oxford 1997.

Abbreviations

AL = *Anthologia Latina*, referred to by numeration of A. Riese (edn. 2, Leipzig 1894–1906).
ANRW = *Aufstieg und Niedergang der römischen Welt* (1972–).
CLE = *Carmina Latina Epigraphica*, ed. F. Bücheler and E. Lommatzsch (Leipzig 1895–1926).

GCN = Groningen Colloquia on the Novel (1988–).
LIMC = Lexicon Iconographicum Mythologiae Classicae (1981–99).
LSJ = H. G. Liddell, R. Scott, and H. S. Jones, *Greek–English Lexicon*, 9th. edn. with revised Supplement (Oxford 1996).
OLD = Oxford Latin Dictionary (1968–82).
PSN = Petronian Society Newsletter (1970–).
RAC = Reallexicon für Antike und Christentum (1950–).
RE = Realencyclopädie der classischen Altertumswissenschaft, ed. A. Pauly, G. Wissowa, and others (1893–1974).
TLL = Thesaurus Linguae Latinae (1900–).

Bibliographies

Schmeling, G. L., and Stuckey, J. H., *Bibliography of Petronius* (Leiden, 1977).
Smith, M. S., *ANRW* 2.32.3.1624 (covering 1945–82).

Other Works

ADAMS, J. N., *The Latin Sexual Vocabulary* (London 1982).
BECK, R., 'Some Observations on the Narrative Technique of Petronius', *Phoenix* 27 (1973), 42.
——'Encolpius at the Cena', ibid. 29 (1975), 271.
——'Eumolpus poeta, Eumolpus fabulator', ibid. 33 (1979), 239.
——'The Satyricon: Satire, Narrator and Antecedents', *MH* 39 (1982), 206.
BLÜMNER, H., *Die römischen Privataltertümer* (Munich 1911).
BODEL, J., 'The Cena Trimalchionis', in H. Hofmann (ed.), *Latin Fiction* (London 1999), 38.
BOWERSOCK, G. W., *Fiction as History* (Berkeley and Los Angeles 1994).
BOYCE, B., *The Language of the Freedmen in Petronius' Cena Trimalchionis* (Leiden 1991).
CAMERON, AVERIL, 'Petronius and Plato', *CQ* 19 (1969), 367.
——'Myth and Meaning in Petronius', *Latomus* 29 (1970), 397.
CÈBE, J.-P., *La Caricature et la parodie dans le monde romaine* (Paris 1966).
CIAFFI, V., *Struttura del Satyricon* (Turin 1955).
COLLIGNON, A., *Étude sur Pétrone* (Paris 1892).
CONNORS, C., *Petronius the Poet* (Cambridge 1998).
CONTE, G. B., *The Hidden Author* (Berkeley 1996).
COURTNEY, E., 'Parody and Literary Allusion in Menippean Satire', *Philol.* 106 (1962), 86.
——*Musa Lapidaria* (Atlanta 1995).

DEONNA, W., and RENARD, T., *Croyances et superstitions de table* (Brussels 1961).

DOVER, K. J., *Greek Homosexuality* (edn. 2, London 1989).

DUNBABIN, K. M. D., *'Sic erimus cuncti', Jahrb. deutsch. Arch. Inst.* 101 (1986), 185.

GOOLD, G. P., *Chariton, Callirhoe* (Loeb Library, Cambridge, Mass. 1995).

GRIFFIN, M. T., *Nero, the End of a Dynasty* (London 1984).

GRONDONA, M., *La religione e la superstizione nella Cena Trimalchionis* (Brussels 1980).

HÄGG, T., *Narrative Technique in Ancient Greek Romance* (Stockholm 1971).

HARRISON, S. J. (ed.), *Oxford Essays on the Roman Novel* (1999).

HEINZE, R., 'Petron und die griechische Roman', *Hermes* 34 (1899), 494.

HENDERSON, J., *The Maculate Muse* (edn. 2, Oxford 1991).

HUBBARD, T. K., 'The Narrative Architecture of Petronius' Satyricon', *AC* 55 (1986), 190.

HUNTER, R. L., 'History and Historicity in the Romance of Chariton', *ANRW* 2.34.2.1055.

JONES, C. P., 'Dinner Theater', in W. J. Slater (ed.), *Dining in a Classical Context* (Ann Arbor 1991), 185.

LAIRD, A., *Powers of Expression, Expressions of Power* (Oxford 1999).

LATTE, K., *Römische Religionsgeschichte* (Munich 1960).

MARQUARDT, J., *Das Privatleben der Römer* (edn. 2 by A. Mau, Leipzig 1886).

MCMAHON, J. M., *Paralysin Cave* (Leiden 1998).

MORGAN, J. R., 'Work on the Fragments of Ancient Greek Fiction 1936–94', *ANRW* 2.34.4.3293.

OTTO, A., *Die Sprichwörter . . . der Römer* (Leipzig 1890), with *Nachträge zu A. Otto, Sprichwörter . . .* (ed. R. Häussler, Darmstadt 1968).

PABST, B., *Prosimetrum, Tradition und Wandel* (Cologne 1994).

PERRY, B. E., *The Ancient Romances* (Berkeley and Los Angeles 1967).

PRIULI, S., *Ascyltos* (Brussels 1975).

RAMELLI, I., 'Petronio e i Cristiani', *Aevum* 70 (1996), 75.

REARDON, B. P., *Collected Ancient Greek Novels* (Berkeley and Los Angeles 1989).

—— *The Form of Greek Romance* (Princeton 1991).

—— 'Achilles Tatius and Ego-Narrative', in J. R. Morgan and R. Stoneman (eds.), *Greek Fiction* (London 1994), 80, and S. Swain (ed.), *Oxford Readings in the Greek Novel* (1999), 243.

RELIHAN, J. C., *Ancient Menippean Satire* (Baltimore 1993).

ROHDE, E., *Der griechische Roman* (edn. 3, Leipzig 1914); referred to by pagination of edn. 2 (1900), recorded in edn. 3.

ROSE, K. F. C., *The Date and Author of the Satyricon* (Leiden 1971).

RUIZ-MONTERO, C., 'Chariton von Aphrodisias', *ANRW* 2.34.2.1006.

—— 'Xenophon von Ephesos', ibid. 1088.

SANDY, G., 'Petronius and the Tradition of the Interpolated Narrative', *TAPA* 101 (1970), 463.

SCHMELING, G. L. (ed.), *The Novel in the Ancient World* (Leiden 1996).

SOLIN, H., *Die griechische Personennamen in Rom* (Berlin 1982).

—— *Die stadtrömischen Sklavennamen* (Stuttgart 1996).

STEINER, G., 'The Graphic Analogue from Myth in Greek Romance', in *Classical Studies presented to B. E. Perry* (Urbana 1969).

STEPHENS, S. A., and WINKLER, J. J., *Ancient Greek Novels, the Fragments* (Princeton 1995).

STÖCKER, C., *Humor bei Petron* (Erlangen and Nuremberg 1969).

SULLIVAN, J. P., *The Satyricon of Petronius* (London 1968).

THOMPSON, STITH, *Motif-Index of Folk-Literature* (Bloomington 1955–8).

TRENKNER, S., *The Greek Novella* (Cambridge 1958).

VEYNE, P., 'Vie de Trimalchion', *Annales ECS* 16 (1961), 213.

—— 'Cave Canem', *MEFR* 75 (1963), 59.

WALSH, P. G., *The Roman Novel* (Cambridge 1970).

WINKLER, J. J., *Auctor & Actor* (Berkeley and Los Angeles 1985).

WISSOWA, G., *Religion und Kultus der Römer* (edn. 2, Munich 1912).

Abbreviations for periodical titles are those of *l'Année Philologique* or more explicit. Chapter-numbers in Roman and Arabic numerals refer respectively to chapters of this book and of Petronius. Fragments of Petronius from the Latin Anthology are also given with the numeration of Bücheler = B and of Müller (Teubner) = M.

Introduction

I hope that the reader of this book will end up convinced that in the novel of Petronius we have a multi-layered book. Such a work presents particularly difficult problems of interpretation, because in an eminent degree it will arouse different responses in different people. How then can any interpretation possess any validity beyond the individual brain and temperament in which it originates? In answer to this question we may apply several criteria. Obviously such an interpretation must be consistent with the text; any interpretation which sees *Bleak House* as a paean of approval for the workings of the Court of Chancery stands self-condemned. Secondly, internal cohesion argues strongly for some kind of validity; I trust that my views on Petronius will be found to exhibit such cohesion. A third criterion brings us to consideration of the contribution which a philological approach, such as is adopted in this book, can make in the case of a work which comes from a culture other than our own.

As I state at the beginning of Ch. II, I consider it important that at one stage of our reading, even with a work already familiar to us, we should make every effort to see each episode in sequential order with fresh eyes and form our impressions of it accordingly. That will be the basis of our own enjoyment (or otherwise) of a work, but in the case of a novel from an alien culture 'our' impressions will not suffice; imagine trying to read *Little Dorrit* in ignorance of the Victorian law of debt! For proper comprehension we need to consider how the author in the culture of his time and his first readers would have regarded and reacted to the situations which he has created, and how they would have seen his style of writing in relation to the literary background with which they were familiar. For the first century AD we have abundant information to help us with the first question, but unfortunately, as Ch. II (i) explains, rather less about the second in the particular case of prose fiction, though, as Ch. VIII (i) makes plain, this is far from being the only genre to enter into contention.

This book tries to put into effect these lines of approach. This means that its purpose is fundamentally historical, not aesthetic; it seeks to provide raw materials to facilitate understanding why I think Petronius wrote as he did. A corollary is the necessity to summarize each episode in sequence; I hope that these summaries will not be found superfluous and boring, since I have endeavoured in each case to present them in such a way that the major nuances implicit in the details of the action emerge. I believe that an authorial intention (a word which I use deliberately), or rather a plurality of such, becomes apparent and gives a validity not limited to myself to my interpretation—this despite the way in which the author only allows us occasional peeps at himself (e.g. at 132.15, discussed on pp. 199–201 below).

Two problems present themselves. First, the author may on the surface pretend to adopt current cultural values while through irony he seeks to undermine them, a process nowadays generally denoted by the facile vogue word 'subversion'. In practice I myself to do not find this to be a great problem; my own experience is that authors have usually left enough indications to testify to their irony, and that when scholars assume irony in the absence of plain signals, they are generally wrong to do so. Second, the author may be striking out in a new direction, setting for himself norms independent of any pre-existing tradition and therefore not appealing to any pre-conditioned response in the reader. The *Satyrica* as a whole has, not without justification, produced this reaction in some readers, but in its parts (and, at any rate in what survives, the parts can give the impression of dominating over the whole) this is not so.

Now I should like to describe the structure of this book and how I think it can best be used. Chapters I–II try to do what can be done to key the reader into the impressions which will have been imparted to the mind of the Roman reader by the now lost parts of the work which preceded the beginning of our text. Chapters III–VII discuss the successive episodes of our text and suggest reactions which each might convey to us and how we should see these episodes linked into an overall design. In many ways these chapters constitute the kernel of the book, and my title 'A Companion to Petronius' is intended to imply a recommendation that after reading a stretch of Petronius novice users of this book should then consider that stretch in the light of my comments; my subdivisions are intended to help this process. Those already familiar with the work can of course read straight through. In general I try to avoid distracting detail except where (a) particularly insightful ideas of other scholars demand acknowledgement (anything which appears in such standard works as Smith's commentary on the *Cena* I treat as common ground); (b) the most frequently used sources, such as Smith, require correction or amplification; (c) I feel that my readers will welcome leads for further investigation. Generally speaking, I think that it will not be found essential to be diverted from the flow of the book by following up as they occur these points of detail with the help of my references; I intend that most of them should be temporarily by-passed. I have tried not to burden the book with superfluous bibliography; most work with which I disagree, as well as some which seems to me to have its value but not to add anything essential to my text, or not to be to my purpose, is passed over in silence. Note too that in an age characterized by what Syme called a 'superfetation of bibliography' I do not consider that we have any obligation to consider unpublished work. Finally Chapter VIII ties together some of the themes which have been remarked in the preceding chapters; VIII (iii) in particular can be brief because it is not intended to introduce much that is by then new, but to recall and link together points already made occurrence by occurrence, so that it can be seen how they pervade the whole novel.

One trap into which I have occasionally seen scholars fall without realizing that they have done so, and against which I should like to warn, is that of interpreting e.g. Trimalchio in terms of factual motivations for his actions, whereas we should think only of motivations which the author Petronius desires to be inferred by his readers. Nevertheless to phrase one's comments so that this is everywhere explicit produces cumbrous results, so I would ask my readers to bear in mind that when I say e.g. 'Trimalchio here intends such and such', I mean this as shorthand.

I have written this book with the thought of appealing primarily to the level of graduate students and young professors (in the American sense), but I shall be pleased if more advanced scholars too derive some profit from it. I have also tried to make it accessible to Latinless readers interested in fiction generally, and with such in mind I have, when possible, preferred to give bibliographical references to works in English and likely to be readily available.

Finally I should like to repeat a contention from my preface to another book, that a good book leaves some work for its readers to do themselves.

I

The Author

In AD 65 the conspiracy of Piso against Nero was detected and suppressed; among those suspected of involvement were Seneca and Lucan, who were forced to commit suicide. In the next year Tacitus records the enforced death of other Roman aristocrats, among them Annaeus Mela, the brother of Seneca and father of Lucan, who was accused of participation in the conspiracy, and a man referred to simply as Petronius by the manuscript of the *Annals* (16.17). Since the other three members of the list are all given a cognomen, there must surely be some corruption here; what it is is better left unsettled for the moment so that judgement is not prejudiced. Having dealt one by one with the other persons in the list, referring to each of them just by cognomen, Tacitus then turns to Petronius (16.18.1) with the words (according to his manuscript) *de C. Petronio pauca supra repetenda sunt* ('I must go back for a few details about Gaius Petronius'). I give the following in the Loeb translation:

He was a man whose day was passed in sleep, his nights in the social duties and amenities of life: others industry may raise to greatness—Petronius had idled into fame. Nor was he regarded, like the common crowd of spendthrifts, as a debauchee and wastrel, but as the finished artist of extravagance (*erudito luxu*). His words and actions had a freedom and a stamp of self-abandonment, which rendered them doubly acceptable by an air of native simplicity (*simplicitatis*). Yet as proconsul of Bithynia, and later as consul, he showed himself a man of energy and competent to affairs. Then, lapsing into the habit, or copying the features, of vice, he was adopted into the narrow circle of Nero's intimates as his Arbiter of Elegance (*arbiter elegantiae*); the jaded emperor finding charm and delicacy in nothing save what Petronius had commended. His success awoke the jealousy of Tigellinus against an apparent rival, more expert in the science of pleasure than himself. He addressed himself, therefore, to the sovereign's cruelty, to which all other passions gave pride of place;

arraigning Petronius for friendship with Scaevinus, while suborning one of his slaves to turn informer, withholding all opportunity of defence, and placing the greater part of his household under arrest.

In those days, as it chanced, the Caesar had migrated to Campania, and Petronius, after proceeding as far as Cumae, was being detained there in custody. He declined to tolerate further the delays of fear or hope; but caused his already severed arteries to be bound up to meet his whim, then opened them once more, and began to converse with his friends, in no grave strain and with no view to the fame of a stout-hearted ending. He listened to them as they rehearsed, not discourses upon the immortality of the soul or the doctrines of philosophy, but light songs and frivolous verses. Some of his slaves tasted of his bounty, a few of the lash. He took his place at dinner, and drowsed a little, so that death, if compulsory, should at least resemble nature. Not even in his will did he follow the routine of suicide by flattering Nero or Tigellinus or another of the mighty, but—prefixing the names of the various catamites and women—detailed the imperial debauches and the novel features of each act of lust, and sent the document under seal to Nero . . . While Nero doubted how the character of his nights was gaining publicity, there suggested itself the name of Silia—the wife of a senator, and therefore a woman of some note, requisitioned by himself for every form of lubricity, and on terms of the closest intimacy with Petronius. She was now driven into exile for failing to observe silence upon what she had seen and undergone.

Who was this man? He is evidently identical with a person mentioned by Pliny, *NH* 37.20 'When the ex-consul T. Petronius was facing death, he broke, to spite Nero, a myrrhine dipper that had cost him 300,000 sesterces', and Plutarch, *Quomodo adulator* 19.60e '(flatterers) will reproach profligate and lavish spenders with meanness and sordidness, as T. Petronius did with Nero' (both of these passages also in the Loeb translation).

The problem about this is the difference in the praenomen given by the manuscript of Tacitus. It would seem therefore that this manuscript is in error both times when the name of Petronius is given; that in 17.1 we should add the praenomen ⟨*T.*⟩ and in 18.1 delete the praenomen *C.*; and that Tacitus' conspicuous avoidance of a cognomen implies that the man had none (P. Petronius, consul AD 19 and attacked by Sen. *Apoc.* 14.2, also had no cognomen). This last fact militates against the

nowadays popular identification of this Petronius with a known
T. Petronius Niger, consul in the early sixties AD.[1]

That, however, is of scant importance; what we have to
decide is whether the T. Petronius known from Tacitus (?),
Pliny, and Plutarch is identical with the author of a surviving
work which in the most reliable manuscripts, with some
unimportant variations, is labelled as *Petronii Arbitri Satyricon*
(this title is also used by 'Marius Victorinus' in quoting fr. 20).
Terentianus Maurus, who perhaps belongs to the second half
of the third century, in adducing fr. 19, and other later writers
quote from an Arbiter, and Fulgentius, probably in the early
sixth century, produces several quotations under the name of
Petronius Arbiter. However, this cognomen has been transferred from the nickname *arbiter elegantiae* mentioned by
Tacitus; Arbiter is a slave-name (clearly the title of a household
function turned into a name) which accordingly becomes a
cognomen of freedmen, and is not found outside this context.
But this very transference implies that someone in the ancient
world, rightly or wrongly, made an identification. The biggest
obstacle to this identification is that Tacitus does not record
any writings of his Petronius, but this is not much of a
problem; mention of a disreputable work of fiction would
consort ill with the dignity of the historian, especially as
prose fiction, as will be shown in Ch. II, was a genre which
carried very little prestige in the ancient world. The *Apocolocyntosis* of Seneca was not beneath the attention of Cassius Dio,
but it was beneath that of Tacitus.

What then favours an identification? One factor that is
relevant, though strictly speaking it carries no probative
weight, is that the dramatic time of action is set in the Neronian
age or shortly before. This is established by mention in the
Cena Trimalchionis of the gladiator Petraites (52.3, 71.6), the

[1] See Rose 50 sqq. He discusses cases where Tacitus omits praenomina, but
does not show that this can happen in a list such as we have here; in a similar
list the editors of Tacitus assume the omission of a name at *Ann.* 15.71.2. Rose
argues that, since the fasti for 58–9 are complete, the Tacitean Petronius will
have been consul at about the same time as Petronius Niger, but there is no
reason why he should not have been consul before 58. Note that there is good
evidence that the praenomen of Petronius Niger was in fact P. (Griffin 272
n. 3; for the publication of the document in question see *Ann. Epigr.* 1989.
681 = *Suppl. Epigr. Gr.* 39 (1989), 1180).

tragic actor Apelles (64.4; he flourished under Caligula, and
Plocamus in his youth heard him), and the singer Menecrates
(73.3). The reservation has to be entered that performers often
assumed the names of famous predecessors (e.g. we know a
plurality of pantomimes called Paris); nevertheless it would be
rash to reject the mutual corroboration given by the occurrence
of three such names.[2] The dramatic time can hardly be much
earlier, since the anecdote in ch. 21 about the execution by an
emperor of the maker of unbreakable glass refers to Tiberius;
and attempts to see allusions to later circumstances have all
failed. A *terminus ante quem* of 60–1 has been sought in 45.8
(see Smith, p. 117); it is possible that this passage was written
before that date, but it is not probable that Petronius fixed the
dramatic date with close precision.

A second factor is that allusions to Seneca and Lucan, about
which more later, provide at least a *terminus post quem*;
probably more than that, since the discussion of Lucan's epic
technique in 118 raises one topic, namely his exclusion of the
traditional epic gods, which does not seem to have remained a
live issue for long (at least the Flavian epic poets declined to
follow him). Here one may remark that the death-scene of the
Tacitean Petronius is presented as what one must call a parody
of the death-scene of Seneca,[3] which itself is modelled on the
death-scene of Socrates; but here is it hard to tell whether
Tacitus has embellished historical fact for artistic reasons.

Thirdly, we seem to catch echoes of competition between
courtiers of Nero in 70.8 (this was first suggested tentatively
by Friedlaender). There a guest's feet are anointed and
perfumed, a procedure which makes the narrator Encolpius
feel ashamed (compare his disgust at 65.1) and to which he
refers as an *inauditus mos* ('an unheard-of custom'). Pliny, *NH*
13.22, tells us that this custom had been introduced by Otho
to Nero before Nero sent him as governor to Lusitania in AD
58 so that he could marry Otho's wife Poppaea.[4] Again, in

---

[2] See Rose 21–2. Smith 139–40 and 179 is characteristically over-sceptical
about Petraites and Apelles, but does not challenge Menecrates.

[3] See Courtney (1991), 12.

[4] Smith 193–4, who raises trivial objections to this interpretation, remarks
occurrences of the practice in Athens (see Athen. 12.553a–e, not just the first
passage there quoted) and Judaea; see too Rose 24, Clarke, *CJ* 87 (1991–2),

57.4 it is likely that there is an allusion to the claim of
Claudius' freedman Pallas, who was dismissed in AD 55 and
supposedly poisoned in 62, to be descended from regal
ancestry.[5] It will be recalled that it was the jealousy of another
courtier, Tigellinus, which brought about the downfall of the
Tacitean Petronius.

More subjective, though not without weight, is the feeling
shared by many that the mental picture which we would be
inclined to form of the author perfectly fits the character
portrayed in Tacitus. First his *elegantia*. See how the narrator
Encolpius continually expresses disgust at Trimalchio's failed
attempts at refinement; the words *elegans* and *elegantia* occur in
this connection at 34.5 and 60.1. Of course we must not
straightforwardly confound, as some ancient sources did (see
below, p. 44), the author with his narrator, but this caveat can
be countered by the observation that *elegantia* plays no part in
the self-characterization of Encolpius anywhere else in the
novel than in the setting of the *Cena*, which is comparable to
the setting in which Petronius' own *elegantia* came into play
with Nero.

These last two observations inevitably raise the question
whether we should see in Trimalchio's feast any veiled allusions to Neronian banquets which lacked the benefit of advice
from the *elegantiae arbiter*; that would imply a criticism that
any refinement possessed by Nero came from others. Some[6]
have indeed seen continual disguised references to Nero in
things said about Trimalchio. It is of course quite possible that
in building up this larger than life character the author could
have taken hints from people known to him, including Nero
himself, but I personally cannot believe that Trimalchio is in
any way intended to suggest to the reader a sustained caricature
of the emperor; rather, as subsequent chapters will show, the

261–2. Cf. the *res nouas* of 27.3 and the *nouum acroama* of 78.5, in both of
which places 'novel' incorporates a sneer.

[5] See Rose 26; Latte, *Philol.* 82 (1932), 266. For the derision here see
below, p. 52.

[6] See Smith's index rerum s.v. *Nero* (here his scepticism is mainly
justified); Walsh (1970) 137–9; Rose 78 and 82. It is possible that there are
uncomplimentary references to Nero in what Agamemnon says in 5.7 and
Eumolpus in 83.8.

grandiose fictional character Trimalchio attempts to assimilate himself to Nero and other emperors.

To return from this digression to the question whether we can see traits of the character depicted by Tacitus in the novel, a second relative factor is the sense of the unnaturalness of contemporary life implied by the underlying symbolic structure of the novel. Discussion of this will have to be postponed to Ch. VIII (iii); here what one may note is the reversal of night and day remarked by Tacitus. Seneca too (*Letter* 122) observes this in some of his contemporaries, calling them *lucifugae*, evaders of daylight; he violently attacks their dissipation and affectation of the unnatural, and speaks (§18) of their *elegantia cenarum*. There can be little doubt that this is aimed at the Petronius described by Tacitus.

Thirdly, one can hardly deny that the author of the novel had a deep interest in sex. The Tacitean Petronius was clearly not a participant in Nero's nocturnal orgies (perhaps Nero feared that he would have found them inelegant, or was not convinced by Petronius' 'imitation of vices'), but he had enough interest in them to ferret out all the seamy details, from a participant, as Nero suspected.

What I regard as a fallacious argument has also been adduced. The capricious behaviour of the Tacitean Petronius in chastising or indulging his slaves has been brought into relation with Trimalchio's treatment of his slaves, but in fact only one slave is beaten during the *Cena* (54.3), another gets off with a minor punishment (34.2), and two are let off altogether (52, 54). He goes so far as to have *tortores*, punishers, of his own (whereas these were usually municipal functionaries; see my note on Juv. 6.480), but they are used only for a sham. The crucifixion of a slave in 53 is part of the mock *acta diurna*, Daily Gazette, of Trimalchio's estates and cannot be taken seriously (this will be discussed on pp. 101–2 below). Trimalchio blusters and poses as contemptuous of his slaves as a cover-up of his own former status, but in fact is a perfectly kind master; contrast the harsh slave-owner Larcius Macedo *qui seruisse patrem suum parum, immo nimium, meminisset*, Pliny *Ep.* 3.14.1 ('He remembered too little, or rather too well, that his own father had been a slave'). Pallas would not even speak to his slaves (Tac. *Ann.* 13.23.2, Dio Cass. 62.14.3).

All the arguments to which I have given weight fall far short of proof, but most modern scholars, I among them, feel that there is enough in favour of the identification for it to be accepted as a reasonable hypothesis.

II

Preliminaries

(i) The Novel Genre as Background

In most genres of literature, and especially fiction, the best way
to appreciate a work is to read it through, picking up as we
proceed the indications by which the author has revealed stage
by stage such things as the conventions which we are to take
into account (i.e. the generic nature of the work), how it is to be
related to other works of literature, how items of information
deliberately held back earlier are illuminated by later passages.
This is what is called a heuristic reading, because the reader is
throughout engaged in progressive discovery. Every successive
rereading is done in the light of the knowledge acquired in the
first process, so that, whereas in our first reading we often had
to look back, we can now fully appreciate e.g. foreshadowing by
looking forward. This is called a hermeneutic reading because
only now can a fully informed interpretation of the work take
place.[1]

Unfortunately we cannot apply this process to Petronius
because we do not possess the beginning of his work. What we
have consists of a series of shorter excerpts (collectively
designated O and preserved in manuscripts of the ninth century and later), a series of longer excerpts (collectively known
as L and preserved in manuscripts and printed texts of the
sixteenth century), and a complete text of the *Cena Trimalchionis* preserved in one fifteenth-century manuscript. These
manuscripts and a few quoting sources give some book-
numbers, which unfortunately are not consistent with each
other.[2] Not to go into this question in detail, the likely

---

[1] The terminology and concepts of this paragraph were applied to the novel
by Winkler 10 sqq. and *passim*; I have used them in an article forthcoming in
Museum Helveticum to interpret the prologue of Lucretius.

[2] See Rose 2–3; Müller (1995) p. xxi; H. Van Thiel, *Maia* 22 (1970), 257,

conclusion is that Book 15 of the work began with the *Cena*, and that in the excerpt tradition it is preceded by part of Book 14. The length of the *Cena* has suggested to some that it filled two or three books,[3] but no convincing break is apparent, and the books of the Greek novels are not on average much shorter, though those of Apuleius are. The rest of the work as we have it may have occupied two or three books; ch. 125 at any rate looks like the beginning of a new book (see below, p. 189). So we have remnants at a minimum of four and a probable maximum of six books. How far the work went, or was intended to go if it was unfinished when Petronius died, we cannot tell.

It is relevant to enquire how much of the continuous text is preserved by the excerpts. Our only way of doing this is by comparison with the continuous text of the *Cena*, in which the excerptor at ch. 37 decided that there was little more to his purpose, so that after this, except for ch. 55, he chooses only a few sentences. Up to that point the long excerpts retain about 90 per cent of the text. Unfortunately this can hardly be representative of the work as a whole; the excerptor must have treated different episodes differently, according to his intentions and taste.

Despite our inability to start at the beginning, we can do a little to recreate the first heuristic reading of a Roman reader. He would have begun with the title, which would have been *Satyrica* or *Satyricon libri*. He would have known not to connect this Greek word with the Latin word *satura*, satire. The two words experience a rapprochement in late antiquity, but had not done so in the first century (not even at Dion. Hal. *AR* 7.72.10–11); confusion about this matter was cleared up by Casaubon in his book *De Satyrica Graecorum Poesi*, published in 1605 (he refers to Petronius on p. 264). The Roman readers will have understood the title to relate to the Greek Satyrs and

and *Petron, Überlieferung und Rekonstruktion* (Leiden 1971) 21; Nelson, *Mnem.* 24 (1971), 80 (improbable); Sullivan 34 and 79; Harrison p. xvii.

[3] Thus e.g. Harrison, *CQ* 48 (1998), 580, divides after 46.8 and 65.2. The former division is acceptable enough, and the latter certainly marks a turning-point in the narrative, but leaves a very abrupt closure to the preceding 'book', though one must admit that book-divisions are not always clearly marked in the novels. I think that he greatly over-estimates the size of the lacunae in the *Cena*.

will have interpreted it to mean 'A Tale of Satyr-like Lust and Depravity' (Plutarch, *Pericles* 13.16 and *Galba* 16.3, refers to men σατυρικοὶ τοῖς βίοις, Satyr-like in their lives). The termination of the adjective will have given him no further clue; the novel of Longus (which probably belongs within the period AD 150–250) may have had Ποιμενικά ('A Pastoral Tale') or an implied Ποιμενικῶν λόγοι as its title or part of its title or one of the titles under which it went in the ancient world, but the form has no particular generic connection (think of e.g. *P. Vergili Maronis Georgicon Libri* or the various poems entitled *Argonautica*).

To translate *Satyrica* into English in the preceding paragraph I had to add the words 'A Tale of'. The first Roman readers would have perceived the narrative form not from the title but from the text, and it would also have been immediately apparent that this was a fictional narrative; not only that, it would at once, or at least very soon, have been apparent that the narrative is couched in the first person. That would have revealed to them that the work was to be classified as what we now would call a novel; what would they have called it? At this point it is necessary to say something about the history of this form in antiquity; I shall sketch the outlines of this complicated subject as I see them, drawing attention to features particularly relevant to Petronius at the expense of others which are not in themselves less important.

When the origin of the Greek novel is discussed, one runs into a point of principle right at the start. Some influential writers about the Greek novel, Perry and Reardon in particular, have been primarily interested in the cultural situation which brought about the birth of this new literary form and in the individual literary impulse, and in a rather reductionist manner have played down any literary inheritance in its creation, which Perry contemptuously refers to as 'the biological metaphor of evolution'. Yet Perry, who on pp. 36–9 strongly denies any evolutionary path leading from historiography to the novel, only a few pages later (42) speaks of 'the peculiar influence exerted by Xenophon's *Cyropedia* as a precedent upon the earliest romancers'; see also 147 'The historical monograph . . . as in Xenophon's *Cyropedia* . . . was the conventional pattern of composition into which the

Greek romancers chose to put their new product with its entirely new orientation', and 173 'Like Ninus, the first Greek romance must have been modelled structurally on the pattern of Xenophon's *Cyropedia*, because the earliest known romance,' [this statement is perhaps a little over-confident] 'that about Ninus and Semiramis, is, as a matter of fact, so constructed, and because the name Xenophon was used as a *nom de plume* by the authors of at least three romances' (the factual allusions in the last sentence will be elucidated below). Similarly Reardon (1989) 6 'For all that, even though literary works do not 'develop' spontaneously as plants do, they do have predecessors that help to shape the writer's thoughts'. To draw a distinction between 'development' and 'literary influence' is mere word-chopping in the interest of the abstract theory that 'one form does not give birth to another' (Perry 14); this dogma is discussed in relation to love-elegy at the end of this chapter. For the purpose of placing Petronius in relation to the Greek novel it is perfectly legitimate not to deal with the motivating idea (in Perry's terms) of the genre, and it is in fact necessary to 'concentrate on the process of creation and the materials used' (Perry 11, disapprovingly).

In these terms I agree with those who see the mainspring of the Greek novel in the *Cyropedia* of Xenophon (see e.g. Reichel, *GCN* 6 (1995), 1), and consider the objections which have been raised against this trivial. One may pirouette on a pinhead whether to call the *Cyropedia* 'historical fiction' or 'fictionalized biography'; even to raise the question shows that Xenophon is moving outside the traditional literary categories (Perry's phrase 'historical monograph' quoted above is misleading). In either case the upshot is the same; Xenophon has taken a historical figure remote from his own time and has written an account of his life with little connection to historical accuracy, but shaped to convey a moral lesson (Cicero, *Ad Q. f.* 1.1.23, speaks of *Cyrus ille a Xenophonte non ad historiae fidem scriptus sed ad effigiem iusti imperi*, 'that Cyrus described by Xenophon according not to historical accuracy but to the image of just rule'). It is possible that some Greek novelists (including Xenophon of Ephesus) adopted his name as a pseudonym in recognition of his status as ultimate founder of the genre.[4]

---

[4] See e.g. Stephens–Winkler 27; Ruiz-Montero 1089; J. N. O'Sullivan,

Xenophon himself (1.1.6, 8.3.1, 8.5.2) describes his literary activity in this work with the verb διηγεῖσθαι, to narrate. It is worth recalling that to Polybius (1.14.6) διήγημα, narrative, means 'history with the truth removed'.

Let us now move on to Chariton, whose work seems to have been entitled something like τὰ περὶ (Χαιρέαν καὶ) Καλλιρόην (ἐρωτικὰ) διηγήματα (The [Love-]Story about [Chaereas and] Callirhoe), with a noun derived from the verb used by Xenophon; the verb itself is used by Chariton in the prefaces to the first and second halves of the work (1.1.1, 5.1.2). Moreover Chariton makes clear allusion to the *Cyropedia* at 6.8.7, and in particular to the story of the love of Abradatas and Pantheia, a pattern of wifely fidelity, as described in instalments in that work, at 2.5.7, 4.1.12, 5.2.4 and 9, 5.3.10, 7.6.7[5] (there are also other less significant recalls; see A. D. Papanikolaou, *Chariton-Studien* (Göttingen 1973) 19–21 and Goold's index s.v. Xenophon). Like Xenophon, Chariton gives his work a vaguely historical base centuries before his own time, though with many anachronisms. In particular his heroine is presented as the daughter of the Syracusan Hermocrates who plays a prominent role in Thucydides, which is why Chariton stakes out a claim not only to Xenophontean but also Thucydidean lineage by describing his work at its close with the Thucydidean verb συγγράφειν, to write a historical account (at 8.1.4 he refers to the last book as a σύγγραμμα); he also puts allusions to the funeral speech of Pericles into Chaereas' exhortation to his soldiers at 7.3.8–9.[6]

In the last paragraph I referred to Chariton's own time; what was this? This question in the past elicited widely different answers, but since O. Weinreich (*Der griechische Liebesroman* (Zürich 1962) 13) put forward the following view it has become widely accepted that a *terminus ante quem* is given by Persius

---

Xenophon of Ephesus (Berlin and New York 1995) 1; G. Schmeling, *Xenophon of Ephesus* (Boston 1980) 16; Perry 167.

[5] See Perry 169 for another Greek narrative on this theme in the first half of the second century AD.

[6] See Hunter 1056, with remarks on other Thucydidean colour on 1056–8; Goold's index s.v. Thucydides; Luginbill, *Mnem.* 53 (2000), 1; for other historical figures see Ruiz-Montero 1013–14, and generally on the historical basis of Chariton Hägg, *CA* 6 (1987), 194.

1.134: 'his mane edictum, post prandia Calliroen do.' Wein-
reich argued that this was to be considered an allusion to
Chariton's work by the name of its heroine, to be dated
before AD 62, when Persius died. I do not believe this.
W. Kissel in his commentary points out that the context is as
follows. Persius appeals for readers such as connoisseurs of Old
Comedy, not people who makes jokes about the sandals of
Greeks, who are proud of petty municipal magistracies, and
who laugh when a whore pulls a philosopher's beard. To such
Persius commends the reading of the praetor's edict (linking
with their magistracies; not a programme for a play or a
gladiatorial show) in the morning, and in the afternoon
during the post-prandial siesta (cf. Catullus 32) a session
with a prostitute like that just mentioned. As Kissel says, one
would hardly suggest the reading of a Greek novel to people
who laugh at the Greeks (even if they admire the biting wit of
Old Comedy; Romans often draw a distinction between classical and contemporary Greeks.)[7]

The only other possible ancient reference to Chariton comes
in the 66th letter of Philostratus (dated in the first half of the
third century), but since I am one of those who believe that the
Chariton there referred to is a contemporary of Philostratus,
not the novelist, I shall not discuss this. So, if there is no
external reference to Chariton from the ancient world, he will
have to be dated by internal evidence; this will be considered
below.

One other Greek novel-writer requires special mention,
Achilles Tatius; unfortunately he too can be dated only in
the broadest terms to the second century AD. His particular
importance for Petronius lies in a considerable number of
thematic parallels (which will be dealt with below under the
individual episodes) and especially in the basic narrative technique. His novel begins with the author-figure looking at the
pictures in a picture-gallery (a setting like that of Petronius
83 sqq.), and specifically at a picture with the erotic theme of
Zeus abducting Europa (a heterosexual theme, whereas those
in Petronius are homosexual). He comments aloud on the
power of Eros, and a young man standing by his side, who

---

[7] See my commentary on Juvenal, p. 28.

turns out to be Clitophon, the hero of the novel, takes the
occasion to recount his own love-story with the heroine
Leucippe. This narrative occupies the rest of the work,
which ends without any authorial coda. The novel of Petronius
also is a narrative by Encolpius of his former adventures, and
there are similarities too in details of technique, which will be
discussed below. Whether Encolpius also recounted his adventures to someone or was represented as writing them down in a
book has been much discussed in relation to ch. 132.15; this
question will be treated at p. 200 below, where the conclusion
is reached that the former option is correct. It must be added
that some of the episodes in Achilles Tatius take the conventions of the novel so far that he has in fact been understood to
be using them sardonically or humorously, which would bring
him even closer to Petronius. One must note in particular that
Clitophon sets out to seduce Leucippe, that she is quite willing
to be seduced and that she elopes with him without any
mention of marriage, which only enters the picture when a
dream warns her (against the wishes of Clitophon, who at 8.5.6
gives her credit for this) to preserve her virginity until
marriage (4.1); as for Clitophon, he goes to bed with Melite
(5.27) and later avoids acknowledgement of this by casuistry
(8.5.7; Melite herself operates with a similar equivocation at
8.11, and we shall see Giton in Petronius acting similarly at
133.1). One can see why the Patriarch Photius regarded
Achilles as salacious. Fusillo in D. H. Roberts and others
(eds.), *Classical Closure* (Princeton 1997), four times on
pp. 220–1 applies the word 'ironic(al)' to Achilles' attitude
towards the erotic novel. Reardon (1994) 80 sqq. = (2000) 243
sqq. (which reads somewhat differently from his earlier views,
(1991) 37–8) thinks that Achilles is still operating within the
conventions of the genre but taking them to their limits
('brinkmanship' is Reardon's term). To myself it seems clear
that, while Achilles is not writing a humorous or parodic
novel, he is treating the topoi, conventions, and outlook of
the genre in a sardonic manner.

One other point. Linkage between Petronius and the Greek
novel will help to account for what must have been the
gargantuan length of the work. Of our extant novels Heliodorus in ten books is much the longest, but Petronius must

have been longer still. A lost work will be a better parallel; the *Babyloniaca* of Iamblichus, who lived in the second century ad, consisted of a minimum of 16 books, and the novel of Antonius Diogenes, who may belong to the same epoch, had 24.

But there is one big difference between Petronius and the Greek novels listed so far; while these do not lack humorous touches, Petronius writes an out-and-out comic novel. At this point it is appropriate to consider what evaluative comments on Petronius himself survive from the ancient world. Unimportant is John Laurentius the Lydian, *de Magistratibus* 1.41, who links him with Juvenal as an abusive writer and says that they transgressed τὸν σατυρικὸν νόμον, the generic norms of satire; in the preceding context he has made it clear that he is using σατυρικός in the Roman sense 'related to satire', and he here means that their vicious attacks violate the *lex operis*. This is based on a misunderstanding (John's knowledge of things Roman is sometimes wider than it is deep); he clearly thought that Petronius was writing a satire and that Trimalchio etc. were real characters satirized by him. More important is Macrobius on *Somn. Scip.* 1.2.8, who links Petronius with Apuleius 'sometimes' (meaning in some of the stories inserted in the *Metamorphoses*, e.g. at 9.22 sqq.) and describes them as writing *argumenta fictis casibus amatorum referta*, fictitious narratives with a strong erotic element. In the Latin here one will note that Macrobius has no distinct term meaning 'novel', and the same is true in Greek; the genre of the novel in Greek can be comprised only under the class of διήγημα πλασματικόν or δραματικόν (in medieval Greek novels can be called δράματα), fictitious or dramatic narrative,[8] which corresponds to *argumentum* in a widespread classification of narrative[9] different from that of Macrobius, though coinciding in this term. In the latter classification, which is based on a scale of truth-content, *argumenta* come between myth and history, covering narratives which did not happen but could have happened, such as the plots of New Comedy, which Macrobius also includes among *argumenta*. Classical canons of taste admitted only history, philosophy, and oratory as respectable prose genres; the

[8] For the terminology see Bowersock 16–19, and Horsfall, *Scripta Class. Israel.* 11 (1991–2), 135.
[9] See Rohde 351–2.

novel never gained any respect among the supercilious, largely because prose is associated with 'truth', and imaginative fiction is regarded as the province of verse. Plautus, *Pseud.* 401–3, humorously employs such concepts of literary theory:

> sed quasi *poeta*, tabulas quom cepit sibi,
> quaerit quod nusquam gentiumst, reperit tamen,
> facit illud ueri simile quod *mendacium* est.

('as a *poet*, when he takes up pen and paper, looks for what does not exist on earth, but yet finds it, and gives plausibility to a *lie*'). For the use of 'lie' in such contexts of literary theory to mean what we would refer to as 'fiction' see Morgan in C. Gill and T. P. Wiseman (eds.), *Lies and Fiction in the Ancient World* (Exeter 1993), 179–81 and 192–3.

The comic nature of Petronius' novel leads on, somewhat indirectly, to a second side of what the Roman reader will speedily have noticed as a feature of the work, namely that passages of verse are interspersed in the prose in which the bulk of the work is written. This literary form is very remark-able in view of the relatively strict compartmentalization of genres in the ancient world; the famous 'Kreuzung der Gattungen', blending of genres, which became quite the fashion in the Hellenistic age in particular and motivated e.g. Callimachus to write an epinician ode in elegiacs, is something very different. The incongruity of the combination would at once mark the work as belonging to a rather low stylistic ambit; the higher genres lay much emphasis on homogeneity of style, so that e.g. historians, with few exceptions, do not quote documents or speeches verbatim even when they have the original wording, but assimilate them to their own style.

This mixed form acquired the name *prosimetrum* in the Middle Ages; it is supposed to have been first used for literary purposes by Menippus of Gadara, who lived in the first half of the third century BC. Practically nothing survives of his writing, but Athenaeus 1.32e tells us that he applied the adjective ἁλμόποτις ('drinking brine') to the port Myndus; especially if the adjective and the name were beside each other, this looks like verse (and original, not quoted, verse). Lucian, *Bis Accusatus* 33, also alludes to his mixture of prose

and verse,[10] and Probus on Verg. *Buc.* 6.31 (3.2.336 Thilo–
Hagen) explicitly attests it (not that he necessarily had first-
hand knowledge).[11] The form was taken up in Rome by Varro
for his *Saturae Menippeae*, and subsequently flourished in both
ancient and modern times. It now universally known as
'Menippean satire' (the term was first so used in 1581),[12] and
I have myself in the past (now I repent) employed this as a
generic term. It distorts the reality, because it never appears in
antiquity as the name of a genre; its only application is to the
satires of Varro. It is noticeable that when Quintilian refers to
the nature of Varro's satires, he has to do so by a clumsy
periphrasis, *alterum illud etiam prius*[13] *saturae genus, sed non
sola carminum uarietate mixtum, condidit Terentius Varro*
(10.1.95). This is translated as follows by M. Winterbottom,
Problems in Quintilian (*BICS* suppl. 25, 1970), 191: 'the other
well-known type of satire—one that arose even before Lucilius
(= *etiam prius*)—was exploited by Varro, but now with a variety
given not merely by metrical changes.' The implication is taken
to be that the satire of Ennius in varied metres (not just the
hexameter on which Lucilius eventually settled, followed in
this by Horace, Persius, and Juvenal) was taken up by Varro,
who added the extra ingredient of prose. In view of all this I
shall avoid the term 'Menippean satire' in favour of *prosimetrum*, because the anachronism which this implies is less
misleading.

There is a faint chance that this form was also employed in
the 'Milesian Tales' translated by Sisenna from the Greek of
Aristides (this sub-genre will be discussed on pp. 137–8 below);
fr. 1 of these consists of the words *nocte uagatrix*, which (as
Bücheler, who included the fragments in his edition of Petronius, remarked) both rhythmically and stylistically looks like
verse. Much more important is the revival of this form by
Seneca for his *Apocolocyntosis*, a satire on the deification of

---

[10] On this passage of Lucian see Relihan (1993) 16, and E. Braun, *Lukian,
Unter doppelter Anklage* (Frankfurt 1994) 350–1.

[11] On a somewhat doubtful testimony of Photius see Relihan (1993) 43 with
n. 28 on p. 232.

[12] See Relihan, *CP* 79 (1984), 226, and (1993) 12.

[13] I share the uneasiness of many about this word; perhaps ⟨anti⟩quius, the
first part of which would easily be lost after *e-tiam*.

Claudius. This must have been produced soon after Claudius' death, perhaps as a squib for the Saturnalia of AD 54. Though it achieved general circulation at least by the latter part of the second century, when Cassius Dio refers to it, this was doubtless not the case at the time, when it must have been just for the delectation of court circles; though Petronius' heyday at court was certainly later, no doubt he was already included in such circles, or at least soon admitted to them. The handling of the form shows some similarities to Petronius (this will be discussed below), and there are also verbal resemblances;[14] it is hard to doubt that this work in some degree influenced Petronius' choice of form, though in sub-ject-matter and treatment it is far from Petronius and much closer to the tradition of Menippus and Varro. It has in common with Petronius that it consists almost entirely of narrative, but no doubt that was also true of some of the works of Menippus and Varro.

However, new vistas were opened in 1971 with the pre-liminary publication by Peter Parsons of Pap. Ox. 3010, subsequently in 1974 given its definitive publication in vol. 42 of the *Oxyrhynchus Papyri*;[15] the handwriting of this seems to belong to the second century AD. In this fragment someone, who is to become a teacher himself, is being taught what a *gallus*, a eunuch priest of Cybele and presumably the teacher, calls mysteries; when he is initiated he will wear female dress. These are of course mysteries of Cybele. This person then goes to a character with the heroic name Iolaus and addresses him, at which point the narrative changes from prose to verse, in Sotadeans (a metre employed by a *cinaedus* (catamite) at Petron. 23.2). He greets Iolaus and tells a *cinaedus* (Nicon?) to be silent, says he has become a *gallus* for Iolaus' sake, and declares that he knows everything about the past of Iolaus, including apparently some seamy episodes and a woman called (if a likely emendation is right) by the Odyssean name Eury-cleia (the nurse of Iolaus, as the original is of Odysseus?). He urges Iolaus accordingly not to hide anything from him; Iolaus apparently intends to engage in a deceitful amour (perhaps by

[14] See Courtney (1991) 11; Maiuri 239; Altamura, *Latinitas* 7 (1959), 48.
[15] See Stephens–Winkler 358 sqq.; Relihan (1993) 199; Morgan 3371; Reardon (1989) 816.

gaining access to a woman through a pretence of being a castrate *gallus*). Then the narrative is resumed in prose. Iolaus receives full instruction from the *gallus*, who evidently has become such at the urging of his friend Nicon. Nicon seems as a mutual friend to have given the *gallus* his information about Iolaus, and his friendship is underlined by a slightly doctored quotation from Euripides' *Orestes* 1155–7 on the subject, there dealing with Pylades and Orestes; perhaps the same sort of mock-heroic contrast as we find often in Petronius is implied. Such a direct quotation bears some resemblance to the use of tags from Homer and Menander by Chariton; in the case of Homer these are direct or adapted quotations except that one or two are integrated in the prose text.

Because of textual mutilation the above reconstruction is open to doubt at a number of points, but it is the best that can be done. There is obviously much in this to remind us of Petronius, in particular (1) the blending of squalid theme and apparently heroic allusion; (2) the mixture of prose and verse; (3) the contrast between correct Greek in the prose narrative and vulgarisms, plus the obscene word βινεῖν, to fuck,[16] in the spoken verse, as in the speech of the guests at the *Cena*; (4) the specific use of Sotadeans in a similar situation, mentioned above; both the Sotadean poems in Petronius make reference to castration, and so perhaps does this one (29 κἀποκοπημ[ ). Against point (2) Parsons himself remarks that it might be due to the fact that *galli* regularly prophesied in verse, and this point is taken up by Pabst 71–3, who compares verse oracles in the novels and argues that consequently the Iolaus-fragment can hardly be called *prosimetrum*; but equally one could hardly call what the *gallus* says either an oracle or a prophecy, and either an oracle or a prophecy in Sotadeans passes belief. If it is argued that what we have is a parody of an oracle or prophecy, then to put it in Sotadeans still means that the author was using what must be called *prosimetrum* form.

In 1981 was published a fragment of another prose narrative[17] about a prophet and *magus* called Tinuphis, with a verse

---

[16] However, primary obscenities are rare in Petronius; see Adams 215 and Ch. VIII (ii).

[17] See Stephens–Winkler 400 sqq.; Morgan 3374; Relihan (1993) 201. Note that the discussion of the metre by West, *ZPE* 45 (1982), 14, was

insert, this time not motivated as quoted speech but carrying on the narrative in the comic metre of iambic tetrameter catalectic allowing hiatus and syllaba anceps at the diaeresis, a feature perhaps due to Latin treatment of this and similar metres (it is e.g. found in a line in Greek in Varro *Satires* 357 B). This papyrus also seems to belong to the second century AD. The style and subject-matter show no affinities to Petronius.

Now we must attempt to draw some conclusions from the material which has just been assembled. First, it is clear that the novel is a genre which did not enjoy much respect among connoisseurs of literature, and was not even thought worthy of a specific name. One can certainly find qualities to admire in the extant Greek novels, particularly in Longus and Heliodorus, but over the genre there hangs an air of effete and etiolated sentimentality which must have made it distasteful to many (as, I have to admit, it does to myself) and would have invited parody. Second, it is obvious that Petronius was in fact writing not just a comic novel but a parody of a serious novel, as originally suggested by Heinze. That is apparent from the appearance of many thematic topoi, usually made ridiculous in some way, and in particular from one inverted theme which must have been clear to the first Roman readers very early in the work, namely the conversion of the heterosexual erotic theme into a homosexual one; these matters will be discussed in more detail presently (for the sexual switch see below, n. 56). Yet even at this stage the simplistic terms 'comic novel' and 'parody of a serious novel' need some amplification. They supply a generic skeleton without which the work would be incomprehensible, but Petronius is too subtle and profound a writer to leave it at that. It will become amply apparent that he has composed a novel with its own coherent approach, depicting characters whose adventures are related to great literature both by themselves and by the author Petronius.

To return to the immediate point, the postulated relationship to the serious novel at once raises two problems.

(i) The first is one of chronology. If Petronius was writing a
inadvertently omitted from the bibliography in Stephens–Winkler (referred to on p. 402).

parody of a serious novel, the serious novel must have existed in his day, and, if I was right in denying reference to Chariton in Persius, that is something which cannot be objectively proved. Even if I was wrong, we would still not be showing that prose fiction had gone much beyond its fountain-head Xenophon in freeing itself from a semblance of historical basis. At this point we must also remember the Ninus-romance,[18] the papyri of which belong to the second half of the first century AD; in fact Stephens–Winkler 26 even suggest that Chariton might be its author. If we may leave this work, which is based on historical characters to the same extent as the *Cyropedia*, out of consideration, Chariton, even if not pre-Petronian, is still almost certainly the earliest of the Greek novelists of whom we have knowledge. Decision of his date must depend primarily on assessment of his language, which shows virtually no trace of the Atticism that began to arise in the late first century AD and prevailed in the second century;[19] it has been argued that he felt that a novel did not demand pretentious Atticism, but this assessment of his style conflicts with his avoidance of hiatus and observance of clausulae, to mention just these. On this ground a dating as early as the first century BC has been proposed, though majority opinion now is probably that he belongs in the second half of the first century AD. This dating would be consistent with the claim that the kicking of the pregnant Callirhoe by Chaereas (1.4.12) alludes to that of Poppaea by Nero, which took place the year before the death of Petronius.[20] Yet even on that dating there is no problem in assuming that other writers had already gone beyond the vaguely historical stage by the time of Petronius; and that is in fact a necessary hypothesis.

(ii) The discovery of what look like two novel-fragments in *prosimetrum* form casts doubt on what was previously a solution perfectly satisfactory in itself, namely that Seneca's *Apocolocyntosis* suggested to Petronius the use of this form. The

[18] See Morgan 3330, Reardon (1989) 803. One respect in which the Ninus-romance moves beyond the *Cyropedia* is in adding a love-theme connected with the principal characters; Xenophon has nothing like this in relation to Cyrus himself.

[19] See Ruiz-Montero 1011–12, 1046–8.

[20] However Perry, 352 n. 25, produces a Herodotean parallel for this theme.

relationship of these fragments to Petronius might be any one of the following:

(*a*) The resemblances might be due to common participation in a variety of narrative types available to these authors, though no longer visible to us, and in 'a style of criminal-satiric fiction already well-established in Greek' (Stephens–Winkler 364(–5) n. 17), such as the *Phoenicica* of Lollianus; then the relationship need not be at all close.

(*b*) These Greek writers might be taking a cue from Petronius; one could support this by the possibly Latin characteristic of the metre in 'Tinuphis', but that is a weak prop.

(*c*) There might have existed already before Petronius a Greek *prosimetrum* novel.

(*d*) There might be no relationship at all, the resemblances being due to coincidence.

At the moment we really have no solid ground for deciding between these alternatives; there is some argumentation on the subject in Stephens–Winkler 365 and 402. Note, however, that on hypothesis (*a*) or (*c*) parody of the Greek novel by Petronius will be easier to comprehend. On the basis of evidence previously available we had to imagine Petronius in one language conceiving the original enterprise of parodying works written in another language, which is not a very easy supposition; now we have reasonable justification for supposing that he had Greek precedent for this aspect of his work. However, in any case we cannot dismiss the Menippean tradition in at least its formal aspect as a factor in the equation which goes to make up Petronius; it is needed, as well as the characterization, to account for the abundant literary allusion discussed in Ch. VIII (i).

If it is right then to assume that in Petronius' day there existed either one specific Greek novel, of the type best known from Xenophon of Ephesus, Achilles Tatius, and Heliodorus, which provided Petronius with the basis of his parody, or (more likely) a plurality of such novels, it is worth while to enquire tentatively what features it possessed or what features were found spread over representatives of the genre. This we will try to deduce from stylistic and thematic coincidences between

Petronius and the later novelists; here only the broad outlines will be sketched, and detailed parallels will be discussed in connection with individual passages. One underlying postulate will be the improbability of supposing that Petronius' parody supplied ideas which later novelists turned to serious use. I should like to add one caveat to this. The resemblances between Petronius and Achilles Tatius are so many and so close that in my opinion students of the latter will have to investigate carefully whether he is in fact influenced by the former, which of course bears on our assessment of the tone of his novel; but in the absence of such an investigation I have in the mean time assumed his independence for the purposes of the following sketch.[21]

In the first place there must have been a heterosexual love affair; this is self-evident. Secondly, the youthful protagonists, usually well-born or at least of bourgeois status, must have been caught up in far-flung wanderings and an assortment of tribulations (listed by Chariton 8.1.4, 'piracy and slavery and trials and fighting and suicide and war and captivity in it'), whether this entailed their separation (and consequently separate adventures) or (as in Petronius and for much of Achilles Tatius and Heliodorus) not; these tribulations may be set in train by Fortune and other persecuting gods, or so at least the characters may think, and may be steered by oracles and dreams. Their wanderings, in which they were accompanied by companions usually faithful but sometimes (e.g. Chaereas in Achilles) treacherous, very likely brought them to Egypt and involved descriptions of storm and shipwreck. Because of the beauty of the lovers there will have been assaults on their constancy to each other,[22] perhaps resulting in fits of jealousy and even attempts at suicide, but usually frustrated by their fidelity in face of force or seduction. Thirdly, it is likely that depictions of erotic themes in the visual arts, giving scope (like the descriptions of storms) to a taste for rhetorical ἔκφρασις,

---

[21] For similar reasons I make little use of Apuleius in this book. He certainly knew Petronius, and if we try to employ him to reconstruct a common original for similarities, we risk confusing the independent and the derived. In passing I will remark a close situational similarity between Ach. Tat. 5.8–9 and Apuleius, *Met.* 2.13–14.

[22] See F. Létoublon, *Les lieux communs du roman* (Leiden 1993), 180.

were employed as a counterpoint to the love affairs of the characters. Fourthly, not only the descriptive rhetoric just mentioned but also emotional rhetoric will have been prominent in the utterances of the characters, and many of the episodes will have been presented in terms drawn from the theatre. Fifthly, the technique of first-person narrative must have been introduced in the genre, which is marked overall by the three threads of love, travel, and rhetoric.

I hope that this reconstruction will not seem too speculative; of course I cannot claim more than that it is all based on reasonable assumption. One may note that a story-pattern with very similar features has been found in Gaelic narratives (Scobie, *Rh. Mus.* 122 (1979), 255).

Consider now how each of the above points is either retained by Petronius as part of the necessary framework or reversed as part of the parody. The love affair which is a continual thread through the novel is homosexual. The protagonists are the *adulescens* or *iuuenis* Encolpius and the teen-age Giton, who belong to a low social milieu; their tribulations are blamed on Fortuna (see below, p. 158) and quite likely set in train by Priapus (below, p. 153), their wanderings seem to have been dictated by an oracle and to have brought them, or to have been intended by Petronius to bring them, to Egypt (below, pp. 145–6). Dreams sent by Priapus bring them into the power of their enemies; they experience storm and shipwreck. They are accompanied by companions, Ascyltos and Eumolpus, of whom the former throughout and the latter initially (not from ch. 100 onwards, despite Encolpius' apprehensions in 100.1–2) make continual assaults on the constancy of Giton, whereas in Xenophon of Ephesus Hippothous, despite the attraction exercised by Antheia, respects his friendship for Habrocomas. These assaults are motivated by the beauty of Giton; Encolpius too is handsome (126.1–2), and this draws him (and the same is true of Giton) into heterosexual affairs, the reverse of episodes in the novels in which the heroes attract other men (Gnathon and Daphnis in Longus, Corymbus and Habrocomas in Xenophon), but never to the point of consummation. Neither Encolpius nor, for the most part, Giton feels any obligation to fidelity; admittedly in our text Encolpius is mostly homosexually faithful, though he tries to be unfaithful at 140.11 and has had sexual dealings with Ascyltos (9.10). There are outbreaks of jealousy and attempted suicides. Erotic art is discussed in a picture-gallery. Descriptive and emotional rhetoric, theatrical references abound. This will be discussed in more detail later; for the moment it will be enough to remark that whereas in the Greek novels misfortunes tend to crush the heroes completely, so that at critical moments they do not act but indulge in a torrent of lamentation, this is not so presented as to make them ridiculous, whereas in Petronius it usually is, often because of implied contrasts with heroic figures of literature or contrasts between the lofty rhetoric and its sordid occasions.

One of the differences between Petronius and the Greek novels which emerges is that in the latter the episodes form a progression towards a resolution of the plot. There must have been, or have been intended to be, some sort of resolution in Petronius, since without one it is hard to see how Encolpius could recount the events of his past life, but as one reads the work it is difficult to feel any sense of this, and in fact the characters seem to be going round in circles of repetitious situations (see below, Ch. VIII (iii)). The succession of farcical incidents provides no emphasis on motivation or continuity. The reason for this is that Petronius has taken parody of the novel as his framework, though introducing extended episodes which break away from this model (see Ch. VIII (i)). But he has conceived the plan of giving much wider literary resonances to his work; his use of the *prosimetrum* form marks it as operating on more than one stylistic level. For that purpose he has replaced the often anaemic characters of the Greek novel with characters who see life in the unrealistic terms of the theatre and grand literature. In this way characterization takes precedence over the thread of a continuous plot.

The evolutionary account of the novel given above will certainly displease devotees of the dogmatic utterances of Perry, so this section may close with a reminder of two episodes of literary history which bear a resemblance (not of course exact in all details) to that account.

First is the way in which the writers of Latin love-elegy are widely, and I believe rightly, supposed to have seen the literary potentialities inherent in the situation experienced by Catullus in his life and described in his poetry, particularly in his 76th poem. Here, as in the case of Petronius, a role in promoting this development had to be ascribed to a lost intermediary, namely Gallus; the difference of course is that we knew objectively of his existence. Confirmation of this in some details turned up with the discovery of a papyrus with a few lines by him, which corresponded in essentials with what had been deduced about him. The creative impulse given by Catullus was enriched by the introduction of themes drawn in particular from epigram, a form used by Catullus himself, and New Comedy. The serious exponents of the genre were followed by Ovid, who turned it into a humorous parody of itself.

Secondly, it is conventional, though often challenged, literary history to ascribe the rise of the English novel to Samuel Richardson at the cost of the earlier work of Daniel Defoe, much of which, one may note, had a historical basis, e.g. his *Memoirs of a Cavalier*. Anyway Richardson's novels have an ethical atmosphere very like that of the Greek novel (see Perry 62 and 83–4), and when *Pamela*, the first of them, appeared in 1740, a parody was produced in 1742 by Henry Fielding, who some years later became a Bow Street magistrate, like Petronius a capable administrator and conversant with the real world, particularly its seamy side. The point of this parody, *Joseph Andrews*, is that we no longer have a servant-girl tempted by her master, but a virtuous footman pursued by his lustful mistress. This of course is not the same sexual switch as we find in Petronius, but the general similarity in the idea of parody by reversal is striking. The parody is maintained by Fielding as far as book I ch. x, and then he gets carried away by his own invention.

Again (in this too, as will be shown, like Petronius) Fielding was a highly literary writer and combined his novel-parody with other literary aims; his title-page expresses obligations to Cervantes, and in his preface he discusses as the literary basis of his work the idea of a comic epic, which he derives from the Homeric *Margites*. Here are some of his words:

A comic romance is a comic epic poem in prose . . . It differs from the serious romance in its fable and action in this: that as in the one these are grave and solemn, so in the other they are light and ridiculous: it differs in its characters by introducing persons of inferior rank and consequently of inferior manners, whereas the grave romance sets the highest before us: lastly in its sentiments and diction, by preserving the ludicrous instead of the sublime. In the diction, I think, burlesque itself may be sometimes admitted . . . as in the description of the battles.

The last sentence refers to Fielding's fondness for describing brawls in mock-Homeric style (we might think of the brawls in Petronius 95 and 108). Behind the epic influence lies the question of the propriety of prose epic as exemplified in Fénelon's *Télémaque* (published in 1699), which was a matter of lively debate among the critics of the day. Though Fielding thus developed his ideas in this respect from contemporary literary criticism, the resemblance between his general design and that of Petronius is remarkable. This is not due to direct influence. Fielding's library included a copy of Burman's 1709 edition of Petronius (in fact he enrolled in Burman's lectures in Leiden in 1728), but none of the Greek novelists, whom, so far as I am aware, he did not know at all (Chariton indeed had not been published when he wrote, and Xenophon of Ephesus had been first published only in 1726). He could not have been expected to realize the intentions of Petronius as I see them, he does not seem to have had much liking for him, and the main classical influence on him was that of Lucian.

Making all allowances for differences, the parallels are striking; we may draw from them some support for the idea that those between the Greek *prosimetrum* fragments and Petronius could be due to coincidence.

(ii) The Employment of Verse

This section will discuss in more detail two points touched on in (i) above. First will be the employment of verse.[23] In this respect I shall say little about the fragments edited in my book *The Poems of Petronius*, since they inevitably lack a context; one of them professes to come from the mouth of a parrot (*AL* 651 = fr. 41 B = 45 M), but it may well have been

---

[23] See Pabst 66–71.

presented in context as a notice on its cage. I shall also say
nothing here about those poems spoken in character by the
poetaster Eumolpus (which perhaps included *AL* 654 = fr.
30 B = 43 M). On much the same level as these is a brief
snatch of verse composed as such by Trimalchio (55.3) and
an epigram which has obviously been composed in advance by
him (34.10). An exceptional position is also taken by what
professes to be a quotation by Trimalchio from Publilius
Syrus (55.6). Other than these specimens the *Cena* naturally
enough has no verse. The scheme of education propounded in
verse, and signalled as such, by Agamemnon (5) has a particular motivation which will be better discussed in its context
(see below, p. 59). Something has been said on pp. 22–3
above about the Sotadeans of the *cinaedus* (23.3), explicitly
labelled as an utterance in verse. Other self-contained utterances are that by the witch Oenothea (134.12) boasting of her
powers, the prayer of Encolpius to Priapus (133.3), and
probably what was no doubt a soliloquy by him in 139.2;
this last however has lost its context and could have been the
continuation of prose. Very likely Encolpius' tribute to the
beauty of Circe in 126.18 was also spoken, in view of her
pleased reaction.

At the other extreme are two passages in which the action is
moved forward in verse, 132.8 and 108. The latter is introduced thus:

in colloquium uenire ausa
    'quis furor' exclamat 'pacem conuertit in arma?'
Tryphaena . . . boldly entered the parley:
    'What madness' cries she 'turns the peace to blows?'
                        (Bracht Branham and Kinney)

It is particularly noteworthy how here prose flows into verse,
which apart from the word *exclamat* consists of Tryphaena's
appeal to the combatants, an intervention integral to the
narrative. The first line here is framed on Ascanius' address
to the Trojan women who are burning the ships at *Aen.* 5.670,
and Setaioli, *Prometheus* 24 (1998), 230, points out that *inquit* is
there sandwiched in the direct speech as *exclamat* is here. The
Vergilian cento in 132.11 may also be said to forward the
action, and so did *AL* 475 = fr. 40 B = 37 M, which begins

with *haec ait et* . . ., as does the poem in Seneca's *Apocolo-cyntosis* 4.1; in the same work the poem in ch. 15, linked to the preceding prose by an initial *nam*, also forwards the action. In the case of eleven poems the narrator simply passes (or twice in the absence of a context may be presumed to have passed) from prose to verse. Two of these are descriptive (131.8, 135.8), the others round off episodes with sententious and/or epigram-matic comments and general reflections on the essence of the action (at least one of these, 80.9, looks like a comment by the narrator subsequent to the action; see below), or give mock-elevation to the action by relating it to mythic analogues, a feature which sometimes appears incidentally in the other poems too.[24] This must be reckoned to be Petronius' pre-dominant use of verse. That his cultivated narrator should have recourse to this medium is not too great a surprise, but it is a bigger surprise when the thug Ascyltos (14.2)[25] and the depraved Quartilla (18.6) do the same. In each case an effect of incongruity is sought; this elevated medium is matched neither by the speaking character nor by the circumstances. When one looks back at the other poems coming from the narrator Encolpius, one generally finds a similar incongruity (which will be better discussed in detail as the individual poems come up in order); in one case (135.8) the incongruity between the verse description and the reality of the hovel of Oenothea has in fact aroused some comment, a matter which will be further discussed on pp. 203–4 below). The incongruity is often underlined by recall of a famous and elevated model in classical verse. A particular group of poems (79.8, 127.9, 131.8) is designed to lead up to a let-down.

The upshot is that Petronius adopts *prosimetrum* not to convey 'Menippean' manner or content, but just as a form suitable for his literary purposes. One striking divergence from Varro and Seneca is that there are no parts in Greek (except for the response of the Sibyl in 48.8) and no mingling of Latin and Greek.

---

[24] This phrasing is taken with some abbreviation from Courtney (1991) 10; I did not there remark on incongruity because the fragments to which my attention was directed lack a context.

[25] At least according to the placement of these verses by Bücheler; where the manuscripts put them they would have to be attributed to Encolpius.

The next section of this chapter will deal with the gap between Encolpius as he participates in the action at the dramatic time and as he subsequently narrates it; here we must consider how this relates to the poems (something more is said about this on pp. 219–20 below). Some of these are certainly envisaged as having been uttered in this form at the dramatic time; 23.2 has just been mentioned, and, as explained below (p. 59), ch. 5 is a pendant to a lost verse improvisation by Encolpius. 133.2 might indicate the same for the following poem, were it not that the word *uersu* is probably corrupt (the emendation *numen auersum* gives a much better clausula than *numina uersu*). But in ch.108, mentioned above, it is plain that Encolpius the narrator is versifying what Tryphaena said at the time (one might compare how Catullus 68.27–9 apparently moulds into his elegiacs words from a letter; see *BICS* 32 (1985), 98). I argue below (p. 205) that the same is true of 136.6, and it might well apply to other poems too. It seems to me likely that the poems put in the mouth of Ascyltos and Quartilla are to be understood in the same way. 79.8 refers to the action at the dramatic time in the past tense, but the following *sine causa gratulor mihi* ('I congratulate myself for no reason') shows that the conclusion *ualete, curae | mortalis; ego sic perire coepi* ('With all your cares, farewell | Mortality! So I rehearsed my dying', Bracht Branham and Kinney) does correspond to thoughts which flashed through Encolpius' mind at the time (I am assuming that *gratulor* is historic present and does not refer to the self-congratulation as it has just been expressed in the narrative).

As for the distribution of the verse, the process of excerpting here robs us of certainty, but it does look as if verse was more abundantly applied in chs. 126–39, in which Encolpius is acting out a role.

It may be useful to list the verse compositions in the *Apocolocyntosis* other than those already mentioned. Two, the speech of Hercules in his tragic role (7.2) and the lament for Claudius (12.3), are spoken in character; two (2.1 and 2.4) are parodically descriptive. Seneca of course does not use any narrator other than the authorial. The reason why he employed this form in this work was as a tribute to Menippus himself, in

whose oeuvre a description of a journey to hell, perhaps even
one to heaven, pretty certainly figured.

(iii) First-Person Narrative

The second question of technique demanding discussion here
is the use of the first-person narrator. Narrative can of course
enter into oratory and philosophical dialogue, but is primarily
at home in history, which is necessarily written in the third
person. We have here to remember that autobiography did not
exist as a literary genre; the nearest approach to such comprised the self-justifying accounts of their careers by politi-
cians, and even in this general area we have to recall that in his
Anabasis Xenophon wrote his account of his doings in the third
person, as did Julius Caesar. First-person narration is suitable
when the persona of the narrator is important, and therefore is
mostly kept for picaresque and fantastic stories, e.g. travellers'
tales;[26] the grandfather of them all is the narrative of Odysseus
in the Phaeacian court, though of course this is required by the
in medias res structure of the *Odyssey* (for the *Odyssey* and
Petronius see Ch. VI (i)). It is also appropriate for the
description of events contemporary with the author and the
reader; by implying personal experience it conveys the impression of reliability (think how poets use *uidi egomet* and the like
in such circumstances, and compare the general import of
Petronius 110.8, where Eumolpus claims that his story is *rem
sua memoria factam*, a thing which happened within his own
memory). A corollary is that events not placed in remote time
or space (*tragoedias ueteres aut nomina saeculis nota* (ibid.),
'tragedies of old or names familiar to the centuries') tend to
be less than grand or dignified (the following story of the
Widow of Ephesus!); these are often closer to the sphere of
the 'comic' as that is exemplified in New Comedy (remember
that in (i) above the association of that with prose fiction in
literary theory was remarked).

Before we turn to Petronius it is worth while to examine how
Achilles Tatius employs first-person narration. In him there is

[26] There are some interesting remarks in this direction in E. Norden,
Agnostos Theos (Leipzig and Berlin 1913) 34–5. The stories in Petron. 61–4 fit
in nicely here.

one such inside another, that of the author-figure who introduces the work and inside this that of Clitophon, who tells his
story to this author-figure. That of course implies contempor-
aneity. The question arises of the length of the interval
between the events which befell Clitophon and his narration
of them. Achilles sometimes reminds the reader of this
interval, but it seems to be small;[27] when Clitophon tells his
story he is still νεανίσκος, a young lad (1.2.1). But the first-
person technique has the potentiality of clashing with the
obligatory separations of the lovers; if the events are narrated
in the strict sequence in which they occur, how can a separ-
ated lover know at the time what is happening to his beloved?
A similar problem arises in interpreting the actions and
motives of other characters; for example, when deceit is
practised, this will only be apparent later. In such cases
what Achilles does is to allow Clitophon to carry on the
narrative like an omniscient author and subsequently reveal
how he came by the knowledge which he disclosed earlier; for
example, at 5.26.12 Melite explains to Clitophon that she has
appealed to Leucippe, who pretends to be from Thessaly, for
magic help, a fact which Clitophon had narrated in ch. 22. At
the end of the work there is a large-scale explanation (8.15.4–
fin.) how Clitophon came by much of the knowledge disclosed
earlier. But problems remain; for example, there is no way
how the hidden love of Chaereas for Leucippe (5.3.1–2) could
be known to Clitophon.[28]

Such problems also arise in the narrative of Odysseus, who
sometimes reveals knowledge which could not have been
known to him at the time of the action. For example, at
9.187–92 what he says about the Cyclops was not known to
him at the point when he relates it, and similarly what he says
about Circe at 10.135–9; the information which he imparts at
10.233 sqq. about the transformation of his companions by
Circe is only learned later partly from Eurylochus, partly from
Hermes, and partly from his own experience. At 12.389–90 he
is forced to explain his knowledge of what went on in heaven by

[27] See Hägg (1971) 126. On Clitophon as narrator and actor see now N. J.
Lowe, *The Classical Plot* (Cambridge 2000) 246–9.

[28] All this is finely discussed with more detail by Hägg ibid. 131–7; see also
Reardon (1994) 81–6 = (2000) 244–9.

communication from Hermes to Calypso and from her to himself.[29]

It is now worth while to examine briefly why Achilles adopts this troublesome technique.[30] There are two main reasons. First, it is very effective in creating suspense because of Clitophon's unawareness at the time of what is happening to Leucippe. Secondly, it convincingly gives a direct representation of the successive extremes of tumultuous emotion experienced by him.

Of these two purposes the creation of suspense is insignificant in the *Satyrica*; much more important are the generic factors expounded in the first paragraph of this discussion. However, psychological realism does play a part in a way rather different from its role in Achilles. Both Clitophon and Encolpius are narrating in the past tense, but in Achilles the interval between the events and their recounting makes no difference to Clitophon's view of those events; in Petronius on the other hand it occasionally becomes clear that Encolpius is looking back at the events with a certain detachment and even amusement, though at the time he presents himself as thinking of them in a semi-tragic light; thus the irony of the narrator, who as such is sophisticated and competent, converges with that of the author. For instance, in 7.1 in desperation he enquires from a stranger if she knows the location of his lodging, a question which he then calls *urbanitas stulta*, a silly witticism; likewise at 126.8 he calls a remark of his a *frigidum schema*, a frigid ploy. Again in 95.1 after the theatrical attempt at suicide of Giton and himself, called a *mimica mors* (death-scene in a farce), he proceeds *dum haec fabula inter amantes luditur* ('While this love-drama was being played out', Sullivan), a remark which surely looks back to recognize the absurdity of the scene. There is another such remark at 41.5. These are comments of the narrator at a distance from the action (and at 65.5 Agamemnon also accuses him of naivety). This narratorial distance implies[31] a chronological gap, perhaps

---

[29] See Heubeck on *Od.* 9.182, 10.210, and (referred to by him) Suerbaum, *Poetica* 2 (1968), 156 sqq.

[30] See Effe, *Poetica* 7 (1975), 150–1; Reardon (1994) 86.

[31] See Beck (1973) (esp. 61, 'the young Encolpius' contrasted with 'the older Encolpius'); (1975); (1982) (esp. 208 'his younger self')—articles which

of sufficient size to permit us to assume that a more mature
Encolpius is looking back at his callow youth (one would guess
that he is in his twenties at the time of the action), but not
enough to bring him to old age.

Nevertheless there is a gap, even if it is to be regarded mainly
as part of a literary technique. That leads on to Petronius'
manipulation of first-person narrative, as best we can grasp it
in the mutilated state of the text. Just as in Achilles Tatius and
Homer, the narrator Encolpius sometimes introduces into the
narrative details which the actor Encolpius did not at the time
know but subsequently ascertained. Thus at 126.4 the geese
which attacked Encolpius are called *sacri* by the narrator,
though the actor did not know this until 137.1–2.[32] In 17.2
Quartilla's tears are described as 'summoned to display grief'
and a 'calculated downpour', but their artificial character is not
apparent to Encolpius and company until 18.7. At 90.1
Eumolpus' poem earns him a pelting with stones, and he,
'familiar with the reception of his talent', covers his head and
runs away from the picture-gallery; but Encolpius the actor
does not know until 90.5 that such a reception is familiar to
Eumolpus. The same feature is found at 33.6 (see Ch. IV n. 25),
83.7 (below, p. 135), and 94.14. (p. 148).

One must, however, note that at least once Petronius goes
beyond this innocuous presumption and, like Achilles, makes
Encolpius aware of things which he has no way of knowing. In
22, while Encolpius and the other participants in the orgy have
fallen into an exhausted sleep, two Syrian thieves enter the
room and in a quarrel create a clatter, which awakens some of
the drunken debauchees; the Syrians, unable to escape, lie down
and pretend to have been asleep like everyone else. Encolpius
has no means of knowing all this, nor can he know that the street
dealer of 15.4 also sometimes acted as an attorney.[33] The

despite some reservations remain fundamental for the distinction between
actor and narrator.

[32] See Courtney (1991) 45 and *MD* 40 (1998), 205, for a defence of the
word *sacri*, deleted by Müller on the explicit grounds that at this stage of the
action Encolpius did not yet know the status of the goose, else he would not
have killed it.

[33] Bracht Branham and Kinney feel so uncomfortable with this that they
insert 'he said' in their translation.

drunkenness of the concierge at 79.6, not known to Encolpius while he was pounding on the door of the inn, may have been represented as coming to his knowledge in the following gap, or may have been let go as an insignificant detail. A motivation which Encolpius could not know is attributed to Ascyltos at 97.7. If the text is right at 104.5 (though probably it is not), it is never explained how the name of the passenger who draws attention to Encolpius and Giton became known to them.

The moral of all this is that we always have to try to distinguish evaluative comments on the action which are instantaneous from those which are to be understood as a product of reflection made at the time when the narrative is represented as being recounted, while recognizing that sometimes this will be impossible or immaterial, e.g. when Encolpius brands his actions as rashness at 82. 4.

(iv) The Identity of the Protagonists

The characters who appear throughout the action of the novel are Encolpius and Giton; at the beginning they are accompanied by Ascyltos, who does not seem to have been in their company for long (10.7) and disappears after ch. 98. It will be convenient to discuss here these three characters and to deal with the others as they appear on the scene.

Who are these people? Conte's answer is that they are *scholastici*, 'declamation-buffs' or 'aficionados', the groupies of the Roman world who hung around the schools of declamation and, as far as they could, aped their style in everyday dealings.[34] This view is essentially based on two passages, 10.6, where Ascyltos says *tamquam scholastici ad cenam promisimus* ('We have accepted a dinner-invitation as' [this word is deliberately evasive; see below] *'scholastici'*), and 61.4, where Niceros says *timeo istos scholasticos ne me [de]rideant* ('I fear that those *scholastici* may laugh at me'); somewhat less specific is Trimalchio's joke (39.5) at the expense of some of his guests, *plurimi hoc signo scholastici nascuntur* ('many *scholastici* are born under this sign'), which is followed by the reaction *laudamus urbanitatem mathematici* ('we praise his astrological wit').

[34] Cf. 6.1; see Conte 2 n. 2, Kennedy, *AJP* 99 (1978), 174–5.

These passages fail to support Conte's theory. Encolpius and
company have been invited to Trimalchio's dinner-party as
umbrae, people not known to the host but brought along by one
of the other guests, in this case the rhetor Agamemnon;
Trimalchio and Niceros, seeing them in his company, just
assume that they are *scholastici*. Hermeros makes the same
assumption when in abusing Ascyltos he refers to Agamemnon
as *magister tuus*, your teacher (57.8, cf. 58.13). As for 10.6, in
Latin of this date *tamquam* can mean either 'as if we were
scholastici' or (so 99.2, 102.13) 'in our capacity as *scholastici*'.
Conte assumes the second, but the first is actually more
pointed; misrepresentation does not matter to these rogues if
it will secure a free meal.[35] Not long before (10.2) Ascyltos had
reproached Encolpius with his willingness to praise
Agamemnon's verses of ch. 5 in order to secure an invitation.

We then recur to the question who they are. First, they have
Greek names, like all the main characters in the novel except
Quartilla,[36] but they are not Greeks; Encolpius disparagingly
describes Puteoli (I agree with the majority opinion that this is
the scene of the *Cena*) as a 'Greek city' (81.3)[37] and a *locus
peregrinus*, a foreign place (80.8), though most of the places
which seem to have been visited are hellenic (including
Marseilles; see below). Though Encolpius can at least spout
the names of Greek classic writers (2.3–8; also Callimachus
135.8), just as Giton can refer to Eteocles and Polynices (80.3)
and Alcibiades and Socrates (128.7), yet his literary culture, a
prominent feature of his characterization, is predominantly
Roman in colour; Giton's references to Greek literary figures

[35] The point is taken by Kennedy.

[36] Circe's name is no doubt a pseudonym. The name Quartilla seems to be
associated with rather upper-class ladies (M. Kajava, *Roman Female Praenomina* (Rome 1994) 131 n. 231), in which case it would be chosen to underline
the contrast between her social standing and her depravity. Novels ancient
and modern are full of women of respectable social standing but concealed
libidinous diversions. There was also the enigmatic Albucia in fr. 6, who
seems to have been of similar character.

[37] In its role as a 'Greek city' Puteoli is Dicaearchia, whereas as a *colonia* in
44.12 and 16, 57.9, 76.10 it is Puteoli. It might also be spoken of as a *Graeca
urbs* because it was overrun by Greek speakers from the Eastern Mediter-
ranean, as Rome itself is so described at Juv. 3.61. The discord between social
classes at Puteoli in AD 58 (Tac. *Ann.* 13.48) fits, though it is not required by,
the complaints of Ganymedes (ch. 44).

are balanced by Ascyltos' references (9.5) to Lucretia and
Tarquin. The characters, in short, have more Roman than
Greek about them; in this way Petronius transfers the social
milieu of the Greek novel, which ignores the contemporary
reality of the Roman empire and, apart from Chariton, leaves
its temporal setting vague, into something more immediate to
his Roman readers. All this leads us to suppose that they are to
be conceived as belonging to the large class of educated freedmen,[38] of undetermined ethnic background;[39] their names
would be those given by their former owners, which would
function as their cognomina when they had been freed.[40]
Confirmation of this is found at 81.4, where Ascyltos is
described as *stupro liber, stupro ingenuus* ('he acquired freedom
and free birth through depravity'), meaning that he had won
his freedom by sexual services to his former owner (*nec turpe est
quod dominus iubet* ['whatever your owner imposes is no
disgrace'], says Trimalchio (75.11) of similar circumstances
in his own life); the wording suggests that the former owner
had colluded with Ascyltos in a legal action in which he
claimed free birth.[41] In the same context reference is made to
a stay by Giton in an *ergastulum*, a slave-prison. A little below
(81.5) we read in Müller's text a seemingly contradictory
reference to Giton's *die togae uirilis*, the day on which he
assumed an adult *toga*, but in the manuscripts this is accompanied by a *tamquam* ('as if' in this case) deleted by Müller
after others; this should probably be retained somewhere, so
that the reference becomes merely a comparison to a similar
stage in the growing up of a citizen boy. On the other side may
be quoted 107–8, where in his defence of Encolpius and Giton
Eumolpus claims that they are *ingenui*, but he is just extempor-
izing in order, as Lichas says (107.10), to create odium. Like-

[38] Suetonius, *De Grammaticis et Rhetoribus*, lists many such; see R. A.
Kaster's edition (Oxford 1995) p. 117.

[39] See the discussion of ethnic origins by J. Christes, *Sklaven und
Freigelassene als Grammatiker und Philologen* (Wiesbaden 1979) 165 sqq. In
view of what will be said in the next section about Marseilles, it may be as well
to point out that 102.14 shows them not to be Gauls.

[40] Greek names were often given to Western slaves; see A. M. Duff,
Freedmen in the Early Roman Empire (Cambridge 1928, repr. with addenda
and corrigenda 1958) 5.

[41] See J. A. Crook, *Law and Life of Rome* (London 1967) 55.

wise when a slave-girl says to Encolpius (113.11) *si quid ingenui sanguinis habes* ('if you have a free-born man's blood in your veins'), that is just an expression of reproach; the slave-girl does not know the biography of Encolpius.

One notices throughout the novel that characters sometimes bear names which seem providentially appropriate, Eumolpus the poetaster for instance.[42] There is also Fortunata, 'Wealthy', the wife of Trimalchio, whose name[43] is introduced with stress on its appropriateness in 37.2, *Fortunata appellatur, quae nummos modio metitur* ('she is called Fortunata, and measures money by the bushel'). Her husband's name too is entirely suitable, as are those of Pannychis, Proselenos, and Oenothea; these will be discussed later. As with Fortunata, the name of Tryphaena (from τρυφᾶν, 'to live luxuriously'), not an uncommon name,[44] has its application underlined when Eumolpus introduces it (101.5 *Tryphaena . . . quae uoluptatis causa huc atque illuc uectatur*, 'Tryphaena who for her pleasure travels hither and thither'; but note that this was not her first appearance in the unmutilated novel). The name Ascyltos, which received its first and unique epigraphic attestation in an inscription published in 1966,[45] is the adjective ἄσκυλτος, untroubled (applied to a man in *Pap. Ox.* 532.14); it well fits this insensitive and swaggering character. Encolp(i)us itself ('bosom companion') is quite a common slave-name,[46] which suggests itself as the name of a *puer delicatus*, a mignon, and it would not be surprising if Encolpius had earned his freedom by the same means as Ascyltos; that aura certainly well fits the character in Petronius.

If in a rationalistic spirit we enquire how such appropriateness could have come about, we can sometimes devise an answer; one could, for instance, envisage Trimalchio's former owner noticing his lordly, Malvolio-like ways and poking fun at

[42] See Priuli 65 n. 219. Since Eumolpus is by no means a 'sweet singer', this name belongs to the category of *antiphrasis*, as large men are still often nicknamed 'Tiny'; see Cèbe 156, J. B. Hofmann and A. Szantyr, *Lateinische Syntax und Stilistik* (Munich 1965) 777, and my note on Juvenal 8.30.

[43] For occurrences of this name see Dessau's index to his *Inscriptiones Latinae Selectae*, III. 1.196.

[44] See Priuli 51.

[45] See Priuli 7; the adjective ἄσκυλτος is of predominantly medical use.

[46] See Priuli 47 and 64, Howell on Mart. 1.31.2.

them by bestowing this name (cf. below, p. 77). But Petronius shows no interest in any such explanation, and it is best to answer this question, which we are simply intended not to raise, by another; what providence arranged that Mr. Gradgrind and Mr. Boundersby in Dickens' *Hard Times* should bear names so fitting to their characters? Such significant names are found in comedy and elsewhere (with Oenothea we may compare Ovid's Dipsas), even, though not a prominent feature, in the Greek novel itself.[47]

(v) The Lost Early Books

Two fragments provide some basis for conjecture about the beginning of the novel. In fr. 1 Servius in his note on *Aen.* 3.57 states that whenever Marseilles suffered from pestilence it was usual for one of the poor citizens to offer himself, after being supported for a year at public expense, to be cursed and driven out of the city,[48] so that the travails of the whole city would fall on his head. This is the ancient institution of the φαρμακός or scapegoat. Servius states that this was referred to in Petronius, and it is hard to see how else it could have been introduced except on the supposition that Encolpius, who speaks of his *tandem expugnata paupertas* ('poverty at long last vanquished') in 125.4 (cf. Ascyltos in 10.4), offered himself as a scapegoat. In 107.15 Lichas actually abuses him as *pharmace*, but, while it is possible that Encolpius and Giton first encountered Lichas at Marseilles, this may simply refer back to Lichas' demand (105.1) for some victim to purify the ship from pollution. It is less likely that it is just a term of abuse (see LSJ s.v.). One may note that in the utopian travel narrative (not a novel) of Iambulus, who perhaps belongs around 200 BC, the protagonist

---

[47] See Rohde 402 n. 2, Ruiz-Montero 1107–9, A. Billault, 'Characterization in the Ancient Novel' (in Schmeling 123–4). One may add the messenger Eudromus in Longus (4.5 draws attention to the appropriateness of the name); a gossip called Konops ('Gnat') in Ach. Tat. 1.20 with reference to incessant droning; Thermouthis ('Asp'), who dies by snake-bite in Heliod. 2.20 (Reardon (1989) 392 n. 46).

[48] The reading *proiciebatur* is not to be altered to *praecipitabatur*; see Bremmer, *HSCP* 87 (1983), 316 n. 1, and for the sense 'banish' Stöcker 25 n. 2 and *OLD* s.v. 7b.

and a companion were made purificatory scapegoats (Diod.
Sic. 2.55.3–5), but there is probably no significance in this.

In fr. 4 Sidonius Apollinaris (*Carm.* 23.155–7; totally misunderstood by W. B. Anderson in the Loeb edition and *CQ* 28
(1934), 22) lists Petronius among writers who would have taken
second place to the father of Consentius:

> et te Massiliensium per hortos
> sacri stipitis, Arbiter, colonum,
> Hellespontiaco parem Priapo.

Here *colonum* evidently means, as it sometimes does in late
Latin (*TLL* 3.1712.24), *cultorem*, worshipper, so that the
translation will be 'you, Arbiter, worshipper of the sacred
stake through the gardens of Marseilles, a match for Priapus
of Lampsacus'; the *sacer stipes* may be either the whole rough
wooden effigy of Priapus, many of which would have been
found in the gardens of Marseilles, or its huge phallus.
Sidonius is clearly equating the first-person narrator Encolpius
with the author; one may, in a general way, compare how,
absurdly identifying Corinna with Julia, he takes Ovid's
Amores as autobiographical (160–1). Closer is Fulgentius'
statement that Petronius declares that he drank an aphrodisiac
(fr. 7; the various confusions in the statement do not affect the
immediate point). Think too how Augustine, *CD* 18.18,
suggests (not with full conviction) that the *Metamorphoses* of
Apuleius may be autobiographical.[49] The epithet *Hellesponti-
acus* Sidonius could have got from Vergil (*Georg.* 4.111), but he
is probably alluding specifically to Petronius' (139.2) borrow-
ing of the word from Vergil; *parem* will mean that Encolpius'
(not Petronius') virility matched that of Priapus, as it certainly
does in much of our text. It is unsafe to go beyond this and
make a connection with the alleged theme of the wrath of
Priapus, which will be discussed in Ch. VI (i); here it need just
be noted that the point will be important for elucidation of
133.3.8–9.

What remains as a conjectural but plausible deduction is that
Encolpius offered himself as scapegoat, and during his year of
public support at Marseilles indulged himself sexually in the

[49] For the phenomenon in bucolic see Reed, *CP* 92 (1997), 264.

gardens of Marseilles (this reminds us of the plane-grove of
126.12 and 131.1 and the *uiridarium* (park) in which Encolpius
and Ascyltos had congress, 9.10; Encolpius seems to like
alfresco love-making); then after his ritual expulsion he will
have begun his wanderings. This supposition would make
Marseilles a suitable starting-point for the narrative, and
would explain why Encolpius calls himself an exile (81.3).
Giton also is an exile (100.4; but Sullivan inclines to delete
the word or alter it to *eum*), and 81.4, though somewhat
ambiguous, may mean that Ascyltos is one and deserves it;
the other possibility is that Encolpius regards Ascyltos as
deserving *relegatio*, a milder form of exile, under the *lex Iulia*
as a penalty for 'adultery' (which, with a characteristic Petronian sex-reversal, will probably mean homosexual infidelity).
At any rate, Encolpius' wanderings seem to have moved east
(and, in a minor degree, south). We know that he was at Rome
(69.9; there is an implication that he was not familiar with
Roman customs); from there he seems to have gone to Naples,
from which he apparently doubled back a few miles through
the *crypta Neapolitana* (fr. 16; for ch. 16.3 see below, p. 65), a
tunnel through a cliff on the shore road, to Puteoli. A setting of
an episode at Baiae, west of Puteoli, has been inferred from
104.2, but in the first place the reading there is uncertain,
though *Bais* does seem to emerge, and in the second, even
accepting this reading, all that is said is that Tryphaena has
been at Baiae, which she could quite naturally have passed
through on her way south to Puteoli, not that Encolpius and
Giton were there with her.

At any rate Encolpius and company take sea-passage from
Puteoli and are shipwrecked near Croton, which is where our
text ends. There is, however, one fragment (37 B = 31 M = *AL*
469) which suggests that farther wanderings were at least
planned. This fragment seems to represent the words of a
prophecy or oracle[50] which states that Encolpius (he is no
doubt intended by the word *iuuenis*) will visit the northern,
eastern, and western ends of the earth, specifically *ultimus
Hister* and the playboy resort of Canopus, which presumably

---

[50] As I pointed out in (1991) 53, there are oracles foretelling the action in
Xenophon of Ephesus and Heliodorus; that in Xenophon prophesies arrival in
Egypt (see below).

represents the south and which would have provided a fine field for his roguery. The latter is interesting, because four of the extant Greek novels at some point bring their characters to Egypt (and so did Iamblichus), for reasons validated in the text only by Heliodorus,[51] though Chariton has the justification that he is basing himself (anachronistically) on an actual historical revolt in Egypt. Fr. 19 describes Egyptian participants in a ritual, but it is not certain that the ritual takes place in Egypt itself. How this prominence of Egypt is to be explained has been a matter of much controversy on which it is here unnecessary to enter. This presumed prophecy or oracle must have come early in the work, and according to an almost certain emendation it describes its recipient as 'a greater Odysseus'; the role of the *Odyssey* in the novel will be discussed in Ch. VI (i). One must, however, feel some doubt about all this, since we have no reason to suppose that Encolpius reached the Danube or the far north, and we cannot suggest any reason why he should have.

Something may be gleaned from references back in the text of the novel. It is clear that Encolpius and Giton have had contact with Lichas and Tryphaena. The wife of Lichas, perhaps called Hedyle (113.3; for the name see Solin (1982) 878), has been seduced, no doubt by Encolpius (106.2); this seduction is coupled with Encolpius' robbery of a sacred robe and a *sistrum* (a rattle used in the cult of Egyptian deities) from the ship (113.3, 114.5),[52] probably from the figurehead (*tutela* 105.4, 108.3; cf. *OLD* s.v. 2b), and also with an elopement (*libidinosa migratio* 113.3). All this is often placed at Baiae, but, apart from the uncertainty about 104.2 discussed above, the space between Baiae and Puteoli seems uncomfortably small to motivate the disappearance of Hedyle from the narrative after the elopement; moreover the word *aliquando* (*amicissimis, familiaritate uobis coniuncti*) in 107.1 and 5 ('at one time close friends, linked to you by friendship') suggests a considerable interval. I should prefer to follow up a hint given above and suggest that Hedyle was seduced by the Priapus-like Encolpius

[51] Xenophon of Ephesus 3.10.4 drags in Egypt in a particularly silly way, perhaps because of abridgement.

[52] The ship will have been called the *Isis*, like others, e.g. that in Lucian, *Navigium*; cf. my note on Juv. 12.28.

at Marseilles and eloped thence with him. Note how Lichas identifies Encolpius (105.9) by the size of his genitals, which probably means that he too had had a sexual relationship with Encolpius (another triangular liaison); this seems to be implied by the stipulation that Lichas is not to investigate where Encolpius sleeps (109.3), which suggests an element of jealousy, and by Encolpius' upset that 'not even' Lichas bestowed a word on him in his ugly state (110.4). However, in the light of this passage it is unwarranted to compare 87.1 and 6 and see a sexual undertone in the earlier *Lichas redire mecum in gratiam coeperat* (109.8; 'Lichas had begun to reconcile himself with me'), even though a little later Lichas' feelings for Encolpius seem to have revived (113.10). We cannot guess what the wrongs (106.2) done to Lichas were.

As for Tryphaena, it is not apparent that she and Lichas have any relationship other than that she is a passenger on his ship (they do not sleep together; 104.2), but, however they met (and the Greek novels are full of coincidental meetings),[53] each clearly has some awareness of the other's involvement with Encolpius and, in Tryphaena's case, Giton. Encolpius has been Tryphaena's lover (113.7–8), but she has been much more involved with Giton, and it is he who has deceived her (100.4, 109.2, implied also 108.10); as a result of her entanglement she has suffered public disgrace (106.4).

Other allusions are less specific (130.2 is not one of them, but merely rhetorical exaggeration), except that to a previous lover of Encolpius called Doris (126.18). At 9.8 Ascyltos hurls some insults at Encolpius. The first is *gladiator obscene, quem de ruina harena dimisit*. The text is suspected here, but with no solid reason; it means that Encolpius had been condemned to fight as a gladiator, but had escaped as a result of (see *OLD, de* 14) the collapse of the amphitheatre; Tacitus, *Ann.* 4.62, describes the collapse of a jerry-built amphitheatre at Fidenae in AD 27, and one might also imagine an earthquake causing such a providential catastrophe. We might link fr. 13 with such an episode

---

[53] For coincidental encounters in the Greek novel see Galli, *GCN* 7 (1996), 33 (e.g. Heliod. 2.11, Xen. Eph. 2.14); in Petronius there are such at 7–8, 12.3, 92.7. The very presence of Encolpius and Giton on Lichas' ship is such a coincidence, brought about by Fortuna (100.3, 101.1), just as Tyche motivates such things in the Greek novel.

if it came from a reliable source. There follow *nocturne percussor* ('assassin by night'), to be discussed in a moment, and aspersions on Encolpius' virility. At 81.3 Encolpius claims *effugi iudicium, harenae imposui, hospitem occidi* ('I escaped the law, cheated the arena, killed my host'). This comes in a rhetorical resumé of past tribulations surmounted in contrast to what seems to be impending doom; such resumés are common in the Greek novel (they will be discussed below (pp. 131–2) and are necessarily veracious (cf. Courtney (1962) 98 n. 1). Fr. 14 clearly comes from such a trial scene, perhaps also fr. 8 if it were reliable. 'I cheated the arena' will allude to the same episode as 9.8, and *hospitem occidi* will also link with *nocturne percussor*[54] there. At a guess, the *hospes* may have been the cruel Lycurgus whose villa they had robbed (83.6 *hospitem Lycurgo crudeliorem*, 'a companion more cruel than Lycurgus'; 117.3); perhaps this name was chosen for him as significant, intended to recall the cruelty of the mythical Lycurgus (ἀνδρο-φόνοιο Λυκούργου, *Iliad* 6.134). Some doubt, however, must be felt about all this because it seems to clash with Encolpius' claim at 133.3.6–7 *non sanguine tristi | perfusus uenio*, 'I do not come stained by grim blood' (perhaps this is meant only to have an immediate reference; see below, p. 154), and with our conception of his fainthearted character, discussed later in this chapter.

Finally in 105.10–11 Encolpius and Giton are referred to as *fugitiui*, runaways, in relation to Lichas and Tryphaena. More-over Eumolpus, who has been informed of the past dealings of Encolpius and Giton with Lichas (101.6), points out that they must not *ultro dominum ad fugientes accersere*, 'take the initia-tive in summoning the owner to runaways' (101.10), and in 113.10 Lichas seeks to treat Encolpius not as *dominus* but as

---

[54] This phrase is followed by *qui ne tum quidem, cum fortiter faceres, cum pura muliere pugnasti* ('Even on your good days you never found a decent woman to have a go at', Walsh). This makes it plain that a sexual pun on *percussor*, 'piercer' is intended (Adams 147), though the sexual undertone can hardly be the primary implication. We can only guess the reference of the rest; my guess would be that Encolpius has had some relations with a woman to whom Ascyltos attributes *fellatio* (cf. 9.6 and Adams 199; Ascyltos is retorting to this insult to himself), not necessarily with truth (see below, p. 224). For military and gladiatorial metaphors applied to sex see Apul. *Met.* 2.16–17, and Adams 158–9.

amicus. Since, if the above reconstruction of the beginning of
the novel at Marseilles is right, even then Encolpius must have
been free (which he certainly is; 81.6), it may be that he and
Giton were in fact freedmen of Lichas, and had run away
without performance of the *operae* (duties, services) which such
owed to their patron.

(vi) Characterization

This section is intended only to outline the background knowledge which the first readers will have had from the earlier
parts of the novel; points made here will be developed in the
coming chapters with more specificity.

When our text begins, Encolpius, Giton, and Ascyltos are
linked in a love-triangle; their relationship is euphemistically
described by the word *fratres*, brothers.[55] While Encolpius and
Ascyltos are each deeply involved with Giton (whom Encolpius
has known much longer than Ascyltos; 10.9), they have also
been involved with each other (9.10), and despite his machismo
Ascyltos had been willing to be the passive partner in a
previous homosexual relationship (81.4). As for Giton, who
is now aged about sixteen (97.2), it was his mother who set him
on his career as a homosexual prostitute, which came in handy
when he was in a slave prison (81.5). Like Encolpius, he is
bisexual;[56] he deflowers Pannychis and has had an affair with

---

[55] See John Boswell, *Same-sex Unions in Premodern Europe* (New York
1994) 67, with some reservations about details, and C. A. Williams, *Roman
Homosexuality* (Oxford 1999) 223–4.

[56] Richardson, *Class. et Med.* 35 (1984), 105, a useful survey of sexual
attitudes in the *Satyrica*, reminds us that this word did not carry in the
ancient world its modern tone of disapproval, but was regarded as the
normal nature of man. This should not be taken to invalidate the point
made in (i) above about the reversal of sexual interest in Petronius as
contrasted with the Greek novel; the change involves both the omnipresence
of consummated sex (or attempts at consummation) and the prominence
given to homosexuality. Sullivan 96, also stressing bisexuality (notorious in
the case of Nero), blurs the issue when he casts doubt on the idea that the
Romans would regard homosexuality as a parody of heterosexuality; the
point is not about sexuality in life, but whether a homosexual narrative is a
parody of a heterosexual one. Moreover the terminology of divorce applied
when the characters split up is a clear indication that deliberate reversal is
intended (79.11, 94.6). For the occasional appearance of pederasty in the

Tryphaena. This affair also had been triangular, involving Encolpius too (see above, p. 47).

The main characters[57] portrayed by Petronius are empty, ineffective, and sterile; they base themselves generally on an inn, have no goal in life and no place in society, and live outside the law (125.4). To anticipate a little, this marginalization applies to all the characters. The upper-class women Quartilla and Circe consort with the dregs of society; the freedmen cannot move above a glass ceiling; Eumolpus cannot gain recognition for his poetry. Encolpius in modern terms might be considered a manic-depressive with wild mood-swings; he has no inner core of personality, and his reactions to events are unstable. The one constant in his character is love of Giton, which requires much self-deception in order to cope with Giton's repeated infidelity. He makes inadequate and comic attempts to understand what he observes, and in many cases is quickly disillusioned. In the *Cena* in particular he moves from being naively impressed to disgust; this shows a certain progress to blasé braggadocio, but he is liable to fall back into nervous and timid reactions (he bursts into tears at least eight times in our text). When he meets a stronger character he becomes submissive, and he is often a passive victim of events or other people. From time to time he is impelled to violence (and indeed he seems actually to have committed a murder; see above) and thoughts of suicide, but generally this comes to nothing.

He is well-educated, but cannot usefully and in a steady way apply this asset (*litterae thesaurum est* ['literacy is a treasure'], says Echion (46.8) illiterately; Hermeros knows that *thesaurus* is correct, 57.9); 10.5, however, suggests that he contemplated regular employment in association with Agamemnon. What he does with his education is to use it as a substitute for realistic efforts to cope with problems and a medium for interpreting and heightening his emotional reactions to events that overwhelm him. This comes out very clearly in many of the poems

Greek novel see Sandy, *AJP* 90 (1969), 299 n. 16. The O-excerpts eliminate pederastic episodes in Petronius.

[57] Much of my phraseology will be found to echo that of H. D. Rankin in his discussion of characterization in Petronius, *Petronius the Artist* (The Hague 1971) 11 sqq. (= *Eranos* 68 (1978), 123).

(see (ii) above), and the histrionic character of many of his
fantasies is accentuated by the dramatic vocabulary in which a
number of them is couched (more on this below, p. 162). The
misplaced poem in 80.9 comments on the play-acting by the
characters. Encolpius, as will be seen, uses literary episodes to ✓
cast himself as first this hero, then that. Petronius may in this
have developed a hint from the Greek novel, in which characters sometimes draw literary parallels[58] in relation to others,
but seldom (Chariton 7.3.5 is one of these rare cases) to
themselves; e.g. in Ach. Tat. 2.23.3 the slave who has drugged
the custodian says to Clitophon 'Your Cyclops' (this word is a
brilliant emendation) 'is asleep; see that you prove yourself a
brave Odysseus', which is particularly interesting in view of
Petronius' use of the same paradigm (to be discussed in
Ch. VI (i)). There is a similar instance in Chariton 5.10.1.
Encolpius' literary culture has a technical advantage for Petronius in that it enables him to integrate verse, whether spoken
by Encolpius or other characters, into the fabric of the novel in
a way absent from Seneca (though Seneca's verses sometimes
have specific motivation in the context) and, so far as we can
tell, the papyrus comic fragments. In the case of Encolpius, we
can at least sometimes interpret the verse as the product of
reflection on his adventures in the interval between the events
and their narration; see (ii) above.

Giton goes through life playing off one partner against
another; in such contexts Encolpius is often placed in the
position of the jealous 'husband' (cf. 81.5). When stirring up
jealousy does not work and quarrels break out that are too
fierce for Giton to control, then he applies moral blackmail by
threats of suicide. Like Encolpius he is well-educated (see
above, p. 40, for his literary references), but he is much more
practical, e.g. at finding his way about a strange town; and this
is consistent with his strong eye for his own advantage.

Ascyltos is more robust, less hysterical and complex than
Encolpius and Giton, but he too is cultured enough to interact
with the rhetorician Agamemnon, to be able to make a living
from his education (10.5), and to make literary references (9.5).
Like Trimalchio, he seems to wish to pose as an *eques* by

[58] See Steiner 128.

wearing gold rings (58.10); Hermeros sees through this and declares that Ascyltos is as much an *eques* as he himself is a king's son (57.4). This is a claim apparently made about Roman slaves from time to time (for Pallas see above, pp. 8–9, and for Nero's freedwoman and mistress Acte see Suet. 28.1, Dio Cass. 61.7.1; more in Nisbet–Hubbard on Hor. *Odes* 2.4.15); indeed this is probably why so many slaves were called Malchio, with the Greek diminutive ending added to the stem Malchus (= 'King'; see below, p. 77) as a subtle undermining of the claim. Malchio seems in fact to have become something of a type name; Martial (3.82.32) applies it to his Zoilus, who shares some features with Trimalchio (Opimian wine 24; his assistant for urination at the snap of his fingers 15–17, cf. Petron. 27.5). Hermeros then ironically uses his true background, namely his voluntary submission to slavery, as if it corroborated his fantasy autobiography against the incredulous.

The nature of the characterization in Petronius is somewhat limited by various factors, and in the first place by the vehicle of first-person narrative, which means that the narrator Encolpius comes across as he sees himself, though, since the action is set in the past, at the time of narration he has the benefit of hindsight, and occasionally displays an amused self-irony at his naivety at the time of the action (some instances have been remarked in (iii) above). The other characters are also presented through the eyes of Encolpius or occasionally those of others (see below, p. 87). Secondly, Petronius is portraying people who are often acting a part, and this tends to expel whatever core of real personality they possess (notoriously this happened with the actor Peter Sellers). Therefore we do not find any deep exploration of character; what takes place is the ironical technique of allowing the characters to reveal themselves in what they say. However, by contrast with the main characters of the Greek novel, one could certainly not say that those of Petronius lack individuality and idiosyncrasy.

To conclude this chapter it will, I think, be interesting to recall some remarks by Northrop Frye, *The Anatomy of Criticism* (Princeton 1957) 308–10, to which attention is drawn by Relihan 4. After classifying the novel as extroverted and personal, the romance as introverted and personal, the confession as introverted and intellectual, he looks for a form of fiction which is extroverted and intellectual, and finds this in what he calls Menippean satire (a term which, like Bakhtin, he uses in a rather loose sense). Here are some of his remarks about this:

The Menippean satire deals less with people as such than with mental attitudes. Pedants, bigots, cranks, parvenus, virtuosi, enthusiasts, rapacious and incompetent professional men of all kinds, are handled in terms of their occupational approach to life as distinct from their social behaviour [I am not sure that I grasp the point of this sentence: E.C.]. The Menippean satire thus resembles the confession in its ability to handle abstract ideas and theories, and differs from the novel in its characterization, which is stylized rather than naturalistic, and presents people as mouthpieces of the ideas they represent . . . The novelist sees evil and folly as social diseases, but the Menippean satirist sees them as diseases of the intellect, as a kind of maddened pedantry . . . [the disjointed narrative form used by Petronius] relies on the free play of intellectual fancy and the kind of humorous observation that produces caricature . . . At its most concentrated the Menippean satire presents us with a vision of the world in terms of a single intellectual pattern. The intellectual structure built up from the story makes for violent dislocations in the customary logic of narrative, though the appearance of carelessness that results reflects only the carelessness of the reader or his tendency to judge by a novel-centered conception of fiction.

III

Book XIV

(i) 1–5, Rhetoric

When our text begins, Encolpius is in the middle of a discussion with a teacher of rhetoric called Agamemnon; it emerges later (27.4–5, 81.1) that the latter has an assistant called Menelaus, from which we infer that they are freedmen who have been given these names by a whimsical former owner (Roman slave-owners were quite fond of such paired names as Amphion and Zethus etc.[1]). The topic of their conversation is the harmful effect of the practice of declamation on Roman education. Many criticisms of this practice are to be found in Roman writers of the first century AD. Cassius Severus is quoted by the elder Seneca (*Contr.* 3 pr. 12 sqq.) as deploring the gulf between declamation and forensic practice (remarked even by Seneca himself, 10 pr. 12; cf. Petron. 1.2), Votienus Montanus made similar observations (Sen. 9 pr., esp. §5), and subsequent to Petronius the *Dialogus* of Tacitus attacks on the same lines.

Encolpius in our text begins by criticizing the unreality of the themes of the exercises, which produce the aforesaid divorce between school and forum; he instances pirates carrying chains,[2] tyrants issuing parricidal edicts (this one goes beyond any of the tyrannical edicts in Seneca), oracular responses ordering the sacrifices of virgins to put an end to plague. This last item has no correspondence in the elder

[1] See H. Solin, *Namenpaare* (Soc. Scient. Fennica, Comm. hum. litt. 90, Helsinki 1990); Agamemnon and Menelaus are not actually attested as such a pair. A reason for the choice of these names is given on ch. 65 (see below, p. 109).

[2] Cf. Sen. *Contr.* 1.2.8 *piratas . . . praeferentes ante se uincula et catenas* ('pirates carrying in their hands bonds and chains'). Petronius will not have forgotten the prominence of pirates in the Greek novels. In fact pirates had been an insignificant problem since Pompey.

Seneca, but it does in the post-Petronian declamations of Calpurnius Flaccus (44, with Sussman's note) and the *Declamationes Minores* which seem to have some connection with Quintilian (no. 384); remedies for plague, *pestilentiae remedia*, are mentioned with scorn in Tac. *Dial.* 35.5, and Quintilian himself (2.10.5) admits the unreality of the theme of *pestilentiam et responsa*, but defends this and the like with reservations as an occasionally permissible exercise. All this seems to indicate that declamation had become more unrealistic since Seneca's day.

The result of this, says Encolpius, is empty polish of diction while the substance is emasculated (cf. 119.25) or hamstrung (*effecistis ut corpus orationis eneruaretur et caderet* 2.2; 'oratory has lost all its vigour and has collapsed', Walsh). Talent was not thus ruined by declamation in the days of the great classical poets and prose writers of Greece. Fine style (*grandis . . . oratio . . . non est . . . turgida*; 'lofty eloquence is not turgid') is elevated by natural elegance; the adjective *grandis*, which is taken up in 4.3 *illa grandis oratio* and applied to Cicero in 5.20, is not here intended in the technical sense of the *genus grande*, the 'grand style', as contrasted with the 'medium style' and the 'unpretentious style'; rather it relates to the concept of ὕψος, 'the sublime', whereas Horace, *AP* 27 *professus grandia turget* ('attempting the grand style he becomes bombastic'), is in the technical sense. This elegance has been corrupted by the recent arrival (*nuper commigrauit*) at Athens of windy Asianic verbosity, and that has caused eloquence to come to a full stop and fall silent. Poetry and painting too have suffered degeneration.

The understanding of this passage has caused great problems,[3] because it is clear that at the dramatic date in Neronian times the quarrel between Atticism and Asianism, which had blown up at Rome essentially because of controversies about the evaluation of Cicero's style, had been pretty much a dead letter for a century, though some declaimers tried to flog a dead horse and called themselves Asianists (Sen. *Contr.* 1.2.23, 9.1.12, 9.6.16, 10.5.21; the last-mentioned 'waged war against all the Atticists'). In this connection since Haley, *HSCP* 2

---

[3] Important discussions are by B. Sinclair in D. F. Bright and E. S. Ramage (eds.), *Classical Texts and their Traditions* (Chico 1984) 231, and D. A. Russell in E. M. Craik (ed.), *Owls to Athens* (Oxford 1990), 293.

(1891), 6–7, it has been usual to adduce a passage from the
treatise *Iudicium de Antiquis Oratoribus* pr. 1 of the Augustan
Dionysius of Halicarnassus, in which he says that, in contrast
to 'the ancient Attic Muse', Asianist oratory arrived 'yesterday
or the day before'. This statement is not intended in any
chronological sense; Dionysius knows perfectly well that
Asianist oratory came into being three centuries before his
own time, though even in a chronological sense 'yesterday or
the day before' is elastic (see Herod. 2.53.1). On the contrary,
the statement is evaluative, intended to characterize Asianist
oratory as an interloper, a Johnny-Come-Lately; this is underlined by the antithesis with the 'ancient' Attic style. There is no
such contextual justification for *nuper* in Petronius. We therefore have to interpret this passage as part of the characterization of Encolpius. His initial remarks on the failings of
declamatory education make perfectly valid points, consonant
with what sensible writers say and no doubt with the personal
opinions of the author Petronius, but then denunciation carries
him off into an interpretation of literary history in which the
shallowness of his knowledge is revealed; he has taken the
statement of Dionysius (or perhaps statements of others in
the same vein) as literally relating to chronology. All that he
says is conceptually a mess; he has dragged in Athens just for
the sake of the Atticist–Asianist contrast, though it has no
relationship either to 'Pindar and the nine lyric poets' whom he
has included in his list of otherwise Attic classic writers nor to
Roman education in the first century AD. In mentioning
Demosthenes he is showing off his knowledge of the standard
point that declamation did not exist in the time of Aeschines
(Sen. *Contr.* 1.8.16), and all the concepts, though not to any
great extent the phraseology,[4] lean hard on similar passages in
Cicero. In short, he is mouthing second-hand, half-under-
stood, and out-of-date platitudes; one notes that he does not
mention one Roman writer as a model of eloquence.

The remarks about poetry illustrate this dependence on
Cicero; with Encolpius' declaration *ne carmen quidem sani
coloris enituit, sed omnia quasi eodem cibo pasta non potuerunt*

---

[4] However, I pick out *Brut.* 22 *eloquentia obmutuit*, 'eloquence has fallen
silent', because of its relevance to a disputed textual point in Petronius 2.7.
See also below n. 10.

usque ad senectutem canescere ('Even poetry has not maintained the brilliance of its complexion unimpaired; it has all been fed on the same diet, and has not been able to survive to grey-haired old age', Walsh) compare *Brut.* 8 *ipsa oratio iam nostra canesceret haberetque suam quandam maturitatem et quasi senec-tutem*[5] ('my oratory had attained a certain ripeness and maturity of age', Hendrickson). This establishes a strong link between poetry and rhetoric in Encolpius' outlook; *sani coloris* takes up §6 *oratio maculosa* (blotchy oratory), and *sanus* (see *OLD* s.v. 4 and *sanitas* 3, to which much, e.g. Cic. *Brut.* 51, could be added) was a partisan term in the Atticist–Asianist controversy. The link is taken up in 118.5, where Eumolpus warns against non-integrated *sententiae* (apophthegms) in poetry with the same metaphor of a healthy shining colour (*intexto uestibus colore niteant*; 'let them shine with colour woven into the fabric'). There too limitations will be found to Eumolpus' literary discernment. As for the irrelevantly-attached remarks about the decline of painting, they also will be taken up in 88 by Eumolpus,[6] with much greater contextual justification.

From all this one must draw the lesson that great care needs to be taken if we attempt to read views of the author Petronius out of the utterances of his fictional characters. There are three places where questions of literary taste are raised from the mouth of Encolpius (here and 132.15) and Eumolpus (118). All three discussions begin with perfectly sensible sentiments, which in 132.15 (see below, p. 200) I believe that Petronius explicitly relates to his own *opus*, but in all three eventually the fictional characters take over and reveal their own shortcomings. Petronius, rather like Horace in the second book of his Satires, to a great extent withholds himself from us, though careful reading and the recognition of a pattern do help us to peep through the veil occasionally; but he does not make this possibility readily available to us, and left no doubt the majority of his expected readers to make what they would of

---

[5] This parallel refutes Fraenkel's deletion of *ad senectutem* in Petronius.

[6] Pliny, *NH* 35.110, also refers to this 'short-cut' in painting; what exactly is meant by it is obscure. See *Der Neue Pauly* s.v. *compendiaria* for some discussions; others are listed in *ANRW* 2.32.3.1655, to which add the commentary of Jex-Blake and Sellers on Pliny loc. cit. and J. J. Pollitt, *The Ancient View of Greek Art* (New Haven 1974) 327.

his material. Modern readers have a bigger problem than he
intended, because from his general characterization one would
think Encolpius the last man in the world to criticize unreality,
and we do not know how Petronius introduced this. Is
Encolpius just trying to impress Agamemnon (he certainly
succeeds; 3.1)? Or did Petronius allow him to step to a
degree out of character in order to put over a topic regarded
by him as important (see below, pp. 61–2)?

Agamemnon does not allow Encolpius' declamation (so this
is a declamation against declamation!) in the portico to last
longer than he himself had sweated in the school (cf. Quintil.
6.4.6 *ambitiosum declamandi sudorem*, 'the ostentatious sweat of
declamation'). He compliments Encolpius on his perceptive-
ness and declares that he will let him into a secret, a secret
which will betray his own cynical disillusionment. It is all the
fault of the teachers (so also says Quintilian 2.10.3), who
pander to the taste of their audiences just as flatterers do to
rich men from whom they look for a dinner invitation; this
topic of dinner invitations recurs in 5.5 and is clearly meant to
show the hypocrisy of Agamemnon, who has cadged an
invitation to Trimalchio's dinner and in 52.7 obsequiously
leads the laughter at a joke of Trimalchio. The teachers feel
obliged *cum insanientibus furere*, to rave along with madmen; in
this phrase Agamemnon matches Encolpius' Ciceronian allusions with one to *Or.* 99, where Cicero describes the orator who
cannot relax his vehemence as seeming *furere apud sanos*,[7] to
rave among the sane, and reinforces this in the next sentence
with a doctored quotation from the *Pro Caelio*. Even the
declaimer Cestius (Sen. *Contr.* 9.6.12) admits *multa dico non
quia mihi placent sed quia audientibus placitura sunt* ('I say many
things not because they please me but because they will please
the audience').

Those who compel the teachers to pander, continues Agamemnon, are the parents, who apply pressure to make the
teachers pass over the austere (the word *seuerus* comes three
times in this and the next chapter) basics too hastily; students
are not given time to soak themselves (this metaphor recurs in
5.21 and 118.3) in wide reading and absorb good models for

---

[7] Cicero is actually alluding to a proverbial phrase, Otto no. 744.

imitation. The result is that schoolboys just play around (*in scholis ludunt*, a bilingual pun, since σχολή means both 'leisure' and 'school'), they make themselves ridiculous when they come prematurely to forensic cases, and the corruption lasts into their old age; oratory is stunted.

Agamemnon ends by stating *ne me putes improbasse schedium Lucilianae humilitatis, quod sentio et ipse carmine effingam* ('So that you may not think that I disapproved of improvisation in low-level Lucilian style, I too shall express my opinions in verse'). What this means (it is often misunderstood, but was correctly interpreted by Collignon 228) is that before our text begins Encolpius had burst into a Lucilian-style stylistically unpretentious improvisation (Lucilius had applied the term *schedium*[8] to his own writings, 1279 Marx), and that Agamemnon is now going to balance this with a poem of his own. It follows that attempts to link the following poem somehow to Lucilius are misguided. On the contrary, the form of scazons followed by hexameters is bound, I suggest, to allude to the recently-deceased (AD 62) and subsequently-published Persius, who introduces his hexameter satires with a choliambic prologue attacking contemporary poets for owing their inspiration to their belly and the hope of cash, themes which find their place in the scazons in Petronius, though we cannot be blind to the irony that the earnest young poet is parroted by the cynical Agamemnon.

In this poem Agamemnon begins by stressing in scazons the need for a base in morality (Quintilian in arguing that the orator must be a good man uses the same word *frugalitas*, 12.1.8); among the things to be avoided is cadging dinner invitations from the powerful, which as we know Agamemnon has done and which Encolpius is also doing (10.2; see below, n. 17). Some of the other prohibitions raise a question whether Petronius had in mind his own situation: be indifferent to truculent palaces with their haughty stares, do not be a claqueur to performing actors. The first might relate to his combination of a certain detachment (see Ch. I) with involvement in Nero's court, but the reference might be quite general, since if *rex* can mean 'patron', *regia* could well mean 'patron's

---

[8] The word is an emendation, but a certain one, in the text of Petronius.

grand house'. Again Nero notoriously organized troups of
claqueurs for his theatrical performances (Suet. 20.3), but he
was not alone in doing so. The surface meaning is adequate,
but that does not preclude the possibility of another level of
concealed meaning.

Agamemnon then passes to hexameters to state that, whether
education is conducted at Athens or Tarentum[9] or Naples (the
home of the Sirens; it is often called Parthenope after one of
them), it should begin with Homer, pass to philosophy (the
Socraticus grex),[10] and then to the oratory of Demosthenes.
Only then should Roman authors be tackled, *in primis* Cicero.[11]
But the aspiring orator should not concentrate just on rhetoric
(Cicero in his *De Oratore* had argued against such narrow
specialization), but should nourish his imagination by reading
about the sudden upsets ascribed by historians to Tyche and
their vivid accounts of battles.[12] In this way, soaked (this
metaphor again) in literature, he will pour forth his words
from his Pierian mind.[13]

This reading-list is of course only an outline, and concen-

---

[9] Tarentum is referred to as a Spartan colony, *Lacedaemonio tellus habitata
colono*; this is a clear reminiscence of Seneca, *AL* 236 (= C. Prato, *Gli
Epigrammi attribuiti a L. Anneo Seneca* [edn. 2, Rome 1964] 2) 1, *Corsica
Phocaico tellus habitata colono*.

[10] He probably has in mind Cic. *De Or.* 1.42 *philosophorum greges iam ab illo
fonte et capite Socrate* ('Droves of philosophers all the way back to their
fountain-head Socrates').

[11] I can make no coherent sense of this passage unless Burman's transposi-
tion of 20, *grandiaque indomiti Ciceronis uerba minentur* ('and let the fine words
of invincible Cicero crash'), to follow 16 is adopted, as it now is by Müller.

[12] The phrase *subducta foro*, 'withdrawn from the forum', seems to recall
Sen. *Tranq. An.* 7.2 *Isocrates Ephorum . . . foro subduxit* ('Isocrates withdrew
Ephorus from the forum'; Ephorus of course turned to history). That *truci . . .
canore* ('savage chant') need not mean that the reference in what follows is to
epic is shown by Cicero's declaration (*Or.* 39) that Thucydides *de bellicis rebus
canit etiam quodam modo bellicum* ('concerning matters of war correspondingly
chants, one might say, in warlike fashion'); but I should not like to deny
altogether the possibility that Vergil might be meant.

[13] The adjective *Pierius* again need not refer solely to poetry in view of
Cicero's assertion (*Or.* 62) in the context of philosophical writing that
Xenophontis uoce Musas quasi locutas ferunt ('They state that the Muses, one
might say, spoke in the voice of Xenophon'). See also Ovid, *Ex Ponto* 2.5.63 *tu
quoque Pieridum studio, studiose, teneris* ('You too, my zealous friend, are in the
grip of zeal for the Muses') addressed to an orator.

trates on the study of authors who will promote oratorical ability. Homer will eminently do this (Quintil. 1.8.5, 10.1.46 sqq.; for starting from Homer as usual see Pliny *Ep.* 2.14.2), so of course will Demosthenes and Cicero. Cicero himself has stylistic reservations about philosophers and historians (*Or.* 62 sqq.), but with similar reservations Quintilian accepts them (10.1.31 sqq., 73 sqq., 81 sqq., 101 sqq.); of course they both regard the moral and cultural influence of philosophy as necessary (so does Agamemnon himself, 4.3). Starting with Greek authors was not unusual (Quintil. 1.4.1; Echion's *cicaro* (46.5) has left Greek behind and is starting on Latin, but at an earlier stage of instruction); however, the reading course here given is an ideal scheme, not something with much relation to the actual educational process, since it compresses into one the provinces of the *grammaticus*, the teacher of reading and literature (who, being mainly concerned with the poets, would deal with Homer), and the *rhetor*, the teacher of oratory (who would cover prose authors, even if in the first century AD he had started to push off on to the *grammaticus* some elementary exercises dealing with prose authors). In fact Agamemnon seems to be compiling a list for personal reading, not something which he envisages as being taught; we should not call it an 'Unterrichtsprogramm'.

As was seen with the 'declamation' of Encolpius, the irony in some of what Agamemnon says is palpable, but at the same time others of his views are such that no sane man could disagree with them, and other writers develop similar themes (e.g. Tac. *Dial.* 30 on premature and restrictive concentration on rhetoric). Bearing in mind what was said above about the primacy of characterization, we still have to recognize that Petronius was under no obligation to base an episode on a rhetorical school. This is one of the themes which he has superadded to the continuous thread of novel-parody.[14] The negative evaluation of conventional school-rhetoric should probably be seen in relation to its omnipresence in the Greek novel (cf. above, n. 2). Petronius clearly wished to raise a bothersome topic for the consideration of his readers; what

---

[14] Varro, *Sat. Men.* 144 B, has sometimes been thought to refer to rhetoric and to be set in a rhetorical school, but more probably it refers to philosophy and is set at a dinner-party (Astbury in Harrison 80 = *CP* 72 (1977), 27).

he did not wish to do was to give them a clear-cut and
authoritative answer.

(ii) 6–11, a Quarrel

When this discussion began Encolpius had been accompanied
by Ascyltos; Encolpius has become so absorbed that he failed
to notice it when Ascyltos slipped away. Now a crowd of
students floods into the portico, coming, as their conversation
shows, from an extempore declamation of someone who had
followed a *suasoria* of Agamemnon; they are full of criticisms of
this declamation. Encolpius grasps the opportunity to slip away
himself and try to find Ascyltos, who, he fears, may be after
Giton. But, being in a strange town, he does not know the way
to his lodgings, and keeps coming back to the same place (the
thematic importance of this will be discussed in Ch. VIII (iii)).
Desperate, he asks a market-woman if she knows where he
lives; she is amused at his silly but politely-addressed question,
says 'Of course' and leads the way; Encolpius follows, aware
that his question was silly but inferring that she has second
sight (*diuinam*). For a joke she brings him to a brothel. As he
rushes out, he encounters Ascyltos, who also has been unable
to find the lodging, and has had experiences which closely
parallel those of Encolpius. A respectable gentleman has
promised to show him the way, has brought him by the back
alleys to the brothel, paid for a room and tried to have his way
with him; Ascyltos however has been able to escape because of
his superior strength. As he and Encolpius now wander
around, the latter sees Giton standing on the sidewalk (he
has no doubt fled from the lodgings to escape Ascyltos after the
assault to be described in 9.4), and with his aid they presumably find the lodging.

Once inside, Giton sits on the bed in tears[15] and eventually
under pressure from Encolpius discloses that just a little earlier

[15] The manuscript reading in 9.2 *lacrimas pollice expressit* ('he squeezed out
tears with his thumb') has sometimes been retained and understood to mean
that Giton is just feigning to be upset in order to provoke a quarrel, and
therefore makes himself cry. That would be quite consistent with the
character of Giton, but the thumb is used to wipe away tears (Ovid, *Met.*
9.395, 13.746, [*Her.* 19.26]), not to squeeze them out. The emendation to
extersit is necessary.

Ascyltos had come into the room and tried to rape him. This probably means that the narrative has been drastically abbreviated before this point rather than that Ascyltos has fabricated his whole story as a cover-up for what he has actually been attempting with Giton, because in that case it would be inexplicable how Ascyltos had turned up in the brothel. When Giton resisted Ascyltos, the latter drew his sword[16] and declared 'If you are a Lucretia, you have found your Tarquin'. At this point we realize that this episode has been a delicious parody of the description of the rape of Lucretia by Tarquin in Livy 1.58. Compare Giton sitting on the bed with Livy §6, where Collatinus and Brutus find Lucretia sitting sadly in her bedroom, *sedentem maestam in cubiculo*; Encolpius' enquiry (*quaesiui*) with that of Collatinus (§7 *quaerenti uiro*); Encolpius' mixture of entreaty and threats with that of Tarquin (§3 *miscere precibus minas*; functionally different); the drawing of the sword with §2 *stricto gladio*. Encolpius' enquiry whether Giton had prepared a meal may also recall Lucretia's preparation of one for Tarquin in Ovid, *Fasti* 2.789–90 *parat . . . epulas*. This is the first place in our text in which the setting of Petronius' rogues against a grand precedent highlights the contrast; just imagine Giton as a paradigm of chastity!

What had happened after that between Giton and Ascyltos we are not told. Now Encolpius and Ascyltos raise their fists and hurl insults (some of which have been discussed on pp. 47–8 above) at each other. These peter out weakly when Encolpius blames Ascyltos for slipping away during the conversation with Agamemnon, and Ascyltos replies (10.2) that Encolpius is a fine one to talk, since he praised Agamemnon's poetry in order to secure an invitation to dinner. This means that he is one of those nicknamed 'Laodiceans', *laudiceni* (Pliny, *Ep*. 2.14.5), as indeed Agamemnon also is (52.7); their Greek name was Σοφοκλεῖς, based on the 'hurrah', *sophōs*, which the guests utter at 40.1, from which we infer that they are all more or less of the same stamp.

---

[16] An obscene amphiboly has often been detected here (see e.g. Adams 21, who himself is hesitant), quite unwarrantably; as travellers Encolpius (79.11, 82.1; 80.10 is interpolated) and Ascyltos naturally have swords available, but the thuggish Ascyltos seems to be in the habit of wearing his (80.1; this is why Giton cannot find it in his lodgings, 94.11).

So the quarrel ends in laughter, but resentment lingers. Encolpius proposes that he and Ascyltos split their belongings and each cope with his poverty in his own way; they have evidently been using their education to earn a living (10.5 *et tu litteras scis et ego*, 'You're a literary man and so am I'; hence their connection with a *rhetor*). Encolpius promises to set up in another profession (*aliquid aliud promittam = profitebor*). Ascyltos proposes (10.6), since they have a dinner invitation for today,[17] to postpone their separation until the morrow, when he will look for another lodging and a *frater* (which here probably means not much more than 'roommate'), but Encolpius insists that it take place at once because he desires to be alone with Giton. After a walk outside, he goes to bed with Giton, but before consummation Ascyltos bursts in, ridicules him, takes the strap off the suitcase which he has packed and gives him a whipping, saying 'this isn't how you should divide with your *frater*'.[18] That means that he is laying claim to a share in Giton; this motif will be revived in 79.12.

(iii) 12–15, the Stolen Cloak

The next episode describes an attempt by Ascyltos and Encolpius to sell a cloak that they have stolen and recover a tunic in the hem of which they have hidden money. They finally recover the tunic but evidently not the money, as is indicated in 15.8 *recuperato, ut putabamus, thesauro* ('after, as we thought, recovering the treasure'), with which cf. 125.2; this

[17] There is a problem here, since their *cena* that evening is prepared by Giton (16.1). Neither this nor 10.2 can refer to the *cena* of Trimalchio. There too there is a problem in the same area; one can get around this by the hypothesis that Ascyltos had still been in the company of Encolpius and Agamemnon at the beginning of ch. 5, and is just assuming Encolpius' praise (of which we hear nothing in the text, though it might have been in the gap which Bücheler marked in 6.1). This is not in itself a difficult assumption (see the *laudatio* which in 35.1 automatically follows verses of Trimalchio), and in any case one does not necessarily stick to known fact in insults. But all this is forced, and on our present evidence I do not see how the difficulty is to be solved.

[18] Either this is a phrase in regular use, here distorted for comic effect, or it is a parody of Sen. *Ep.* 88.11 *quid mihi prodest scire agellum in partes diuidere, si nescio cum fratre diuidere?* ('What good does it do me to know how to divide a small estate into shares, if I do not know how to divide it with my brother?').

is foreshadowed at 13.3 *illa est tunicula adhuc, ut apparet, intactis aureis plena*, 'that is our tunic still, apparently, full of untouched cash'. This is clearly the sequel to an earlier, lost episode, and in its present state of mutilation the details of the action, the relevance to the plot, and the connection with the literary themes of the work cannot satisfactorily be made out. It will therefore not be discussed here, though in the next section I shall try to forge a link with the following episode. It may be as well to say that attempts to identify the stolen cloak with the vestment taken by Encolpius from the figurehead of the ship of Lichas, an episode discussed on p. 46 above, for a number of reasons will not work.

(iv) 16.1–26.6, Quartilla and an Orgy

When they return to their lodgings, even though they seem to have neglected to do the shopping as they had intended (14.3), Giton has prepared a meal, as Encolpius had expected him to do for an earlier meal in 9.2. Suddenly there is a thunderous and terrifying knock on the door; the bar falls down of its own accord.[19] The visitor identifies herself thus: 'I am the maid of Quartilla, whose ritual in front of the vault (*cryptam*) you disturbed.' She announces that Quartilla herself will be arriving soon, which she duly does, accompanied by a young girl; she sits down on Encolpius' bed and bursts into a flood of tears, which with hindsight the narrator Encolpius realizes to be of the crocodile variety. She accuses them of *fabulas etiam antecessura latrocinia* ('thievery that would outdo even the story-books'), which might be a hit at the fondness of the Greek novelists for brigands; in the plot, however, it probably refers to the stealing of the expensive cloak in the previous

---

[19] Rationalistically, this is presumably due to its weakening when Ascyltos battered open the door at 11.2, but no doubt we are meant to understand that the startled companions see it as a traditional sign of an epiphany; see O. Weinreich, *Religionsgeschichtliche Studien* (Darmstadt 1968) 234, Pease on Cic. *De Div.* 1.74, Norden on *Aen.* 6.81 and Horsfall on 7.620. The maid's reassurance *nolite perturbari* ('Do not be disturbed') also fits into the context of an epiphany; see e.g. Hom. *Il.* 24.171; *Hom. hymn* 5.193; Gospel acc. to Luke 1: 13 and 30, 2: 10; Matthew 28: 5 (and also Matthew 14: 27, Mark 6: 50); Revelation 1: 17.

episode (attributed to *latrocinium* 12.2, 14.5, 15.3; two of these
references have aroused unmerited textual suspicion), especially since in the manuscript text of 16.3 (which again it is
imprudent to alter) the maidservant is identified as the woman
who had recognized the cloak at 14.5,[20] and her first words here
are 'Thought you had fooled me, did you?' Quartilla pities
them[21] for leaving themselves open to punishment for seeing in
the chapel of Priapus nocturnal rites (i.e. a *peruigilium*) they
were not meant to see; whether there is a theme of the 'Wrath
of Priapus' running through the novel and, if so, whether this
episode relates to it, will be discussed in Ch. VI(i). Quartilla
states that she personally is not seeking revenge and thinks that
they have just committed a youthful indiscretion; this is all
hogwash intended merely to gain their confidence, since on the
above reconstruction she must know about their theft of the
cloak. She herself was so upset that she has fallen into a tertian
fever and has looked for a cure in a dream (it was supposed that
one could command dreams on a desired topic; see L. Deubner,
De Incubatione (Leipzig 1900) 30, R. MacMullen, *Paganism in
the Roman Empire* (New Haven 1981) 61); she has been
instructed to search out the trio and cure her illness by a
subtle method revealed to her. This again is just hogwash; the
dream is fabricated like those in Longus 3.17 and Heliodorus
7.11, in both cases by women trying to seduce men. As for the
subtle cure, it turns out to be the following orgy! But, she says,
her main concern is that they should not reveal the rituals
which they have seen (now at last she discloses her actual
purpose), rituals that hardly a thousand human beings
(*homines*, not *uiri*) know. This number has to be understood
as a slip of the tongue; she wants to impress on the trio the
exclusivity of their knowledge, but instead inadvertently lets
out the true scale of involvement in these doubtless highly
immoral rites. It seems a pity to eliminate the humour and the

[20] I think that the actual words *quae cum rustico steterat* in 14.5 are likely to
be interpolated from 16.3; they do not seem to present any problem in the
latter place. Cf. Pardini, *A e R* 41 (1996), 187.

[21] As a point of characterization Petronius makes her use the masculine
oath *mediusfidius* here (its transmitted occurrence from the pen of Circe in
129.6 is open to grave doubt). This is a masterful woman, menacing and
sexually dominating.

oxymoronic combination with 'hardly' by altering 'a thousand' (*mille* = M) to 'three' (*tres* = III).

Encolpius cheers her up by promising to abstain from disclosure and to help with any other cure for her fever prescribed by the god;[22] little does he know what he is letting himself in for by the latter promise. Quartilla grants them forgiveness, and says that if they had not agreed she had a mob ready to avenge her tomorrow; as we read on it becomes apparent that tomorrow she will use this mob anyway. Her tears turn to applause (a sign of glee, repeated at 24.2 and by the maid at 20.6) and laughter, in which she is joined by her two attendants; Encolpius and company, unaware of what is in store for them, react with apprehension and bewilderment. She reveals that she has hired the whole inn for the day (*hodie* must mean 'for the rest of today', since it is now evening) so that she can receive the cure for her fever without interruption. This again strikes apprehension into Ascyltos and Encolpius, but the latter reflects that the three of them are surely a match for three weak women.

The narrative now becomes very fragmentary, but we find the maidservant (now given the name Psyche) spreading a blanket on the floor, someone (Quartilla?) stimulating Encolpius' inert genitals, Psyche binding his and Ascyltos' hands and feet with two ribbons;[23] a potion of *satyrion* intended for both has been drunk in its entirety by Encolpius. *Satyrion* is a variety of orchid (so called because its tubers resemble the testicles, ὄρχεις) used as an aphrodisiac (Pliny, *NH* 26.96–9, and McMahon 88); it had been mentioned in the brothel context at 8.4 and will again be mentioned in 21.1.[24] The

---

[22] This is referred to as *diuina prouidentia*, the design of the gods, in an ironical use of the technical vocabulary for such situations; O. Weinreich, *Antike Heilungswunder* (Giessen 1909), 135.

[23] This perhaps is part of a magic ritual, like the *licium* (cord) at 131.4, to restore their flagging virility.

[24] C. A. Faraone in J. Tatum and G. M. Vernazza (eds.), *The Ancient Novel* (1990) 114, claimed that a double dose of an aphrodisiac would have been considered likely actually to produce impotence. Perhaps Encolpius' impotence at 20.2 was caused by having drunk this double dose, though this is only discovered now; but it may have been due simply to fear. However, Faraone now (*Ancient Greek Love Magic* (Cambridge, Mass. 1995) 125) corrects this view and argues that a double dose would be believed to cause

reader will of course link the name with the title of the novel; in fact sexually stimulating drugs were called *satyrica* (recorded in Lewis and Short, with a false reference which should be Cael. Aurel. *Acut.* 3.18.175 p. 410, Drabkin, but not in *OLD* nor in LSJ). All laugh at him, including Giton, whom Quartilla's young girl embraces and kisses; Giton's willingness to accept these kisses foreshadows his 'marriage' to Pannychis in 26.3. A *cinaedus* ('drag-queen', Bracht Branham and Kinney) arrives and sexually assaults them, *extortis nos clunibus cecidit* 'he belaboured us with his grinding buttocks', a phrase often misunderstood (cf. the same *cinaedus* with Ascyltos on the next day, 24.4 *clunibus eum basiisque distriuit*, 'he wore him down with his buttocks and kisses'). The oddity of the phrase has been remarked by Adams, *LCM* 7 (1952), 88; it consists in the fact that the verb *caedo*, which normally indicates the action of the penetrator with an undertone of punishment (Adams, *Latin Sexual Vocabulary* 145–6), is here applied to the penetrated. Adams calls this 'a characteristic Petronian adaptation of a current sexual metaphor', but the word 'reversal', frequently applied in this book to the sexual situations in Petronius, would more precisely indicate the point.

After 21.3 (in this I agree with Ciaffi 31 sqq.) there is a sizeable gap in the narrative within which both time and place change; time to the next day, place to Quartilla's house (23.2). When the narrative resumes, masseurs enter and refresh the companions after the bath which they have been presumably taking, then they move into a dining-room and have such a hearty meal[25] that they are on the point of dozing off, until Quartilla announces that an all-night vigil is due to Priapus. Yet the whole company is so exhausted that they all fall asleep, only to be awakened by the racket caused by the two Syrian thieves (discussed above on p. 38); the feast is resumed.

Next the *cinaedus* whom they had encountered yesterday enters; he is described as *homo omnium insulsissimus* ('the most tasteless character imaginable'), probably with reference to the

satyriasis, in which case no link can be forged with the narrative of Petronius as we have it.

[25] This is apparently their second meal of the evening (cf. 73.5) in view of *cenatoria repetimus*, 'we put on our dinner-clothes again' 21.5.

verses which he is about to recite (see Barchiesi in Harrison
134). By this time we are feeling that all these entries and exits
are like nothing so much as a stage performance,[26] and we are
right; the impresario Quartilla has scripted all this in advance.
This *cinaedus* in Sotadeans (the use of this metre has been
discussed above on pp. 22–3) issues an invitation, of course
meant only rhetorically, to all *cinaedi* to participate. He climbs
on the couch on which Encolpius reclines at table and despite
his resistance sexually assaults him; the phrase (23.4) *immun-
dissimo me basio conspuit* ('he spluttered over me with a filthy
kiss') recalls *nos . . . basiis olidissimis inquinauit* (21.2; 'he
besmirched us with filthy kisses') from yesterday. He apparently elicits no physical response (*frustra* 23.5). Encolpius
appeals to Quartilla, saying that she had ordered (note the
staging again) for him an *embasicoetas*, by which he had
thought that she intended a kind of goblet (Athen. 11.469a)
used for nightcaps. She explains that she had actually meant its
sense as a slang nickname for a *cinaedus*, who also of course can
put one pleasantly to sleep (naturally she had deliberately
intended to mislead); the name must have on reflection
appealed to Encolpius, who takes it over at 26.1. Encolpius
protests that he is being unfairly singled out while Ascyltos is
left unmolested, and Quartilla to even things out sends the
cinaedus over to assault Ascyltos.

All this time Giton has been standing by, laughing heartily as
he had yesterday (20.8), but Quartilla has not taken any notice
of him. Now she does, on enquiry finds out that he is the *frater*
of Encolpius, kisses him, feels his genitals, and declares that
she will sample them as an hors d'oeuvre tomorrow because
today *post asellum* she needs no more daily rations. *Asellus* here
is in two senses; first it means the fish hake, second it refers to
the notorious sexual vigour of the ass.[27] From this we infer a
fact which has been eliminated in the excerpting, namely that
she had had intercourse with Encolpius, whose impotence can
only have been temporary; intercourse was considered effica-
cious against fever (Pliny, *NH* 28.83; Weinreich, *Heilungswunder* [above, n. 22] 183), and this was the cure at which she has

[26] There is much interesting detail corroborating this point in Sandy 340;
note *mimico risu* (laughter at a farce), 19.1.
[27] See my note on Juvenal 9.92, and Winkler 174.

been hinting since 17.7. One must, however, recognize the possibility that it is Ascyltos with whom she has had intercourse. It is striking that in Achilles Tatius 5.26.2 Melite asks Clitophon to make love to her as a cure for her fever, and after he has done so he speaks of himself as having 'healed' her (6.1.1).

Psyche now whispers in Quartilla's ear the suggestion, eagerly adopted by her, that this would be a good occasion for the deflowering (*deuirginatur*) of the seven-year old girl Pannychis by Giton, who is aged about sixteen (97.2). Her name is a real one found on inscriptions (Priuli 51), but it is also appropriate to the vigil, *peruigilium* (21.6), in which they are engaged; both παννυχίζειν (Henderson 153; Dickie in *Papers Leeds Latin Seminar* 9 (1996), 334 n. 5) and *peruigilare* (Catull. 88.2; see also *OLD peruigilium* 2 fin.) are used with erotic connotations. In fact Lucian, *Dial. Mer.* 11, introduces a courtesan called Pannychis, and there is a concubine so called at Joseph., *Bell. Iud.* 1.25.6.511. Petronius at this point is perhaps thinking of Aristophanes, *Thesm.* 480, where the disguised Mnesilochus alleges that a friend με διεκόρησεν οὖσαν ἑπτέτιν ('took my virginity when I was aged seven').[28]

The idea meets with general approval, but is disapproved by Encolpius, who protests that Giton is a modest young boy (at the moment this may be an opportunistic claim, but it is actually how the starry-eyed Encolpius sees Giton) and the girl too young for intercourse. Quartilla counters this by declaring that she herself was just as young when she had her sexual initiation. So a mock wedding is celebrated with proper Roman ritual; when the girl is put to bed Quartilla, inflamed with lust, leads Giton into the bedroom. The door is shut, but

[28] The mention of this age in particular is connected with the common ancient division of life into 7-year periods (see my note on Juv. 14.10); the point then would be the transference of sexual activity from the beginning of puberty at 14 (though girls were usually reckoned to be sexually mature at 12) years to the end of infancy. Heliodorus 2.30.6 refers to a girl aged 7 as almost mature. According to Hellanicus (fr. 168b) Helen was abducted by Theseus at the age of 7; other authorities gave a higher age (see Jacoby's note). Beard, *JRS* 68 (1978), 202, notes three inscriptions which to all appearances indicate marriage of a 7-year old girl. For the position in such under-age marriages see S. Treggiari, *Roman Marriage* (Oxford 1991) 41.

Quartilla plays the voyeur, peeping through a crack (a time-honoured pornographic motif appearing e.g. in [Lucian], *Asinus* 52; see Kay on Mart. 11.45.6); she also pulls Encolpius over to watch and kisses him when their faces touch each other. A very similar scene will be enacted in 140.11.

IV

The Feast of Trimalchio

(i) 26.7–31.11

The last sentence preserved of Book 14 is 'casting ourselves on our beds we spent the rest of the night without fear'. After this the excerpts naturally mark a gap, since the next extract comes from 27.1; but the probability is that this was in fact the last sentence of Book 14, and was directly followed by the first sentence of Book 15 ('Finally the third day had arrived, that is the prospect of the last meal of the condemned, but, pierced by so many wounds,[1] we felt more like running away than resting'; 26.7). What I have translated as 'the last meal of the condemned' actually refers to the dinner of gladiators on the evening before their appearance in the amphitheatre; the gladiatorial metaphor takes up 21.2 *iussit infelicibus dari missionem* ('She ordered that we poor fellows receive our discharge'). This presumably means that, Quartilla's abuse of them having already lasted two days (if we follow Ciaffi), they are expecting another ordeal today (Quartilla looks forward to this with her reference to 'tomorrow' at 24.7). But a slave of Agamemnon arrives and informs them that their host this evening is to be Trimalchio, which provides them with an escape; it is not clear exactly what hold over them Quartilla has. The slave reports (with what motivation is uncertain, since there seems to be a gap in the text) that Trimalchio keeps a clock in his dining-room and a trumpeter[2] who would blow at

---

[1] The phrase *uulneribus confoss-*, pierced by wounds, recurs in the epic on the Civil War (124.260); its use here is an instance of the theatrical and literary terms in which the characters see themselves. Cf. Ch. VI n. 9, and also p. 128 below on 79.10.

[2] This trumpeter, like the clock, would be a hydraulic one; see *Aetna* 293–5, Vitruv. 9.8.5, and Meerwaldt, *Mnem.* 49 (1921), 407, taking *horologium et bucinatorem subornatum* to mean *h. bucinatore s.*, a clock equipped with a trumpeter. In fact Magnusson, *Eranos* 98 (2000), 116, unaware of Meerwaldt's article, now proposes to emend the text to exactly this.

every hour, so that at intervals he may know how much of his life he has lost. This is the first hint of black undertones to the *Cena*; note how a link is established between luxury and death by the placing in the dining-room, and that a trumpet-blast regularly accompanied funerals (see below, pp. 121–2 and n. 69). This hint is given extra point in 77.2, where we find that Trimalchio has learned from an astrologer exactly how long he still has to live (30 years, 4 months, 2 days). Since *etiamnunc* in that context must mean 'even now', not (as it perfectly well can) 'even then', it must follow that since the prophecy was given to him Trimalchio has been keeping careful count.

So they go to the baths with Giton acting as their slave, as he has been doing in the preceding narrative and will do in the *Cena*; the invitation as guests is strictly for Encolpius and Ascyltos, who alone have been in contact with Agamemnon. They are wandering around in the exercise room when they suddenly see (more than see; he is a show, *spectaculum* 27.2, just as he puts on a show in his *Cena*) an old man[3] dressed in a red tunic with a green ball; Trimalchio likes to wear vivid colours, and so do his slaves (e.g. 28.8, 30.11). The form of the preceding sentence reproduces that of the Latin, in which Trimalchio is introduced with the *cum inversum* which stresses the subordinate rather than the main clause (for the 'suddenly' cf. *cum subito* 34.1); *cum Trimalchio* becomes a signal for turning-points in the *Cena* (32.1, 47.1, 64.2), though it also appears at less critical points. One aspect of his arrangements which they observe[4] is singled out as *res nouae* (27.3), a novelty, a phrase that carries with it a supercilious implication that he is transgressing societal norms.[5] That is taken up by the following

---

[3] He is hardly very old in fact, but seems so to these *iuuenes*.

[4] The verb *notare*, observe, occurs with significant frequency in the *Cena*, in which Encolpius and company function as spectators much more than as actors. One indication of his retreat into the background is that only at 49.7 and 69.9 (72.5 is different) does he report a remark by himself in direct speech; structurally the three remarks are very similar (Laird 220 n. 20). Even his private thoughts are seldom reported (Laird 227–8 notes an instance at 41.1, to which one might add 36.7, 54.3). The general passivity of his character facilitates this retreat into the background

[5] For this implication of *nouus* in the *Cena* see 31.10, 78.5, and compare *inaudito more* (see above, p. 8) 70.8.

has miraremur lautitias ('We were admiring these refinements'),
meant of course ironically as sometimes in the *Cena*, whereas
the slave of Agamemnon had in naive sincerity described
Trimalchio as *lautissimus homo*, a very refined man; it is
significant that the words *lautus* and *lautitia* occur only twice
outside the *Cena*, both times in connection with meals (so the
introduction by emendation at 117.2 does not seem very
probable). At this point Agamemnon's assistant Menelaus
comes up to Ascyltos and Encolpius and identifies the man as
their host for the evening. Thus the *spectaculum* which he
offered is the prelude (*principium*) to the Cena, which is to be
full of *spectacula*. After relieving himself (without however
stopping his game) in a chamber-pot held by a eunuch, and
washing his hands, Trimalchio dries them on the hair of a
slave, thus treating him as an instrument according to an
outlook common in higher social strata (Aristotle's 'animate
tool', Varro's 'articulate tool' *RR* 1.17.1); only when he is
drunk does he allow a different attitude to emerge (71.1).
Another reference to wiping one's hands on another's hair,
with similar overtones, has been introduced by plausible
conjecture in 57.6. It is yet more insulting, after blowing the
nose, to wipe one's hands on another's hair (Aristoph. *Knights*
910).

After the bath proper and the rub-down with oil Trimalchio
is wrapped in a scarlet robe and carried off home in a litter
preceded by four couriers, with his old and unattractive *deliciae*
(mignon) following him in a rickshaw (old is another relative
term, old for a *puer delicatus*); Trimalchio is following the
upper-class fashion for keeping such *pueri delicati* (he has been
one himself, 75.11), but characteristically does so in a form
lacking refinement. He is accompanied by an oboe-player, who
plays all the way quietly so that only Trimalchio can hear.
Throughout the *Cena* the fondness of Trimalchio for music,
often shrill and out of tune, is stressed (cf. 53.12–13, where he
speaks as if there were such a thing as Latin oboe-playing;
Sedgwick 145 amusingly quotes from the Autobiography of
Berlioz §13 'Of course I whistle in French, monsieur'); however, he was not alone in this at the time,[6] and within the novel

---

[6] See L. Friedlaender, *Darstellungen aus der Sittengeschichte Roms* (edn. 10,

the taste for it is shared by Plocamus (64.2–5), if not by the more refined narrator Encolpius. In the *Cena* new courses are often heralded by an outburst of music; at 32.1 and 34.1 this is introduced in the form of the *cum inversum* mentioned above.

The trio with Agamemnon follow, full of *admiratio* (an ambiguous word, like *miraremur* above, which can denote either admiration or amazement). Here and in 30.5 the admiration is spoken of as if it were itself food (*saturi, repleti*, both indicating repletion), which gives us a hint that the point of the meal is to impress as much as it is to feed.[7] Trimalchio's door has a notice on it threatening punishment to any slave who goes out without the owner's permission; this is part of his bluster towards slaves, which, as remarked above (p. 10), he practically never puts into effect. It also marks Trimalchio's dominion as a self-contained world (guests too find it difficult to get out; 73.10); compare his aspiration to travel to Africa without leaving his own property (48.3). Consequent on this, Trimalchio dominates the action in the *Cena*, and Encolpius withdraws from the centre to the periphery as a mere spectator (cf. above n. 4). On the compositional plane too one observes that the *Cena* is exceptionally self-contained, and that Trimalchio has no function in any other episode (the same seems to apply to Circe). At the entrance stands a doorkeeper in multi-coloured dress shelling peas in a silver dish; this detail is meant to indicate the lavishness with which even humble tasks are conducted in this household, and Hermeros later (37.8) shows himself impressed by the abundance of silver in the doorkeeper's room. This all affects Encolpius with such *stupor* that he takes for real a painting of a huge dog, with the common inscription 'beware of the dog',[8] and almost falls over

Leipzig 1922) 2.175–6 = Eng. tr. *Roman Life and Manners* (1907–13) 2.349–50; Horsfall, *G & R* 36 (1989), 198, and *MAAR* 41 (1996), 112.

[7] For a discussion of the way in which the 'conspicuous consumption' at Trimalchio's feast is directed less to alimentary purposes than to display, so that the food becomes essentially a representation of affluence, see Tony Tanner, *Adultery in the Novel* (Baltimore 1979) 52, and, following him N. Bryson, *Looking at the Overlooked* (Cambridge, Mass. 1990), 48. For my purposes this sociological side of the meal is less important than the trickery involved, but it is certainly not unimportant.

[8] These inscriptions occur on floor-mosaics, not on paintings. Veyne (1963) 59 points to a wall-painting of a dog in *trompe l'oeil* style in the

in fright; even though he is in a daze, we must take this as a sign of his naivety, but it is also the first time (there will be many others) we encounter things that are not what they seem. The actual dog, by antiphrasis (as in the case of Eumolpos; see Ch. II n. 42) called 'Puppy', will reappear in 64.7 and 72.7.

Aroused to attention, Encolpius peruses the other paintings on the wall, which show a slave-market and the youthful Trimalchio with long hair (cf. 63.3; like his own page-boys at 27.1 and Hermeros coming to Puteoli at 57.9) holding a herald's wand (this assimilates him to Mercury) and entering Rome, escorted by Minerva. Next the painter, with explanatory titles, showed him learning to reckon (an accomplishment which Minerva would patronize; Livy 7.3.6 says that she was the inventor of arithmetic) and becoming a paymaster. At the far end of the entrance-hall Mercury,[9] the god of gain (77.4), whose emblem is the just-mentioned herald's wand, is lifting him by the chin on to a high platform (cf. 71.9; a mark of his promotion to be *seuir Augustalis*, a member of the board for maintaining the municipal cult of the emperor). Near at hand is Fortuna with a cornucopia and the three Fates spinning golden threads of destiny, like those which Seneca (*Apoc.* 4.1.9; a work which Petronius had read) makes them spin at the opening of Nero's reign.[10] This picture of Trimalchio's career is balanced

---

vestibule of the house of M. Casellius Marcellus at Pompeii, and (66) the discovery of another.

[9] The figures of Trimalchio and Mercury on this picture are interestingly related to depictions on tombstones by Bodel in J. Tatum (ed.), *The Search for the Ancient Novel* (Baltimore 1994) 246, though I cannot feel that at this point this in itself conveys a funereal atmosphere. For depictions of Fortuna with cornucopia and Mercury see *LIMC* s.v. Mercurius 265–6, 271–4, and Tyche 130–4. The lifting by the chin (*mento leuatum*) is presumably because tilting the head back so that the chin is prominent is a sign of pride, as Mussolini well knew; but 43.4, which doubtless refers to keeping a drowning man's head above water, should not be compared. However, the phrase *leuatum mento* remains under heavy suspicion; Fuchs has proposed *(porticu) ⟨sicut⟩ leuatum uento*. I can agree with the diagnosis of Neumann and Simon, *WJA* 23 (1999), 115, but not with the emendation *momento*.

[10] As with other cases mentioned below, this should not be taken to mean that we are to see a caricature of Nero in Trimalchio. It is better to understand it in a metatextual way, as if Trimalchio had read Seneca's flattery of Nero and was assimilating himself to the imperial destiny; thus there is a side-swipe at Seneca too.

at the end of the *Cena* by an autobiographical account by Trimalchio himself (75.10–77.5), some items of which I shall here relate out of order. He came as a small boy from Asia (i.e. Asia Minor, like Ganymede in 44.4); hence his name. Malchus and Malchio are semitic names from a root meaning 'king'[11] which also appears e.g. in Melchior (one of the Three Magi) and the god Moloch. For Malchio as a slave-name see Solin (1996) 603 and in *ANRW* 2.29.2.677, 680, 729–30; his previous owner must be presumed to have been amused by his bumptiousness and added the intensifying prefix, 'King to the power of three'.[12] He was the *deliciae* of his owner, presumably succeeding the *deliciae* mentioned in 63.3, for fourteen years,[13] a fact of which he is now somewhat ashamed; but he also performed sexual services for his owner's wife (we may think of the bisexual Giton, now of comparable age, and his entanglement with Tryphaena, discussed above (p. 47)); from this we see that triangular relationships are not confined to Encolpius and company. This former owner was called C. Pompeius, as we learn from Trimalchio's formal nomenclature C. Pompeius Trimalchio in 30.2, 71.12; the former passage is a legal notice, in the latter, which is Trimalchio's self-composed epitaph, he has added the extra name Maecenatianus. Such an agnomen would normally mean that he had been the slave of Maecenas before being that of C. Pompeius; chronologically that is hardly possible, and it is nowhere implicit in the narrative. He has simply usurped the name, for a purpose clarified by J. H. D'Arms, *Commerce and Social Standing* (Cambridge, Mass. 1981) 111. The conferment of the sevirate on him in his absence and his refusal of status, mentioned in the context (see below), are characteristics of a rank in society higher than his own, namely that of *eques*, and

---

[11] Porphyry, *Life of Plotinus* 17, and Eunapius, *Vit. Soph.* 456, remark the equivalence; see too John Laurentius the Lydian, *De Mensibus* 4.118. Cf. Bremmer, *Mnem.* 34 (1981), 395.

[12] For such formations, which are common in comic diction, see Marx on Plaut. *Rud.* 734 and *RAC* s.v. *Drei* 293; one may compare Hermes Trismegistus. For the name see further above, p. 52.

[13] This is the natural interpretation of the manuscript reading, and both the reading and interpretation are correct. As Richardson, *Phoenix* 40 (1986), 201 realizes, only so can the following *tamen* be explained; 'I tried to make my beard grow more quickly, *but nevertheless* I was my owner's *deliciae* for fourteen years.' Trimalchio repeats his experience with his own *deliciae* Croesus.

Maecenas was the pattern of an *eques* who refused to move up;
see e.g. Prop. 3.9.2 *intra fortunam qui cupis esse tuam* ('You who
desire to remain within your station'), Tac. *Ann.* 3.30.2, and in
general my note on Juv. 4.111–12, and R. J. A. Talbert, *The
Senate of Imperial Rome* (Princeton 1984) 77. So all this is a
mark of inverted snobbery as far as concerns the character
Trimalchio, but in relation to the author Petronius, who
himself probably had no cognomen, it may well also mock
the growing aristocratic habit of polyonymy.

Trimalchio so took his owner's fancy that on the death of the
latter he became co-heir with Caesar, and built up a business
empire despite some setbacks; by now he had migrated to
Campania, since he speaks of sending a cargo of wine to
Rome (the epitaph which he produces for himself at 71.12
states that he could have been a member of every club of public
officials at Rome, but declined; for the snob-value of this see
Bodel, *CP* 84 (1989), 227–8). Finally he retired from trading
and used his freedmen as agents for money-lending, while also
of course enjoying his revenues from the estates about which
we have already heard (compare how Eumolpus pretends to
have his investments in *fundis nominibusque* (real estate and
money-lending) 117.8, and also Pliny *Ep.* 3.19.8). Such a move
from trading to land would confer respectability (Cic. *De Off.*
1.151; see Veyne (1961) 238–9); but Trimalchio is so dominated by the speech-habits of his slave days that he still refers
to his fortune as *peculium* (the pocket-money which a slave was
allowed to retain), as does the freedman on *CIL* 3.6998 (Veyne
233; see other instances in *TLL* 10.1.931.45, and p. 120 below
on 75.3 and 76.7).

Now to return to the narrative at 29.7. In the portico Encolpius
also saw a team of those couriers who had escorted Trimalchio
from the baths (28.4) exercising under their trainer.[14] In a large
cupboard which holds the Lares as well he sees a statue of
Venus (because it was his owner's love that gave Trimalchio his

---

[14] It is amusing to see how Blümner 466 n. 12 takes this as factual
information. It is of course part of the fictional character Trimalchio's attempt
to elevate his household to imperial scale, and the trainer is like those for the
imperial post (*cursus*) mentioned in the inscriptions referred to by Blümner.
Handbooks on Roman antiquities often take fantasy for prosaic fact.

prosperity) and a sizeable gold casket containing, as he is told, the first clippings of Trimalchio's beard. It was not unusual to dedicate such first clippings of both beard and hair, but it is almost imperial ostentation to use gold for the casket, as Nero did (Suet. 12.4, Dio Cass. 61.19.1) and later Domitian's *deliciae* (Stat. *Silv*. 3.4.91; the *pyxis* is specifically mentioned in the preface to the book). The point, however, is not that we should see a caricature of Nero in Trimalchio, but again (above, n. 10) that Trimalchio apes imperial procedures; there will be more about this below.

At this point there seem to be gaps in the text, as there not seldom are in the manuscript of the *Cena*, though they are not due to a process of excerpting. In respect to an enquiry by Encolpius, the porter (they are now apparently in the *atrium*, the entrance-hall) explains that some pictures show the *Iliad* and the *Odyssey* and the gladiatorial show put on by Laenas; this is meant to prepare us for the mixture of vulgar enthusiasms and pretensions to culture that will characterize Trimalchio (cf. the scenes on his goblets at 52.1–3). Note that Encolpius seems unable to decipher the Homeric pictures without the captions of 29.3; this suggests that the Homeric narrative was as distorted as Trimalchio's later versions. When they arrive at the dining-room itself, they find fasces and axes affixed to the doorposts, with an inscription indicating that a steward Cinnamus had put them up in honour of Trimalchio's sevirate (this board predominantly consisted of wealthy freedmen and was in part a vanity office; cf. 57.6, 65.3); at 71.12 we are told that he had been complimented by being elected in his absence (this has been discussed above). The sevirs were entitled to fasces, but not to axes; this again is vanity, but, as Friedlaender shows (see also Veyne (1963) 62(–63) n. 3), not unique to Trimalchio. The difference between the social milieu depicted by Petronius and that which we usually encounter in Roman literature is highlighted by the fact that nowhere else in Roman literature is there any mention of the Augustales, abundantly attested by inscriptions as a vital ingredient in small-town life in Italy.

There are also two notice-boards. One is an appointment calendar for Trimalchio with the announcement 'on December 30 and 31 our Gaius is dining out'; the use of the praenomen is

not, as Smith has it, a sign of over-familiarity of the household
towards Trimalchio, but, as Maiuri 157 shows from Pompeian
inscriptions, a perfectly normal form of expression. This is
intended to give long advance notice[15] to Trimalchio's usual
guests that he will not be holding his regular dinner-party on
those dates, and therefore to convey that his lavish meal is a
nightly occurrence,[16] and that he moves outside his self-
contained world (see above, p. 75, on 28.7) only on the last
two days of the year. The other board[17] shows the course of the
moon, with the favourable and unfavourable days of the lunar
month marked, and pictures of the gods representing the seven
planets (i.e. Jupiter, Saturn, Mars, Venus, Mercury, sun and
moon, the gods of the seven-day week which in our record
appears at Rome first at Tib. 1.3.18; see *RE*, *Hebdomas*
2573–4). This is designed to introduce us to Trimalchio's
superstition, and especially his belief in astrology; Encolpius
sarcastically refers to all this as *uoluptates*. The superstition is
underlined by the admonition of a slave that they must enter
the dining-room with the well-omened right foot.[18]

As they are about to enter, a slave who has been stripped
ready for a whipping entreats them to rescue him from punishment for failing to watch the clothes of the steward at the baths.
So they intercede; the steward, no doubt the above-mentioned

---

[15] 53.2 shows that the dramatic time is late July or early August; though
there has been a cold snap (41.11) there is also a drought (44.2). One must
admit that perhaps Petronius did not bother about exact timing.

[16] The same implication is conveyed by 'yesterday' 34.7. P. Tremoli, *Le
iscrizioni di Trimalchione* (Trieste 1960) 16, adduces *CIL* 4.8352 *III Non(as)
Mai(as) III Non(as) Iunias Pompeis. pr(idie) Non(as) Iunias P[uteo]li(s)*
('On May 5 and June 3 at Pompeii, on June 4 at Puteoli'); since this is in a
kitchen, it looks like a cook's record of when his master will be at home and
when away.

[17] The clearest idea of the appearance of this may be gained from the
drawings of a similar board (now lost and known only from reconstructions)
in S. Eriksson, *Wochentagsgötter, Mond und Tierkreise* (Stockholm 1956) 18,
and *Inscriptiones Italiae* 13.2.56 (pp. 308–9); see also *RE* s.v. *Parapegma*
1362–3 and *Planeten* 2169, H. G. Gundel, *Zodiakos* (Mainz 1992) 45, Eriksson
40. A similar poster calendar has been found at Dura-Europos (Snyder, *JRS*
26 (1936), 12 and pl. 5 after p. 141); Snyder's plate is reproduced in J. Rüpke,
Kalender und Öffentlichkeit (Berlin 1995), 589, with the other board on 590
and discussion of the whole topic. See ibid. 456 for the seven-day week.

[18] See Deonna–Renard 68 and my note on Juvenal 10.5.

Cinnamus, condescendingly says that the clothes were an
expensive gift of a dinner-suit from a client (of Trimalchio,
of course), made of Tyrian purple even if they had lost some
value through having been once to the cleaners, but it is not so
much their loss that annoys him as the carelessness of the
worthless slave, whom nevertheless he will forgive at their
request. When they enter the dining-room the same slave
rushes up to them, plants a shower of kisses on them and
promises to serve them the best wine; he seems to be using a
proverbial expression here,[19] so we should not take his words
too literally and infer that Trimalchio is one of the notorious
hosts who provided poorer wine for the less distinguished
guests (in 34.5 sqq. he serves what professes to be Falernian
wine to everyone).

The point of all this is to give us a foretaste, based on the
converse of the axiom *qualis dominus, talis et seruus* (58.3; like
master, like slave), of the atmosphere of the house of Trimalchio. First of all is the condescension of the *dispensator*, who is
himself a slave, both to the free guests and to another slave; he
is a Trimalchio (who himself had learned to keep accounts and
be a *dispensator*, 29.4) in the making, and mirrors the manner in
which Trimalchio, himself an ex-slave, speaks of his slaves in
order to distance himself from his former status (compare
30.10 *nequissimi serui* (worthless slave) with 34.5 *putidissimi
serui* (filthy slaves); cf. *nequissimi serui* in the mouth of Bargates,
certainly himself a freedman, at 96.6). Secondly, the clothes,
like those of his master, are of vivid colours, specifically of
expensive Tyrian purple, the wearing of which various emperors tried without success to restrict (see my note on Juvenal
1.26). Thirdly, in lordly fashion he pretends that the pecuniary
loss is not the main thing in his eyes, here too adopting the
attitude of his betters (Trimalchio himself in 64.11, Eumolpus
pretending to be a rich man in 117.7, all three times with the
phrase *iactura mouet* ('the loss upsets') in various forms).
Fourthly, he apes Trimalchio's habit of forgiving slaves for

[19] For Greek and oriental parallels see Jacobson, *CP* 66 (1971), 183, and the
articles quoted by him (note particularly Aristoph. *Knights* 1205 adduced by
Zielinski), Bauer in *Festschr. R. Muth* (Innsbruck 1983), 17 and 19, Fehling,
Glotta 58 (1980), 20. It is sometimes said that the slave's words constitute a
senarius, but *ministratóris* is not a legitimate iambic shortening, whereas
ministrátor would be.

transgressions on the intercession of guests (49.6, 54.3); this will be discussed below (pp. 97–8).

Finally they get to recline (sit down, in modern terms). Young slaves pour refrigerated water on their hands, chiropodists (*ad pedes*) remove their hangnails (not something that they enjoy). All the time they sing; Encolpius, wishing to find out if the whole household sings, asks for an aperitif, which is duly served with song which Encolpius compares to the chorus which would accompany a pantomime. This brings to our attention the strong element of theatricality in Trimalchio's presentation of his meal, which has been excellently discussed by C. P. Jones 185. Then come very nice hors d'oeuvre, still in the absence of Trimalchio, for whom an unconventional (*nouo more*; cf. 27.3 and n. 5 above) place is reserved, apparently *summus in summo* rather than the usual *summus in imo*.[20] One of the hors d'oeuvre introduces the theme of deceptive foods which will become prominent in the *Cena*. Sizzling sausages are served on a silver dish, beneath which are damsons and pomegranate grains; the idea is that they should look like hot coals.[21]

(ii) 32.1–36.8

At last Trimalchio himself appears to a fanfare, but his appearance is so absurd that the unwary among the guests are surprised into laughter. He is wearing a scarlet coat, a scarf with a broad purple stripe and a fringe of tassels,[22] a gilt ring on the little finger of his left hand and on the next finger a smaller gold ring studded with iron stars.[23] Most of this is meant to

[20] Smith 66 gives a diagram of the seating arrangements. Bauer 19 compares πρωτοκλισία in Matthew 23: 6, Mark 12: 39, Luke 20: 46.

[21] As Avery, *Hermes* 107 (1979), 120, points out, *prunum* means 'plum', *pruna* 'live coal'; there is no etymological connection, nor did the Romans make one.

[22] Marmorale quotes Suet. *Iul.* 45.3 *ferunt usum lato clauo ad manus fimbriato* ('They say that he used a broad-striped tunic with fringes down to the hands'); perhaps another case of Trimalchio modelling himself on a (nearly) imperial precedent. See also Mart. 4.46.17 *lato uariata mappa clauo* ('a napkin marked with a broad stripe').

[23] For his rings see also 71.9. I have encountered the statement that he would have been entitled to wear a gold ring during his tenure of the sevirate, an office held for a limited term (annual?), though renewable; but I have not

hint at, without actually claiming, the status of a senator (the purple stripe, which he does not venture to have on a toga) or an *eques* (pure gold rings were the mark of free-born *equites*). After using a silver toothpick, he says that he did not yet feel like coming to table, but he had done so so that his guests would not be kept waiting any longer. This is of course a social gaffe in that, while professing to oblige his guests, he actually puts them in an awkward position. He asks indulgence to finish his solitaire game, played on a board of expensive materials and (which really impresses Encolpius; *rem omnium delicatissimam*, the height of refinement) with gold and silver coins instead of black and white counters, and swears heartily when the dice do not fall as desired.

Meanwhile a dish is brought in with a nest in which a wooden hen lies as if hatching her eggs; two slaves (to musical accompaniment, naturally) search through the straw and find not hen eggs (which were sometimes presented at table in this manner; Juv. 11.70) but peahen eggs,[24] which they serve up. Trimalchio diverts his attention from his game to this piece of theatre, *scaena*, as Encolpius sees it; we infer that Trimalchio is the impresario, and as the *Cena* progresses it will become more and more apparent how he has tried (not always with success) to plan it to impress. Trimalchio pretends to fear that the eggs, which are actually made of pastry,[25] have already hatched, and Encolpius is about to reject his in disgust when he hears a guest who is an old hand (cf. 36.8) say 'there must be some goody here', and finds inside a plump fig-pecker (a little bird which is still a favourite Italian delicacy) coated in real egg-yolk with pepper. This is the second, more elaborate and more explicitly drawn to our attention, instance of foods which are not what they seem to be (a feature recurring with pastries in 40.4, 69.6). This recurrent theme of unreality and deception reaches its

been able to find any evidence for this. The iron stars are a diluted reminder of the iron ring ordinarily worn by freedmen (58.11) among others (see my note on Juv. 11.129).

[24] Avery [above, n. 21] 120–1 points out that peahens' eggs, which are larger than hens' eggs (Colum. 8.11.12), were regularly hatched by hens (Colum. loc. cit. etc.).

[25] At the moment (33.6) when the narrator Encolpius conveys to us that the eggs were of pastry the actor Encolpius did not yet know this. This feature of Petronius' narrative technique has been discussed on p. 38 above.

height later in the cook Daedalus (70.1–2), who can make any
food into any other; of course he derives his name (sometimes
given to slaves; Solin (1996) 328) from the mythical Daedalus,
also a master of deception, who in Trimalchio's muddled brain
(52.2) shut Niobe inside the Trojan Horse, another symbol of
deception which will again play its part in the *Cena* (ch. 49).

While the hors d'oeuvre are being removed, a silver dish is
dropped, a slave is pummelled for picking it up, and it is swept
away with the trash. This is meant to show Trimalchio's lordly
indifference to valuable property once it has been damaged; we
are reminded how his steward's suit of Tyrian purple lost value
in his eyes (though not so much as the silver in Trimalchio's
eyes) once it had been cleaned, and indeed how balls which had
hit the ground were not picked up (27.2). Then two 'long-
haired Ethiopians' enter and before the next course instead of
water pour wine over the hands of the guests from wineskins
like those used for sprinkling the sand in the amphitheatre, a
comparison which reinforces the feeling that Trimalchio is
making a spectacle out of the meal. 'Long-haired Ethiopians'
is a contradiction in terms; these are the long-haired pages
common in Roman households (27.1, 57.9, 70.8; Trimalchio
himself 29.3, 63.3) with blackened faces (cf. 102.13), another
case of things which are not what they seem. Actual Ethiopian
slaves were a popular form of ostentation (see Barsby on Ter.
Eun. 165). The guests praise Trimalchio for his *elegantiae*, but
right away this is exposed as empty. For wine-jars are brought
in with labels stating that this is 100-year old wine dating from
the consulship of Opimius in 121 BC (i.e. the labels claim to
have been affixed in 21 BC). This famous vintage was already
undrinkable in Cicero's day (*Brut.* 287), and in Petronius' time
could only be used to fortify younger wines (Pliny, *NH* 14.55).
Since this wine is not undrinkable, and since Trimalchio later
(48.2) specifically claims that he never buys wine but produces
all that he serves on his own estates, one must infer that all this
is empty ostentation, despite his give-away remark 'I serve up
REAL Opimian wine'. It has also been pointed out that at the
date of Opimius local designations of wine were not yet applied
(Pliny, *NH* 14.94; Bicknell, *AJP* 89 (1968), 347), so the
originator of the labels (i.e. Trimalchio) has betrayed himself
with *Falernum*. Trimalchio adds 'I served up less good wine

yesterday, though the guests were of a much better class', again
a piece of social ineptitude which simultaneously compliments
and insults the company. They, however, discharge their social
obligation by conscientiously (*accuratissime*) praising the lavishness (*lautitiae*, a word which Encolpius used without sarcasm in 32.1; cf. *lauta* 31.8).

Anyway the wine provokes gloomy comments from Trimalchio: 'Wine lives longer than man, so let's drink heartily, wine
is the stuff of life.' This will immediately put the readers in
mind of some tomb inscriptions, such as *CLE* 243 'While I
lived, I enjoyed drinking; drink up, you who are alive' (see also
my *Musa Lapidaria* nos. 169–71 with my notes). The funereal
atmosphere is heightened when a jointed silver skeleton is
brought in and thrown on the central table several times to
produce grotesque shapes. This is the famous 'skeleton at the
feast', a reminder of mortality deriving ultimately from Egypt[26]
though, unlike the Egyptian mummy, this has something of the
puppet-show about it. It elicits from Trimalchio a mournful
three-line epigram, in the sub-literary form (as at 55.2) of two
hexameters and one pentameter, which has obviously been
composed in advance—another instance of staging. Trimalchio
is so proud of his ability as a poet (others would with more
justice call him a poetaster) that he later has a slave recite some
of his compositions (41.6). There has been a hint of dark
undertones in 26.9; now they are brought out much more
clearly.

After the guests have praised (cf. 39.6, 41.8, 52.7–8) this
mediocre epigram, the next dish to arrive seems disappoint-
ingly small, though novel. It resumes from 30.4 the theme of
astrological superstition, consisting as it does of a round platter
displaying the signs of the Zodiac, with an appropriate food
placed by each, e.g. a slice of beef by Taurus.[27] Most of the
items take the form of a rebus, which Trimalchio again adopts

---

[26] See Dunbabin 186 sqq., esp. 196 sqq. and (for Egypt) 208; Wöhrle,
Hermes 118 (1990), 292 sqq. (esp. 297). See also Polemon, *AP* 11.38 = Gow–
Page, *Garland of Philip* 3350, where again we find the link between death and
drinking.

[27] This is not quite so novel as the guests think; a similar dish with a partial
Zodiac is described by Alexis fr. 263 Arnott, and see also *AP* 9.822 (late and
anonymous).

in 56.8–9. The guests are disappointed by the mediocre food,[28] but Trimalchio urges them to eat; '*hoc est ius cenae*'. When the lid is lifted delicacies are disclosed, some of them again in deceptive form (a hare with feathers attached to look like Pegasus, fishes in sauce as if swimming). Now the guests grasp the point of Trimalchio's feeble pun on *ius*, 'law' and 'sauce'. So the slaves break into applause (cf. 50.1; they have been trained to do this like the claqueurs often organized for theatrical performances), and the guests with laughter take the hint and do the same, to Trimalchio's delight.[29] Applause too is something which will put us in mind of the theatre; so also at 50.1, where it is coupled with the specifically theatrical term *automatum*, conjuring trick. At this point we will recall that Agamemnon (5.7) had advised against becoming a hired applauder in the theatre, which is exactly the role that he himself plays in the *Cena*!

Trimalchio calls out a slave, who carves up these delicacies, needless to say, to musical accompaniment, which is compared to that at a gladiatorial show, so that the display of art takes precedence over the function of carving. This slave is named Carpus (quite a common name), so that the vocative *Carpe* is identical with the imperative *carpe* of the verb *carpo* 'carve', and this provides Trimalchio with the material for another feeble pun. Encolpius is so dim-witted that he has to have this explained to him by a veteran guest (cf. 33.8; 'veteran' is *qui saepius eiusmodi ludos spectauerat*, 'who had often watched shows of this type', which takes up the gladiatorial comparison); he is so disgusted that he cannot touch a morsel more. This then is the critical point at which he begins to find it hard to stomach Trimalchio. Note the implication that Trimalchio has perfected his tricks at feast after feast, so that the veteran guests are perfectly familiar with them.

(iii) 37.1–41.8

Turning to his neighbour (Hermeros, as the combination of 57.1 and 59.1 indicates,[30] Encolpius enquires about the woman

---

[28] There are some problems about this, very likely caused by a gap in the text; see Smith on 35.6–7.

[29] The point of all this was explained by Avery, *CP* 55 (1960), 116.

[*See opposite page for n. 30*]

running around hither and thither. In the first of the *Cena*'s long freedmen speeches, the character of which will be analysed in (iv) below, Hermeros identifies her as Trimalchio's wife Fortunata. What is remarkable in this speech is that it is a description of one character from the mouth of another who by his words also reveals himself; it was brilliantly analysed in these terms by E. Auerbach (*Mimesis*, Berne 1946, Eng. tr. Princeton 1953, ch. 2), who points out that the nature of Trimalchio's circle is thus illuminated from within and its vulgarity is made apparent by the standard which it itself sets, namely that wealth is the greatest good, and that any means of obtaining it is respectable, even the generally despised profession of undertaker (38.14); Stöcker 150 remarks how many of the characters in the *Cena* are introduced by a statement of their wealth. We may note that Hermeros hopes even in death to find pride in the material acquisitions of his life (57.6).

Auerbach's second point is the impression that is conveyed of dynamic social mobility (he might have remarked the pride that Hermeros takes in his rise at 57.11); all four characters mentioned by Hermeros have their past contrasted with their present, and bank-balances can go up (Trimalchio, Fortunata, C. Pompeius Diogenes, whose name shows that he is literally a fellow-freedman, *collibertus* (38.6), of C. Pompeius Trimalchio) or down (Iulius Proculus). In particular we may note the phrase 38.7 *de nihilo creuit* ('He started out with nothing') compared with 43.1 *ab asse creuit* ('He started out with a penny'), 71.12 *ex paruo creuit* ('He started from small beginnings'); we also note the craving for assimilation betrayed by the phrase *hominem inter homines*, a man of the world, 39.4 (here with a special point; see below) compared with 57.5, 74.13.[31] The reservation must be entered that this social mobility has its limits; as a freedman Hermeros can rise so far and no farther. Auerbach concluded that in the presentation of the guests at the *Cena* Petronius 'is closer to our modern conception of a realistic presentation than anything else that has come down to us from antiquity', a statement which of

[30] The identification is confirmed by the recurrence of some turns of speech, particularly *in rutae folium conicere* 37.10, 58.5 ('to throw into a leaf of rue', an obscure expression).

[31] For the Greek equivalent see Herodas 5.15 and Ch. VII n. 9.

course does not intend to deny the larger than life traits in the personality of Trimalchio himself.

Fortunata, reports Hermeros, has risen from the gutter and now exercises control over Trimalchio, whose wealth is so great that he can aim at self-sufficiency in which everything will be home-grown (Trimalchio himself makes this point at 48.2); for example, he fetches bees from Athens so that he will not have to buy Attic honey, and (a surrealistic climax) he has sent a message to have mushroom-seed imported from India. All this is summarized, from Hermeros' viewpoint, as bliss of mind, *animi beatitudo*! At this point we will recollect that Nasidienus was given the epithet *beatus*, which can refer either to mental or material happiness, in the very first line of Horace's poem discussed below (pp. 91 and 103). As far as Encolpius is concerned, he sarcastically designates Hermeros' information as *tam dulces fabulas*, pleasant gossip (39.1).

By now the last course has been removed, and Trimalchio reminds the guests that they should know him better than to suppose that he is concerned only with the food which he serves; '*sic notus Ulixes?*' ('Don't you know Ulysses any better?'), a Vergilian tag coming from the context in which Laocoon warns against the tricks of Ulysses, specifically the Trojan horse. 'One must' he says 'even while dining pay attention to culture (*philologia*); thank God for my ex-owner who made me a man of the world, au fait with everything'. 'Man of the world' is *hominem inter homines*, here with the point of suggesting a novel interpretation of the cultural ideal of *humanitas*, Trimalchio's mastery of which has enabled him to produce the Vergilian quotation. The remark alerts us to various recurrent themes, the most important one for the moment being the parody of the learned discussions recounted by many writers as having taken place at symposia; prominent surviving representatives of the sub-genre 'Symposion-literatur' (see *RE* esp. 1278, *OCD*, and *Der Kleine Pauly* s.v.) are the *Deipnosophists* of Athenaeus, the *Saturnalia* of Macrobius, and the *Quaestiones Symposiacae* of Plutarch (the last of these in fact emphasizes φιλολογία (Courtney 1962) 97; for φιλόλογα, cultural conversation, at dinner cf. Cic. *ad Att.* 13.52.2). Trimalchio's immediate purpose is to explain the Zodiac dish of 35.1–5. He starts with Aries, a sign under which are born

men with hard heads and countenances that know no shame; it
is the sign of *scholastici*, a joke at Agamemnon and his *umbrae*
which they take in good part. The other signs and the corresponding foods are similarly explained, with another shot at
Agamemnon when *rhetores* are said to be born under Pisces; it
is as if Trimalchio has heard Agamemnon's metaphor of fishing
for students at 3.4 (one might to some extent compare the
metatextual reference to Seneca discussed in n. 10 above),
though he has astrological justification (Grondona 24(–25)
n. 61 adduces Firm. Mat. *Math.* 8.30.7 for orators and
Pisces). As far as Trimalchio's own sign Cancer is concerned,
Connors 113 adduces an observation by T. Barton, *Power and
Knowledge* (Ann Arbor 1994) 193 n. 79, that his placing only of
a garland, not an item of food, over it carries imperial overtones. At the end the guests again shout 'bravo' (*sophōs*, a form
of acclamation used in the theatre) and proclaim Trimalchio
the king of astronomers.

Now the slaves bring in coverlets showing hunting scenes,
hunting dogs rush into the dining room,[32] and a tray with a
huge boar wearing a cap is carried in; it is surrounded by pastry
piglets placed as if they were suckling, another illusion but not
really meant to deceive since the guests see clearly that the boar
is not a sow. A burly, bearded man dressed as a hunter cuts
open its side, and out fly thrushes, which are captured by bird-
catchers with limed rods and brought to the guests. Presumably when each guest has inspected his bird, they are to be
taken away and cooked, but later (65.2) capons are served
instead. Here the theme introduced in subtle fashion at 39.3
is picked up; this theatrical course was known as a Trojan Pig,
porcus Troianus (Macrob. *Sat.* 3.13.13, quoting the orator
Titius of the second century BC). Encolpius tries in vain to
deduce why the boar is wearing a cap. Hermeros again has to
explain; yesterday the main course had laid claim to the boar
(*uindicasset*, in two senses, one suggesting that the boar is being
claimed as a slave), but it had been sent back by the guests
(*dimissus est* meaning also that it had been let go free, cf. 66.7
pernae missionem dedimus 'We gave its discharge to the ham'),
so today it returns to the feast wearing the cap of a freedman,

---

[32] C. P. Jones sees this as intended to recall an animal-hunt (*uenatio*) in the
amphitheatre.

which naturally is something that has significance for the host
and most of the guests. Encolpius' reaction to this explanation
is to curse his own stupidity and resolve to make no more
enquiries; already he has had to force himself (*duraui* 41.2),
whereas he had felt no shame in asking for the first time (36.7).
Petronius emphasizes the parallelism of these two episodes by
etiam hoc ('this too') in the answer of Hermeros, and by the
repetition of *interrogare* and *at ille*. Encolpius therefore is afraid
that he may seem never to have dined in respectable company.
This is of course ironical; Trimalchio had spoken of having had
'respectable company' to dinner yesterday (34.7), but it is an
odd kind of 'respectable company' which can be expected to
key into such 'freedman-humour'. This line of humour is
continued when a handsome boy enters dressed as Bacchus
and assuming his aspects as 'the Uproarious', 'the Loosener',
'the Clamorous'; he carries grapes around and in a high-pitched
voice delivers Trimalchio's poems. Trimalchio says to him
'*Dionyse, liber (Liber) esto*', of which the most obvious sense
is 'be free' (cf. 54.5), as if he were being freed like the boar, the
less obvious one is 'be Liber', in contrast to the other aspects of
the god already portrayed by him. The boy acts out this pre-
rehearsed charade by snatching the cap from the boar and
putting it on his own head. Trimalchio then points out that he
has *Liberum (liberum) patrem*, which on the surface means that
he owns *Liber Pater*, the slave Dionysus, but also slyly insin-
uates that he has now acquired a free father and has therefore
become of free birth (of course he and the company enjoy the
complicity in knowing this to be untrue). These elaborate puns
elicit the usual eulogy (*laudamus*) from the guests.

(iv) 41.9–46.8, *Conuiuarum Sermones*

The phrase quoted at the head of this section is pretty clearly a
reader's marginal heading which has been incorporated into the
text to mark the intermezzo 41.9–46.8. Trimalchio leaves the
table to attend to a call of nature; the guests feel that they have
gained 'liberty without a tyrant', a phrase which indicates the
control that so far Trimalchio has exercised over the proceedings, but also continues the preceding puns by laying claim to
the same freedom as the slave Dionysus. The first symptom of

this freedom is that Dama requests more to drink (apparently; unfortunately the text is corrupt), whereas this previously was only done with Trimalchio's permission (34.1). Here we catch an echo of another dinner with an obnoxious host, namely Nasidienus in Horace, *Satires* 2.8.77–83, where the host leaves the room, a buzz of whispered conversation breaks out, and Vibidius' requests for more wine are ignored by the slaves. On looking back we can pick up more echoes. In Horace 92–4 the host explains the origins and nature of all the food, so that in disgust the guests refuse to eat; likewise in 37.1 Encolpius is so disgusted by Trimalchio's feeble punning that with the same verb (*gusto*) he too refuses to eat anything more. The dish of Petronius 36.3, which has fish as if swimming in gravy (*ius*, previously introduced by Trimalchio in a pun; see above, p. 86, on 35.7–36.4) and soaked with peppered *garum*, fish-sauce, is suggested by that at Horace 42–50, which has an eel surrounded by scampi 'swimming' in a *ius* of which *garum* and pepper are ingredients. In Horace too the events of the party are related by a participant in the tone, a mixture of disgust and amused superiority, to which Encolpius eventually comes; one of the guests, Maecenas, like Agamemnon brings along two *umbrae*; and dishes are served with comparable ceremonial pomp. There will be more.

Five guests now give a speech each on topics such as a funeral that has taken place today, the character of the deceased, the high price of bread, the general deterioration in the state of the town and the inferiority of present-day officials to their predecessors, the upcoming gladiatorial show which will put a miserable previous one in the shade,[33] a public meal which will win electoral favour for its donor, and some scandalous gossip. These speeches constitute a structurally important element in the elaborately symmetrical scheme which Bodel 45, adjusting Hubbard, has laid out for the *Cena*, as they form the hinge or turning-point after which earlier episodes are recalled in reverse order; and this repetition is functional in that it contributes to the increasing sense of tedium and satiety communicated by Encolpius.

---

[33] Echion remarks on *familia non lanistica, sed plurimi liberti*, 'not just a hack troupe of gladiators but freedmen for the most part' (Sullivan), as if he were not a freedman himself.

Finally (46.1) Echion realizes that Agamemnon is becoming bored with this chatter and feels himself of a different social class, entitled to mock the words of his inferiors; this shows his own insecurity about the way he talks. His retort is that they all know that Agamemnon has been crazed by learning, and that Agamemnon should visit his modest (a diminutive in the Latin) place, where Echion will scratch together a meal;[34] this mock-modesty about his material prosperity is his answer to his cultural insecurity. He also states that Agamemnon will have Echion's own *cicaro* attending on him. This word at 71.11 appears to mean Trimalchio's slave-born foster-child, and it pretty certainly means the same here, as Booth, *TAPA* 109 (1979), 16, argues. This has the advantage of accounting for the typical slave-name Primigenius and Echion's statement *habebis ad latus seruulum*, 'You'll have a little slave at your side' (if Echion's own son were meant this would have to be taken as figurative); Booth compares the boy in Stat. *Silv.* 5.5, but this 'parallel' turns round and bites him, since Statius emancipated that boy in infancy (73). Anyway this is a studious boy (cf. the slave-boy at 75.4), whose studies, however, Echion wishes to direct to practical ends, not literature but law, to help run the family business (*domusio*; just as Trimalchio learnt *in domusionem litteras* 48.4 according to a pretty certain emendation); failing an inclination for that, he will be trained for a good trade as a barber or auctioneer or in the last resort (*certe*) an attorney. Romans with conventional views would have thought no more of the first two professions than of that of undertaker, which Hermeros, reflecting much the same values as Echion, had regarded as an honourable trade, *honesta negotiatio* (38.14). To such Romans the profession of attorney (which is why he will need Agamemnon's instruction, if that is what is meant) would have seemed a step up the social scale, not a second-best as it is to Echion, who evidently regards it as likely to bring in less money; Juvenal agrees with this view (7.106 sqq., where see my note), and we all have heard about plumbers who make more than some lawyers. Nevertheless

[34] He adds 'even if stormy weather has ruined everything this year'; if Petronius was writing this towards the end of his life, as he very likely was, this could be a reference to the great storm of AD 65 in Campania (Tac. *Ann.* 16.13.1).

Echion tells the boy 'whatever you learn, you learn for yourself' (a parody of Sen. *Ep.* 7.9) and holds up the attorney Phileros (not the Phileros who spoke ch. 43) for a model as one who has risen in the world because of his profession (here we see the same sense of social mobility as in the speech of Hermeros); the climax of his exhortation is 'learning's a treasure, and a trade stays with you for life'.

The point of all this small-town talk is clearly that the absent Trimalchio, who has been portrayed mainly in his own right up to this point, should now be set against a social background of the municipal society within which he circulates, and that, as with Hermeros, this society should come across through the mouths of its members. The first speakers show how their world is dominated by trivialities. Echion deepens the picture by his more explicit value-judgements and his belief that education derives its value from the income which it produces; as he says in strikingly concrete fashion, 'law brings in the bread, and he's tainted enough by literature'. This could not be said in the presence of Trimalchio, who has recently (39.2–4) stressed culture and whose tone towards Agamemnon in ch. 49 after his return is quite different from that of Echion here. Echion is acting in what he sees as the best interests of the boy and feels pride in him (even if it is absurd to be proud that he can divide by four; Trimalchio's pet slave-boy can divide by ten, 75.4, which is less easy with Roman numerals than in our decimal system); however, his resultant actions come over as stifling to any attempt at creativity and independence. That is exactly how Petronius wishes us to see Trimalchio and his society, often well-meaning but with inevitably Philistine values. One may add that suppressed hostility to Agamemnon breaks out again from Hermeros, who in 57.8 is quite polite about him, but as he gets angrier abuses him as Ascyltos' teacher at 58.13 (by now his rage has been diverted from Giton to Ascyltos; this happened at 58.7, where Friedlaender was perhaps right to suppose a gap in the text).[35]

The Latinity of these speeches has naturally aroused much interest, and indeed its comic quality has sometimes been allowed to overshadow more significant aspects of the *Cena*.

[35] There is a discussion of the characterization of all the guests in R. J. Ball (ed.), *The Unpublished Lectures of Gilbert Highet* (New York 1998) 126.

It is not central to the theme of this book to analyse this in
detail; useful starting-points for its study can be found in
Smith's appendix ii and in Boyce; see too Müller-Ehlers (ed.
3) 497, and N. Slater, *Reading Petronius* (Baltimore 1990) 147–
51. I should, however, like to stress that modern linguistic
perspectives demonstrate the accuracy of Petronius' observation of vulgar language, in that he makes his characters conform to linguistic trends which were not recognized as such
until modern times, and which can be seen establishing
themselves as the Latin of the lower orders turns into the
Romance languages. I mention in particular, since Smith and
Boyce do not draw special attention to this, that there seem to
be some expressions which have analogues in the Romance
languages but not in classical Latin, not only (if rightly
emended) *disparpallauit* (46.2; see A. Stefenelli, *Die Volks-
sprache im Werk des Petron* (Vienna 1962) 97), but also
(admittedly of uncertain interpretation) *tantum auri uides*
(37.7), which has been compared (Zucchelli, *WS* 28 (1906),
167) with Italian *tant' oro*. By contrast Heliodorus 8.15 comments on the bad Greek of Bagoas, but reports it in perfectly
good Greek; this is a sign of the difference of approach between
the serious novel and Petronius' comic version.

Overall the speeches are marked by an abundance of
Grecisms (and hybrid words produced by combining Greek
and Latin elements), slang expressions and clichés (including
more or less proverbial phrases), expressions that reveal the
impress of a slave past (such as appeal to a superior's *genius*),
morphological and syntactical vulgarisms (the former in particular often paralleled by Pompeian graffiti). Boyce (48–9, 52,
83) remarks that Trimalchio and Echion are particularly prone
to hyperurbanisms, the type of error which makes so many
people nowadays say 'between you and I'; that is, errors due to
over-correction in one direction of what is vaguely recognized
as a tendency to err in the opposite direction. In Trimalchio
this chimes perfectly with his attempts at culture; in Echion it
is a mark of his love–hate relationship towards education.
Finally we must note in these speeches a tangy, pungent quality
which comes from a sense of vivid feelings and engagement in
the topics, trivial though they may seem to outsiders; these
feelings, expressed in vigorous phrases and lively ellipses,

contrast with the trite clichés in a way strikingly true to life.
When J. B. Hofmann was writing his classic book on conversational Latin, he began by seeking a criterion which could define
conversational language in general, and found this in 'Affekt';
that is exactly the quality which we see in these speeches.

There is one more notable speech by a freedman in 57–8,
where Hermeros bursts into a tirade against Ascyltos and
Giton for their bad manners in openly deriding Trimalchio's
arrangements. Tension between the freedmen and those
regarded by them as *scholastici* has been apparent at 46.1 and
will reappear at 61.4. Encolpius himself indicates that Hermeros is quite justified (57.1 *intemperantis licentiae*, 'unrest-
rained and ill-behaved', 58.1 *indecenter*, 'inappropriately'); the
modern reader, however, will feel that a wider question is
raised both here and in Horace's *Cena Nasidieni*. That is
because we have developed the concept of 'snobbery', for
which Latin does not even have a word (*fastidium* is probably
nearest). The amused superiority which I have remarked in
Horace is the attitude of insiders to an outsider (in Horace this
attitude is present throughout, in Petronius Encolpius comes to
it only gradually); Trimalchio and his guests are such outsiders
who do their best to boost their status until they come up
against its boundaries. It is easy to mock the language and
attitudes of such men and allow this mockery to obscure their
qualities and achievements, but nowadays one can hardly
admire the mocker. Was Petronius such a mocker? It seems
quite likely that the *arbiter elegantiae* as a historical person was,
but the question is irrelevant; what we have in his novel are the
attitudes of his narrator. The mockery has to be seen against
the background of the cultural pretensions of Encolpius; he can
look down on these people, but equally they would be entitled
to dismiss him as an underachiever. As far as Trimalchio is
concerned, he aspires to a certain extent to the cultural values
of the narrator, but only as a decoration; essentially he is stuck
in the freedman values of wealth, luxury, and status.

(v) 47.1–65.2

Most of the central themes and motifs of the *Cena* have now
been introduced, so for chs. 47.1–65.2 it will not be necessary

to follow the method of sequential exposition employed so far. Instead the occurrences of these themes and motifs will be noted grouped together; note that sometimes two are combined and cannot be neatly sorted into separate compartments.

First is the theme of death, which was unobtrusively introduced at 26.9 (Trimalchio's clock which tolls out the hours of his life) and followed up at 34.10 with the skeleton and at 42–3 (a funeral which Seleucus has just attended). One of the guests, Julius Proculus, is an undertaker (and of course later Habinnas, who makes funeral monuments, appears). At this point we may review the attitudes to death revealed by the characters. In the *Cena* the word *mors*, the primary word for 'death', is found only at 71.6 (though the verb *morior* is quite common), and the euphemisms *uitali* [*lecto*] ('bed of life', i.e. bier; cf. *uitalia* 'grave-clothes' 77.15) and *abiit ad plures* ('he has gone to join the majority') appear at 42.5–6. Yet death is in the thoughts of the characters; Echion's praise of his boy has to be tempered by *si uixerit* ('if he lives') 46.3, and only Orcus, the god of death, can take away his accomplishments (§7, cf. 34.10). Short life-expectation in antiquity would make such thoughts spring naturally to mind, but what is significant in the *Cena* is their quantity. The commonest reaction is that we must enjoy life while we can (34.7 and 10, 43.1 [provoked by the preceding talk about a funeral], 72.2 [similarly], 75.7), i.e. by sensual pleasure (69.2), which is the only thing that one can bring with one into death (43.8; for this conception see my *Musa Lapidaria* no. 169 with the notes). For there is a sort of continuum between life and death (57.6, 74.17, 78.3), hence it is important to have a fine funeral and tomb (42.6–43.1, 58.12, 71.7, 78.2). One may observe also that a soldier is 'as strong as Orcus' (62.2), with which Otto 1306 and Friedlaender compared the Song of Solomon 8: 6 'Love is as strong as death', perhaps one of the Semitisms which have been detected in the speech of the freedmen.

It is noteworthy that there are direct links between thoughts of mortality and luxurious feasting. For this compare the words of Seneca to the glutton, *Ep.* 77.18 *mortem times: at quomodo illam media boletatione contemnis! uiuere uis: scis enim? mori times: quid porro? ista uita non mors est?* ('You fear death; but how you despise it in the act of savouring mushrooms! You

wish to live; is that because you know how to? You are afraid to
die; well then, is this life of yours not death?'). See too ibid.
60.4. The clock that tolls out the hours of Trimalchio's life is
placed in the dining-room (26.9); the cock whose crow foretells
a death ends up in a saucepan (ch. 74). Note too the observations of Dunbabin quoted on p. 115 below.

Within the section that concerns us in this chapter death and
fear come out strongly in the stories about the werewolf and the
witches (61–3); the former is the party-piece of Niceros
(Sandy, *ANRW* 2.34.2.1547, points out a subtle recall of
Vergil's eighth and ninth Bucolics), and Trimalchio, who has
previously heard it, persuades him to repeat it, as ever mana-
ging the entertainment (61.2, cf. 64.2). The same theme
appears in Trimalchio's story of seeing the Sibyl in a bottle
at Cumae; when boys ask her what she wants, her reply is 'I
want to die' (48.8; question and answer are naturally in Greek,
since the Sibyl did not know Latin). This builds on the account
of Ovid, *Met.* 14.129–53 (see Bömer's note on 147), where the
Sibyl reveals that in extreme old age she is doomed to be
reduced to an invisible particle with only the voice remaining
recognizable. Pausanias 10.12.8 says that her bones were
preserved in an urn at Cumae, and [Justin] *Cohort. ad Graecos*
37 p. 35E says that her 'relics' (*leipsana*) were there kept in a
bronze flask. All this of course belongs to the familiar pattern of
'the imp in the bottle'.[36] In rationalistic terms Petronius
probably wants us to understand that Trimalchio has been
taken in by an illusionist tourist attraction, the proprietors of
which will have dictated the question to be put to the Sibyl.

If we do so understand this, that introduces the next theme,
that of trickery and deception. In 47.8 Encolpius, by now
conditioned to look for tricks, expects the pigs which have
been brought in (with harnesses, as if they were equine; for the
bells cf. Phaedr. 2.7.5, Apul. *Met.* 10.18) and the men who
bring them to be performing animals[37] and acrobats (acrobats
eventually arrive in 53.11), but is disappointed in this; here we
have a double bluff. In 49 a pig served up appears not to have

---

[36] See Campbell Bonner in *Quantulacumque, Studies presented to Kirksopp
Lake* (London 1937) 1; Stith Thompson, index s.v. Bottle; G. Anderson,
Fairytale in the Ancient World (London 2000) 136.

[37] The *portenta* which he expects the pigs to do are θαύματα (cf. LSJ s.v.
I 2), tricks.

been disembowelled, and the cook is stripped for a whipping. Most of the guests intercede in his favour; clearly they understand that they are to play their regular role in a pantomime of begging off slaves from punishment so that Trimalchio can display his magnanimity. The same thing happens in 52.6 and 54.3, by which time Encolpius has learned his lesson, and as we look back to 30.9 (where we meet the same verb *despoliare*, 'strip') we can see how the slaves have learned to take advantage of this feature of the household and how the paymaster has adopted the lordly ways of his master. On this occasion, however, Encolpius is not disposed to mercy; he characterizes himself as *crudelissimae seueritatis*, showing ruthless severity, which is how he sees his actions at the time from his subsequent viewpoint as narrator, when he can perceive how he was taken in. It should be remembered that such requests by slaves for the intercession of friends or guests of the owner were apparently not unusual; 'since the master's treatment of his slaves was part of his public image, the slave might acquire some leverage on his master through the guests; not only that, but the etiquette of hospitality included deference to a guest who urged leniency for a slave threatened with punishment' (W. Fitzgerald, *Slavery and the Roman Literary Imagination* (Cambridge 2000) 55). The jurist Paulus, *Dig.* 21.1.43.1 speaks of *qui ad amicum domini deprecaturus confugit* ('A slave who takes refuge with a friend of his owner in order to seek pardon'; *deprecor* appears in this context in Petron. 30.9, 49.6), and the comic poets use the word *precator* (*TLL* s.v. 1150.57), intercessor; with 49.6 *postea si fecerit, nemo nostrum pro illo rogabit* ('if he does this again none of us will intercede for him') compare Ter. *Ph.* 142 *posthac si quicquam, nil precor* ('if after this (he does) anything, I do not intercede'). Here, as is remarked below (p. 115) on 71.12, we have to see Trimalchio as social reality writ large.

Anyway on this occasion when the 'forgiven' slave goes to 'disembowel' the pig, out pour sausages, a display that is called an *automatum* (50.1, cf. 54.4; not to be taken as an adjective with *plausum*), a conjuring trick (this too a word relating to spectacle, cf. Suet. *Claud.* 34.3). The cook now has a silver crown presented to him, as if he had been victor in some theatrical contest.

In 54, which has just been referred to twice, an acrobat falls on Trimalchio, an event which Encolpius, remembering ch. 49, suspects to be leading up to a pre-arranged *catastropha*, a 'coup de théâtre'.[38] He feels that his suspicion is justified when Trimalchio issues a 'decree' that the acrobat be freed (Trimalchio can do this, since 53.12–13 imply that he owns the acrobats), so that nobody can say that such a great man was injured by a slave. The 'decree' is not the only way in which Trimalchio here accentuates his greatness; a slave is beaten for applying a white bandage, not one of imperial purple (cf. 38.5). The reflections of the guests on the instability of Fortune again invite Trimalchio to three lines (unfortunately textually defective[39]) of subliterary verse which end with an injunction of the funereal type to 'eat, drink, and be merry'; this recalls 34.7–10, leading up to the first specimen of Trimalchio's subliterary verse (there the moral is introduced with *ergo*, as here with *quare*, both meaning 'therefore'). Trimalchio represents this as improvisatory. He says that the event (*casus*, a pun, since it also means 'fall'; the same pun in Hor. *Sat.* 2.8.71, see below, p. 103) must not pass without *inscriptio*, that is ἐπίγραμμα (55.4), and this is intended as a parody of the mini-genre of epigrams on non-fatal accidents (see Citroni on Mart. 1.12). The whole episode seems like a metatextual (see above, n. 10) recall of a mishap at the dinner-party of Nasidienus (Hor. *Sat.* 2.8.54 sqq.), when the hangings fall down and the host is comforted by reflections, which we might think disproportionate to the occasion, on the role of Fortune in human affairs. Was Encolpius right in his suspicion that all this has been staged? Looking back on the incident as narrator he certainly thinks so, and we cannot go against this.

In 60.4 a pastry Priapus holds fruit in his bosom *more uulgato*, in the common style, but when this fruit is touched it squirts saffron, which was regularly so squirted in the Roman theatre (hence this is described as a new opening of the games,

---

[38] Theatrical metaphors in Petronius will be discussed below, p. 162. Plut. *De Cupid. Divit.* 528b applies πομπή ('parade', cf. Petron. 60.5), θέατρον, δρᾶμα to dinner-parties of the rich.

[39] Others think that their metrical defect may be due to improvisation, as Trimalchio represents it; this would imply that the accident was not staged. If it was staged, then he has composed the verse in advance.

noua ludorum commissio [the last word a likely emendation][40])
and at sacrifices. This is not without precedent in Roman
luxury. Sallust, *Hist.* 2.70 Maurenbrecher (= 2.59 McGushin)
describes a meal *scenis ad ostentationem histrionum fabricatis,
simul croco sparsa humus et alia in modum templi celeberrimi.
praeterea tum sedenti* (sc. *Metello*, whose victory over Sertorius
is being celebrated) *transenna demissum Victoriae simulacrum
cum machinato strepitu tonitruum* (compare with this the preceding narrative in Petron. 60.1–3, discussed below);
McGushin's translation is 'Stages were erected for the shows
of the actors, the floor was strewn with saffron, and other
features recalled the magnificence of a temple. In addition to
that, when he was seated, a statue of Victory, let down by a
rope and accompanied by the artificially produced sound of
thunder . . .' It looks to me as if Petronius, who knew his
Sallust, is thinking of that actual occasion (cf. below, n. 52).
The actors for whom a stage was constructed would very likely
be performers of comedies, which refined hosts favoured, but
not Trimalchio, who prefers Atellan farces (cf. 68.5); Hadrian
'according to circumstances' put on either (*Historia Augusta*
1.26.4). Here the guests misunderstand the saffron and rush to
show their loyalty to the emperor; their misunderstanding is
due to Trimalchio's status as an Augustalis. The very phrase
noua ludorum commissio implicitly compares Trimalchio to the
magistrate presiding over the games, and thus introduces the
next heading.

Third comes the theme of the continuing attempts by
Trimalchio to assimilate himself to the high and mighty. His
'decree' in 54.5 has just been mentioned. In 47.1–7 on his
return to table he explains that he has recently been suffering
from constipation; he gives permission to the guests to fart at
table (that, he says, is what doctors advise) or to leave the table
for his well-furnished lavatory. He claims to know many who
died attempting to hold themselves in, because they 'refused to

[40] The Acta of the Secular Games of Septimius Severus (*Ann. Epigr.*
1932.70 p. 21; I (= G). B. Pighi, *De Ludis Saecularibus* (edn. 2, Amsterdam
1964) 161) after the heading *ordo ludorum honorariorum* (programme of the
games) list first a *commissio noua* consisting of pantomimes, so we probably
have another theatrical metaphor here. The whole episode is carefully
analysed by Miller, *Hermes* 117 (1989), 192.

face the facts' (this is Walsh's translation of *dum nolunt sibi uerum dicere*). The point of this is double-edged. First, he is assimilating himself to the imperial precedent of Claudius (again Smith is characteristically sceptical about this), who is said (Suet. 32) to have contemplated issuing an edict permitting farting at banquets, because he found that someone had been endangered by holding himself in (*continentia*, cf. *continere* twice in Petronius). Secondly, it is a comic distortion of Seneca, *Tranq. An.* 1.16 *quis sibi uerum dicere ausus est?*, 'Who has dared to tell himself the truth?' (in the context Seneca is talking about people who flatter themselves into believing that they have attained wisdom and into overlooking their faults, a matter which has a wider relevance to Trimalchio); physical in place of moral introspection, as Maiuri wittily puts it. One may compare the transference from vulcanology to physiology in fr. 39 B = 35 M = *AL* 473 (see Courtney (1991) 57).

Then in 47.13 Trimalchio threatens his cook, who is thus reminded of Trimalchio's *potentia*, with demotion to the company (*decuria*[41]) of the *uiatores* if he fails to perform satisfactorily. By this he means the couriers of 28.4 and 29.7; by calling them *uiatores* he suggests the official attendants on lesser magistrates (cf. *CIL* 12.4448 = *ILS* 6973 *exs decuria lictorum uiatorum*, 'from the company of lictors and couriers', and *OLD*, *uiatorius* 2). Again in 48.4 we are told about his twin Latin and Greek libraries, which mimic the set-up of the imperial public libraries of Rome (Starr, *Hermes* 115 (1987), 252). The most striking instance comes in 53 with the reading of the Daily Gazette of Trimalchio's estates; however much this has been disputed, and however unrealistically the numbers, which are all suspiciously round, are exaggerated, this must be taken to cover only one day (see Rose, *CP* 62 (1967), 258, and Smith 142; the criticism of Rose by R. Duncan-Jones, *Economy of the Roman Empire* (edn. 2, Cambridge 1982) 239, is niggling in some points). We are reminded of Pompey's freedman Demetrius (*RE* no. 50), who had the number of his slaves reported to him daily (Sen. *Tranq. An.* 8.6). This Gazette records the alleged crucifixion of a slave Mithridates for

[41] For such *decuriae* Baldwin, *Acta Classica* 21 (1978), 93, compares *CIL* 4.1604 = E. Diehl, *Pompeianische Wandinschriften* 496; see other instances in *TLL* 5.223.84.

cursing Trimalchio's *genius*, which is like an act of *maiestas*, treason, towards an emperor, the banishment (*relegatio*) of a porter to Baiae[42] (which is as much a punishment as banishment to e.g. Acapulco), and judicial proceedings (cf. 70.5) involving other slaves. What has caused the desperate attempt to see the Gazette as covering six months is Trimalchio's surprise at hearing that he owns a park at Pompeii, the reader's explanation that it was bought last year and has therefore not yet been entered in the books, and Trimalchio's reply that such purchases must be reported to him within six months. But this again is all pre-rehearsed playacting to impress the guests with the magnitude of Trimalchio's properties, and is not to be taken literally any more than the statistics. Likewise in 47.11–13 he pretends not to know the cook, whom he actually knows very well (70.1), just in order to show that he has *decuriae* of slaves.

One episode which is hard to interpret because of a gap in the text comes in 60.8–9. Here three slaves enter, of whom two place images of the Lares on the table; the gap follows, after which Trimalchio says that one is called Cerdo, the second Felicio, the third Lucrio. These are materialistic names (the first is common, for the second and third see Solin (1996) 93 and 66); we may compare the name of Trimalchio's *deliciae* Croesus, and indeed Fortunata herself, as well as the invocations of *Lucrum* and *Felicitas*, Gain and Prosperity, in Roman houses, for which see my notes on Juv. 14.204 and my *Musa Lapidaria* no. 135. Then the guests kiss an accurate likeness, *uera imago*, of Trimalchio. The three names are usually taken to belong to the Lares, but there would only be two Lares; these are clearly the names of the three slaves. The *uera imago* of Trimalchio would be a statuette of his *genius* with his own features; such a statuette is often found placed between two Lares (Wissowa 173). The kiss then would be that regularly given to an effigy of a god as a sign of respect (the *locus classicus* is Cic. 2 *Verr.* 4.94; see further Miller [above, n. 40] 203 n. 48); but the fact that the statuette has the features of Trimalchio clearly elevates his status.

Fourth are Encolpius' reactions to the proceedings and an

---

[42] Patrons at Rome could banish (the same verb) their freedmen to Campania (Tac. *Ann.* 13.26.2).

increasing sense of oppression; the latter comes through in the statement (47.8) *nec adhuc sciebamus nos in medio, quod aiunt, cliuo laborare* ('We did not yet know that we were toiling half-way up the hill, as the proverb has it'). Similarly the theatrical carving of 59, described in 60.1 as *tam elegantes* (this of course ironical) *strophas* ('tricks', originally a wrestling term but by now a dead metaphor), is followed by the resonant opening of the ceiling panels and the trembling of the whole room as if in an earthquake, which scares Encolpius;[43] the other guests, as Encolpius interprets their reaction, look up in expectation of a celestial omen. In fact a huge hoop with little perfume-jars to take away is lowered. Then the saffron of 60.6, already mentioned, is referred to as *molestus umor*, annoying liquid; Trimalchio's ostentation has misfired, because the saffron becomes unpleasant when it is squirted in the face. Finally in 65.1 Encolpius states that even the recollection of the savouries disgusts him.

Fifth come recalls of Horace's dinner-party of Nasidienus, one of which has already been mentioned. In 47.7 the guests stifle their laughter with swigs of wine, as Varius in Horace (63) does with his napkin; in 58.1 Giton is unable to stifle his. In 48.1 Trimalchio, like Nasidienus (16), offers to change the wine if the guests so desire. At 52.4 a servant drops a cup; Petronius is taking a hint from Horace, who envisages such a mishap (72). There will be one more striking recall at the end of the *Cena*. More generally, the *Cena Nasidieni* is also recounted by a participant playing little part in the action, which the host attempts to dominate.

   A reminiscence of another *Symposion*, that of Xenophon, will be discussed in a moment. Here one may remark that the acrobats in 53.11 recall the acrobat girl in Xenophon 2.7–22, but that Socrates enjoys the music (2.2) more than Encolpius. More significant is one of Plato's *Symposion* (the importance of

---

[43] The manuscript specifies his fear as *et timui ne per tectum petauristarius aliquis descenderet* ('and I was afraid that some acrobat would come down through the ceiling'). This is so feeble that I think it must have been interpolated by someone who had 53.11 sqq. in mind. The passage reads excellently without it: *consternatus ego surrexi, nec minus reliqui conuiuae mirantes erexere uultus* ('In consternation I rose, and likewise the other guests in amazement lifted up their countenances').

which will emerge in (vi) below), detected by Citroni, *Maia* 27 (1975), 301, in 61.4, where Niceros, about to recount his werewolf story, says 'I am afraid that these schoolmen' (i.e. Agamemnon, Encolpius, and Ascyltos) 'may laugh at me . . . better to be laughed at than laughed down' (this is Sullivan's translation of the play on words in the Latin). This recalls the remark of Aristophanes prior to his comical account of the origin of love in Plato, *Symp.* 189b, that he is afraid his words may be considered not γελοῖα but καταγέλαστα, not laughter-provoking but laughable. In Petronius the debasement of the context is underlined by the following epic tag *haec ubi dicta dedit* to introduce the far from sublime story. In 56.7 Trimalchio is by now even putting the philosophers out of business, a clear hint to us of the parody of the philosophical symposion; this is the sequel to a series of questions of the 'what is the most *x*?' type, such as were often discussed in the symposion (see *RE*, *Rätsel* 110–11), and a gnomic reflection on the mingling of bitter with the sweet. At this point I suggest that we are intended to recall that those speakers who address the whole company at the *Cena* are Trimalchio, Dama (he is too drunk to say more than a little, 41.10–12), Seleucus, Phileros, Ganymedes, Echion, and Niceros, seven in number if we leave out those who speak on a one-to-one basis; and there are exactly seven speeches in Plato's *Symposion*. B. Snell, *Leben und Meinungen der Sieben Weisen* (edn. 4, Munich 1971) 62 (see also his *Gesammelte Schriften* (Göttingen 1966) 115), suggests that Plato may have been influenced by a 'Dinner-Party of the Seven Sages'; he sees traces of the existence of this in the fifth century in skolia and a hexameter fragment preserved on papyrus. For other indications of the existence (not necessarily pre-Platonic) of such a work see *RE*, *Sieben Weisen* 2252–4. Controversial though the growth of the traditions about the Seven Sages is, at any rate we will note the discussion of such riddles in Plutarch's work of that name, 152f sqq.; a collection of riddles is associated with Cleobulus, one of the Seven, by Diog. Laert. 1.89.

In one respect the *Cena* resembles Plato more than Horace. In Petronius as in Plato each guest makes a speech and then falls silent (Trimalchio of course excepted); on an individual basis Hermeros interacts with each of the trio Encolpius,

Ascyltos, and Giton, but there is no general conversation round the table as there is in Horace. This is of course because Trimalchio imposes his dominance more than Nasidienus can do.

There are some other links to the tradition of symposion-literature, which has regularly appearing generic episodes just as do the novel (see Ch. II (i)), the epic (e.g. description of decorations of a shield), New Comedy, and most genres of ancient literature. Such motifs are the quarrel in 57–8, the θεάματα in 53.11 (discussed above), and the ἀκροάματα (the word in 53.12, 78.5) in 59.3 (discussed below); these Greek words were taken into Latin to indicate visual and oral entertainments at Roman dinner-parties.

Sixth, we have the intermittent attempts to keep up culture. In 48.4 Trimalchio asks Agamemnon what controversy he declaimed today, backing up his request with his claim to an interest in literature; and indeed he does know the technical term *peristasis*, the circumstances presumed as background of a declamation. Agamemnon starts off 'A rich man and a poor man were enemies', which gives Trimalchio a chance to enquire in pretended naivety 'What is a poor man?' This is a parody of a declamatory ploy found in Sen. *Contr.* 9.6.10–12, where a young girl accused of complicity in poisoning her half-brother asks 'Mother, what is poison?' and 'Father, what is a defendant?' 'A witty remark', replies Agamemnon; given his acceptance of the role (52.7) of praising Trimalchio's jokes, it is likely that this is to be understood as having been rehearsed. But, more than that, this role reproduces that of Philip in Xenophon's *Symposion* (1.14; he 'immediately tried to say something witty, so that he might discharge the function for which he regularly used to be invited to banquets'). After Agamemnon has expounded the *controversia*, Trimalchio dismisses it with a crude dilemma: 'if this happened, it can't be a *controversia*' (because *controversiae* were based on fictions); 'if it didn't happen, it's nonsense'. This sally meets with the usual obsequious praise from the guests, which encourages Trimalchio to ask if Agamemnon knows about the Twelve Labours of Hercules, or how, as he says he used to read as a boy in Homer, the Cyclops tore off Ulysses' thumb!

In the same vein Agamemnon gives a cue (50.1), by careful

examination of a dish of Corinthian bronze, for Trimalchio to claim that he alone possesses real Corinthian bronze. Encolpius looks for Trimalchio to boast that he imports his bronze from Corinth (which, since the real Corinthian bronze was no longer made there, would show his gullibility), but the explanation lies in Trimalchio's third pun on a name, that he buys it from a bronzeworker called Corinthus. Then, so that his guests may not consider him an ignoramus, he explains the origin of Corinthian bronze as due to the mixing of metal objects burnt by Hannibal after the capture of Troy[44] (an episode about which a listener called Agamemnon should surely know something!). He continues by describing vessels which he has, one showing Cassandra (!) killing her children: 'the boys lie dead so that you would think that they were alive', a phrase which comically misuses a commonplace of art criticism.[45] Another has Daedalus shutting Niobe inside the Trojan horse (a mixture of three separate stories), others the gladiatorial fights of Hermeros and Petraites (a let-down here; cf. the conjunction in 29.9 of the *Iliad* and *Odyssey* with the gladiatorial games of Laenas). His final comment is 'I wouldn't sell my connoisseurship for any money'!

In 55, after Trimalchio has improvised some verse (probably a pretence; see above, p. 99), the conversation, in which the guests (?) confuse Mopsus[46] with Musaeus or Orpheus, turns to poets in general, and Trimalchio asks Agamemnon what he sees as the difference between Publilius Syrus and Cicero. This is of course a ridiculous pairing, and we have to do with a

[44] Isidore, *Et.* 16.20.4 (quoted by Müller (Teubner) p. xxxi), takes this seriously! To Trimalchio heroic Greece, historical Greece (since he has in mind the capture of Corinth by Mummius in 146 BC), and Magna Graecia (since in 59.4 he has the Trojans fight the Tarentines, the latter name a certain correction) all merge into one. He also seems to be vaguely conscious that Carthage and Corinth were sacked in the same year. The mention of Hannibal is due to a confused recollection of the pyre in which the Saguntines immolated themselves and their valuables.

[45] See my note on Juv. 6.436, and Kay on Mart. 11.9. Petronius probably has in mind particularly Ovid, *Met.* 10.250 *uiuere credas* ('you would think it was alive'; the statue made by Pygmalion), with more references in Bömer's note.

[46] Most of the guests probably, like Trimalchio himself, come from Asia Minor, and they would know the name of Mopsus as founder of the famous oracle at Klaros, and also from the Cilician town Mopsuhestia.

parody of such comparisons in literary discussions (see my note on Juv. 6.436). Without waiting for an answer Trimalchio gives his own, which is that Publilius expresses finer sentiments, and he then quotes a moralizing passage, which he claims to be by Publilius, against expensive imported fowl and jewellery. His admiration of such verses contrasts as ill with his own luxury as Agamemnon's praise of frugality and independence in ch. 5. This poem poses a problem discussed in my *Poems of Petronius* 19–20, where I reject the views that it is actually by Publilius, that Trimalchio has composed it himself, or that it is a real quotation from someone other than Publilius misattributed by Trimalchio. I reached the conclusion, now accepted by Walsh, that Petronius composed the piece himself and, while he linked it to themes of the work, did not intend it as a literary composition to be related to the characterization of Trimalchio. Instead, I suggested, he is taking the opportunity to parody the quite frequent use of quotations from Publilius by Seneca to illustrate his moral teaching, and the piece is itself a parody of such moral tirades. There is a subtle recall of it in 67.9–10 (see below, p. 111). To a certain extent the description of the house of Oenothea (135.8) as I understand the point of that (see below, pp. 203–4) is comparable.

Then in 59 we have the entry of the Homeristae, a profession which gave theatrical performances of scenes from Homer[47] (Artemidorus 4.2; one is described in Ach. Tat. 3.20). While they are conducting their dialogue in Greek, Trimalchio reads out aloud a Latin translation for the guests and then, assuming that they have not followed the story, despite his claim to have read Homer as a boy (49.7), gives another of his mythologically garbled accounts of the narrative, in which Dio-medes appears as one of the Dio-scuri and has Gany-medes as his brother. The climax of this is that Ajax goes mad (because of the marriage of Achilles and Iphigenia!), and he, says Trimalchio, will complete the story. A boiled calf wearing a helmet (as if it were Odysseus, whom Ajax wished to kill) is brought in, and a carver dressed as Ajax cuts up the beast and serves it to the

---

[47] The material on these Homeristae is collected in full by Heraeus, *Rh. Mus.* 79 (1930), 397–402; see also *RE* suppl. 3.1158, C. P. Jones 189, and Starr, *Latomus* 46 (1987), 199. They are of course another theatrical element.

guests; thus the recitation is followed by a sort of performance of the same episode.

At the end of this episode, when Encolpius reports that his head was starting to swim with the wine (64.2), Trimalchio begins to lose control (64.8 sqq.). Two pups fight, breaking expensive crystal, he gives his *deliciae* Croesus, whom we first met in 28.5 and whose name again emphasizes the importance of material wealth in this household, a ride on his back, at the same time playing a game like morra,[48] and he orders a drink for the slaves of his guests (see Friedlaender on 64.13), which Encolpius sarcastically calls *humanitas* (65.1). Dramatically this means that his attempts to keep his distance from slaves are breaking down as he becomes drunker; this will be taken up in 71.1.

Finally *matteae*, sweetmeats, are served (65.1–2). This would normally happen at the end of a meal, and presumably offered some hope to the disgusted Encolpius that the ordeal of the meal is nearly over, or, to put it in his language of 47.8, they have reached the top of the hill. Not a bit of it; more food arrives in the next section, and there are more antics to come.

(vi) 65.3–78.8

Now comes the climax of the *Cena*, for which it will be necessary to return to sequential exposition.

A lictor knocks at the door of the dining room, and a reveller (*commissator*, that is κωμαστής) with a great train of followers enters. Encolpius is terrified by his lordly appearance (*maiestas*), takes him for the 'praetor' (a name sometimes used to dignify the office of municipal *duouir*[49]), and is on the point of rising (whether as a gesture of respect or because he has a guilty conscience and wants to get away) when Agamemnon stops him and says it is just a *seuir*,[50] the stone-mason Habinnas.

[48] See Smith on 64.12. This game is of great interest to South African scholars because of a similar one played there; see e.g. Hewitt, *Acta Classica* 3 (1960), 90. For other countries see Ullman (cited by Smith), and Collin in *Studier tillegnade E. Tegnér* (Lund 1918) 369, Winstedt, *Folk-Lore* 60 (1949), 395.

[49] See *RE, municipium* 617.37; for Puteoli specifically see *CIL* 10 p. 183b.

[50] For his lictor see p. 79 above on the fasces at 30.1.

Now relieved, Encolpius contemplates him more closely; he is drunk, leans on his wife's shoulder, wears garlands, and perfume is flowing down into his eyes; a queer kind of *maiestas*! He sits in the *praetorius locus*[51] and immediately asks for wine and warm water.

All this is an elaborate recall of the arrival of Alcibiades in Plato's *Symposion*, best discussed by Averil Cameron (1969). Some features derive from traditional precedents; the arrival of an uninvited (ἄκλητος) guest who turns up late goes back to the arrival of Menelaus (*Il.* 2.408) after Agamemnon has invited other Greek leaders to the sacrifice, which in Greek religious practice would be followed by a meal; the fact that this is a stock motif does not justify Smith 181 in casting doubt on the relationship to Plato.[52] Plato's *Symposion*, the dinner of Nasidienus in Horace, and the *Cena* are all recounted by a guest (in the case of Plato at second hand), as is common in the minigenre of the symposion. When we cast our minds back, we can see earlier foreshadowings. With the narrative of 26.8–10 we can compare how Socrates after his bath meets Aristodemus and says that he is going to dine at Agathon's house, hence (unusually for him) he has dressed up (cf. 26.10 *amicimur ergo diligenter*, 'So we dressed carefully'); he then invites Aristodemus to accompany him as ἄκλητος (174b–c), like Menelaus at the sacrifice and meal of Agamemnon. Petronius in fact has probably chosen the names Agamemnon and Menelaus to prepare for the Platonic setting, though those who bear them do not play roles corresponding to their Homeric namesakes; a

---

[51] This name is found also at Sen. *Contr.* 9.2.2; both here and there it is an adaptation to circumstances of the usual *locus consularis*, since Flamininus, the subject of the *controuersia* reported by Seneca, is consistently referred to by the speakers as praetor, for reasons which I do not understand, though the episode in fact is supposed to have taken place while he was consul in Cisalpine Gaul in 192 BC.

[52] In Xenophon's *Symposion* the buffoon Philippus is such an uninvited guest (1.11–13). Plut. *Brut.* 34.8 reports that Favonius, the crude imitator of Cato, after his bath forced his way uninvited into a dinner-party of Brutus. Brutus ordered the slaves to bring him to the *lectus summus* but he insisted on the more honorific *medius* (the *locus consularis* was *imus in medio*). There followed παιδία οὐ(κ) ἀφιλόσοφος, mirth and jest in philosophical vein. I wonder if Petronius knew of this incident. Another anecdote about a meal from Roman history was mentioned on p. 100 above. Perhaps the *elegantiae arbiter* had made a study of banquets for his use in setting up those of Nero.

role has likewise been shifted at 65.8, where it is the host Trimalchio who calls for larger cups, whereas in Plato (213e–214a) Alcibiades does this.[53] Later the host Trimalchio's impulses to versify (34.10, 55.3) correspond to that of the host Agathon (197c). Another reminiscence has been remarked at 61.4 (p. 104 above), and there will be another striking one at the end of the party.

Habinnas bears an otherwise unattested name which appears to be Cappadocian (69.2; though it may be that we have there a semi-proverbial expression not meaning literally that he is from Cappadocia); he is certainly not, as has sometimes been supposed, Jewish, since he dislikes circumcision (68.2). He explains that he has come from a memorial feast, *cena nouendialis*, laid on by Scissa (another unattested name) in honour of a dead slave (death again!); in response to the enquiry of Trimalchio, who is naturally interested in food, in the style of Old and Middle Comedy[54] he reels off the gargantuan menu, with some difficulty in remembering it all. It emerges that he too has a pet slave-boy, for whom he has stolen two apples in his napkin (66.4), because otherwise the petulant boy will give him a hard time. Encolpius has done the same for Giton (60.7), to whom he is in the same sort of semi-subjection. Now we can see the thematic function of the Platonic recall, the refinement of which casts a lurid light on these proceedings. The aristocratic Alcibiades is one of those people who become more charming as they become more tipsy, in all respects the opposite of Habinnas. The view of love, the central theme of the *Symposion*, represented by Habinnas and the boy-slave, and for that matter by Encolpius and Giton, could not be farther from that represented by Alcibiades and Socrates, which Giton later (128.7) uses as a reproach against abstinence by Encolpius.

After Habinnas' report of the menu, he asks why Fortunata is not present. Trimalchio replies that she is characteristically keeping an eagle eye on the serving, but at Habinnas' insistence has her summoned. She arrives, naturally in polychromatic attire, and goes over beside Habinnas' wife Scintilla; thus

---

[53] For another role-shift see above, p. 63 on 9.3.

[54] We may compare also the dithyramb Δεῖπνον of Philoxenus (Page, *Poetae Melici Graeci* 836).

Petronius, having previously shown Trimalchio in relation to
his cronies, now fills out the picture of him and Habinnas by
turning attention to the wives. Fortunata shows her jewellery
to Scintilla, and Trimalchio insists on having it weighed to
validate its value, while pretending to complain about its
expense. Scintilla too takes earrings from her locket[55] for
Fortunata's admiration, and Habinnas, like Trimalchio, pretends to grudge the expense. Connors 59–60 (making some
other far-fetched connections) has related this passage to the
'Publilius' poem in 55 and its criticism of pearls. Scintilla's
earrings are called *crotalia*, castanets; Pliny (*NH* 9.114) says
that earrings have this name because the pearls rattle against
each other. I add that 'Publilius' describes emeralds as 'expensive glass', and that Scintilla has pestered her husband to buy a
'glass bean' for her. So we here see the high sentiments of
which Trimalchio had approved in 55 given the lie by the
realities of his life. The women are by now tipsy and kissing
each other. Habinnas quietly rises, grabs Fortunata's ankles
and flings her legs up on the couch, so that her petticoat (her
dress is tucked up, 67.4) flies up over her knees; she hides her
blushes in her scarf. The crassness of this vulgar horseplay,
which shows the emptiness of Habinnas' 'courtesy' at 67.1–3,
does not need to be underlined.

Trimalchio then (68.1) orders *mensae secundae*, which in
ordinary parlance would mean 'dessert'; instead the slaves
bring in a second set of tables. All this too has obviously
been pre-arranged to give Trimalchio the opportunity for
another feeble pun, which he draws to the attention of his
guests. The slaves scatter sawdust tinted with saffron (see
Sallust quoted on p. 100 above), vermilion, and powdered
mica, a blend which will put the reader in mind of circus
spectacle (see Smith's note). A slave of Habinnas, prompted, as
Encolpius guesses, by his owner, begins an unmelodious recital
from Vergil, with verses from Atellan farces (cf. 53.13) interspersed; this and the preceding imitation of animal noises[56] are
called *ludi*, stage performances. Habinnas remarks that the

[55] She calls this Felicio 'Lucky Boy' (cf. 60.8), as if the jewel-box had
personality for her.

[56] Cf. Phaedrus 5.5 and Plut., *Quaest. Symp.* 5.1.674b–c, the story of
Parmeno's pig.

slave has had no formal instruction, but that he had trained him
by sending him to the street performers, so that he can now
imitate muleteers or street performers (what a qualification for
reciting Vergil!). He can also turn his hand to many occupa-
tions, but has two flaws, that he is circumcised and snores. This
indicates that Habinnas has experience of him in bed; the
circumcision would be a flaw because Greek homoerotic
vase-paintings show a preference for elongated foreskins.[57]
Scintilla's jealousy is aroused by this (cf. already 67.11), but
Trimalchio retorts that Habinnas is right to enjoy himself
while he is alive, for no one will give this to him when he is
dead (cf. 43.8 in the context of a funeral); that women too are
not paragons of fidelity, and he himself used to 'bang' his
mistress (he again refers to this at 75.11) until his owner
became suspicious and sent him off to supervise a country
estate. The slave, as if he had been praised, took a clay lamp out
of his 'pocket' and used it to imitate a trumpet (as Trimalchio
had done at 64.5), with Habinnas chiming in, then employing
broken reeds he imitated an oboe-player, finally in costume
mimicked muleteers until Habinnas called him over and
kissed him.

  All this afflicts Encolpius, but finally the dessert, ordered by
Trimalchio at 68.1, is served, consisting entirely of foods which
imitate other foods, pastry thrushes, quinces with thorns stuck
in them to look like sea-urchins, a goose surrounded by fish and
gamebirds, at which Trimalchio remarks that everything the
guests see is made of one substance. Encolpius, referring to
himself with ironical hindsight as *scilicet homo prudentissimus*
('being of course quick on the uptake'), and declaring that he at
once realized what was happening, presumes this substance to
be wax (? this is a textual supplement) or clay, like fake foods
which he had seen at Rome at the Saturnalia. Wrong again!
Trimalchio explains that they are all made of pork; his cook has
the knack of turning any food into any other,[58] and therefore
has been given the name of the supreme trickster Daedalus,

[57] See Dover 125–9, Henderson 111 n. 17, T. Hopfner, *Das Sexualleben der
Griechen und Römer* (Prague 1938) 219.

[58] Cf. (ii) above. He was not unique in this; see Livy 35.49.6–7, Horace's
Cena Nasidieni 28 with Muecke's note, Kay on Mart. 11.31, and Rosati in
Harrison 95; add Cic. *Ad Fam.* 9.20.2 as emended.

whose trick of presenting a wooden figure as a bull has been
alluded to in the garbled account of 52.2.

A brawl between two slaves follows, but it is all a pantomime; despite all that Encolpius and the other guests have
seen, they still fail to realize this. The point is double: first to
stress the grandeur of Trimalchio, who issues a formal judgment between the slaves (cf. 53.10); second, to motivate the
breakage of the jars which the slaves carry, out of which spill
oysters and scallops. Then comes the anointing of the feet
discussed on p. 8 above. By now the women, already tipsy at
67.11, are thoroughly inebriated, so that Fortunata is willing to
perform the dance which she had declined at 52.8–10. Trimalchio too now abandons his dignity towards his slaves and in
Saturnalian fashion invites them to recline at table, which they
do, almost pushing the guests off the couches; the cook even
challenges Trimalchio to a bet on the next circus races.
Trimalchio, becoming expansive with this rivalry, says to the
company 'Slaves too are human beings' (*homines*, taking up
humanitas in 65.1), 'yet while I'm still alive they will soon taste
freedom, for I free them all in my will' (a comic self-
contradiction). 'I proclaim this so that my household may
love me now as if I were dead' (a remark whose implications
he might have avoided had he been sober). All this is clearly
written in relation to Seneca, *Ep.* 47, in which Seneca commends Lucilius for his treatment of his slaves: *'serui sunt', immo
homines* (§1) . . . *rideo istos qui turpe existimant cum seruo suo
cenare* (§2) . . . *(seruum) admitte . . . in conuictum* (§13) [' "They
are slaves", on the contrary human beings . . . I laugh at those
who think it disgraceful to dine with their slave . . . admit a
slave to a convivial occasion']. Seneca goes on to say (§15) that
only slaves whose good character merits this should share the
meal. As Smith states, Petronius is not here parodying Seneca,
who of course is talking about occasions when Lucilius is
dining alone; the point in Petronius is to show Trimalchio
reducing this *ad absurdum*.

Prompted by all this, Trimalchio sends for his will and reads
it out. Then he turns to Habinnas (now we see why Petronius
made him a stone-mason) to discuss his tomb and its sculp-
tures, which are to include his dog,[59] garlands and perfumes to

[59] The monument and its representations are discussed by Whitehead in

recall his feasts,[60] and all the combats of the gladiator Petraites
(already referred to at 52.3), so that Habinnas may provide
Trimalchio with posthumous life.[61] He is also to show the ships
that carried Trimalchio's merchandise (76.4 sqq.[62]) and Trimalchio wearing his official robe, *toga praetexta* (see below,
n. 66), and five gold rings, sitting on a platform and scattering
coins to the populace, plus a representation of a public meal
laid on by him (like that of Mammea, 45.10; see further
Donahue, *CP* 94 (1999), 68). All these prescriptions find a
close parallel in *CIL* 13.5708 = *ILS* 8379, which clearly consists of instructions given in a will but copied on to the actual
tomb, which was to be surrounded by orchards, *pomaria* (cf.
Petron. 71.7). Trimalchio's monument itself has long been
compared with those of C. Lusius Storax from Chieti and
M. Valerius Anteros Asiaticus (*CIL* 5.4482) from Brescia,[63] the
former showing gladiatorial games and Storax on a platform
(he wears three rings in contrast to Trimalchio's five), the latter

P. J. Holliday, *Narrative and Event in Ancient Art* (Cambridge 1993), 299.
For dogs represented on tombstones see there 303, and J. M. C. Toynbee,
Animals in Roman Life and Art (London 1973) 109 sqq.; there is one on the
tombstone which gives us the name Ascyltos (Priuli tav. 1–2).

[60] Cf. 60.3, 65.7. But again we have the convergence of feast and grave, for
garlands and perfumes are common offerings at graves (see my *Musa
Lapidaria* 183.45), and garlands and perfume vessels are often shown on
funeral monuments (Whitehead 305).

[61] For representations of gladiators on tombs see Dentzer, *MEFR* 74
(1962), 554, and T. Wiedemann, *Emperors and Gladiators* (London 1992)
17.

[62] Whitehead 309 points out that while Trimalchio knows the significance
of the ships in his biography, the reader does not yet, and will for the moment
understand the ships as those frequently shown on funeral monuments with
symbolic significance; they link with such topics as 'the haven of eternal rest'.
The funeral altar of C. Munatius Faustus at Pompeii has a ship under full sail
on its side.

[63] For the monument of Storax see Whitehead 306, 310, and fig. 91;
B. Andreae, *The Art of Rome* (New York 1977) 62 and fig. 195; D. Kleiner,
Roman Sculpture (New Haven 1992) 148; *Cambridge Ancient History* (ed. 1)
plates 4 (1934) 190d; for that of Asiaticus Whitehead 310 and fig. 93; for both
J. Ronke, *Magistratische Repräsentation im röm. Relief* (Oxford 1987) 109, 140,
and Abb. 3–9. There are illustrations of both in *Dial. Arch.* 1 (1967), figs. 1–4,
and in *Studi Misc.* 10 (*Sculture municipali dell' area sabellica*) tav. xxx–xxxix
(Storax) and iv (Anteros). For Storax (the name of an aromatic gum, like
Cinnamus in 30.3) as a slave-name see Solin (1996) 161.

Valerius on a platform scattering largesse and a procession of
seuiri escorted by lictors.

As well as these official representations, there are to be
private ones: Fortunata holding a dove and leading a puppy
on a leash, Trimalchio's *deliciae* Croesus (referred to as *cicaro*;
cf. 46.3), wine-jars, one of them broken with a boy weeping
over it (obvious symbols of mortality), and a sun-dial, consultation of which will oblige the public to read Trimalchio's
name. Such a sun-dial is also of course a reminder of the
passage of time and hence of mortality (see above, pp. 72–3, on
26.9). Dunbabin 206–8 draws attention to a sarcophagus which
shows a skeleton, a meal, and a sun-dial, and remarks 'The
allusion to what is to come serves as a reminder . . . to enjoy
the pleasures of this life . . . Such a merging of the imagery of
the banquet with that of the grave is a familiar feature of
funerary iconography in many other respects also; similar
parallels exist between the epigraphy of the grave and the
epigrams of the feast.' These remarks are of wide applicability
to the *Cena* (the ambiguous message of the garlands and
perfume at 71.6 has just been mentioned); for funerary
epigrams in particular see my comments above (p. 85) on
Trimalchio's verses at 34.10.

Finally Trimalchio dictates his inscription, which begins by
inflating his name (see above, pp. 77–8), records his official
career, his virtues and wealth, and ends 'and he never attended
philosophy lectures'. There are two points of interest here.
First, Trimalchio was not alone in having his wealth recorded
on his tomb; editors quote *CIL* 11.5400 = *ILS* 7812 and
Horace, *Sat.* 2.3.84 sqq. We always have to remember that
while in many respects Trimalchio is surreal, in others he is
simply social reality writ large, and beneath the exaggeration
Petronius intends us to see him as representative of a certain
stratum in society with a soulless outlook. The actual amount
mentioned, 30 million sesterces, is not particularly large; he
lost this much in a shipwreck (76.4). If we bear in mind that at
the moment he cannot possibly foretell his bank-balance at his
death, we will understand that he is just filling in a temporary
blank with the amount which in general terms makes one a
'millionaire' (it is specified in this sense at 88.8). Secondly,
whereas Trimalchio in his way respects 'philology', which is

part of the culture of the class to which he aspires, he has no use
for philosophy (cf. 56.7) which is not an integral part of that
culture. A boast that one never succumbed to some fault or
other is often found in epitaphs; here Trimalchio's achievement is to be untainted by philosophy![64]

After this Trimalchio himself and everyone else begin to
weep (narrated by Encolpius in mock-elevated style), even
Encolpius. But Trimalchio puts an end to this with a sudden
mood-swing: 'We know that we shall die, so let's enjoy life'
(this recalls his poem in 34.10), and he takes everyone off for a
hot bath (we cannot but be reminded of the funereal commonplace *balnea uina Venus* 'baths, wine, and love'; see e.g. my
Musa Lapidaria nos. 170–1). Such hot baths, intended to
promote digestion and therefore renewal of appetite, were by
now quite common, and a favourite target of moralists; see my
note on Juvenal 1.143. Encolpius cannot bear the thought of
this, so he and Ascyltos agree to abscond. Giton guides them
(this function of guide is one that has to be presumed between
9.1 and 9.2, and he will be seen exercising it again in 79.4; its
thematic significance will become plain in Ch. VIII(iii)).
When they reach the door, the chained dog Scylax, which
they have encountered in 64.7, barks so loudly that Ascyltos
falls into the pool; note the significant contrasts that Ascyltos is
afraid of a real dog, whereas the naive Encolpius had feared a
painted one (29.1), and that here the dog prevents exit from the
house whereas the painted one had discouraged entry. In
attempting to rescue him, Encolpius too, now thoroughly
drunk, is pulled into the same 'flood', *gurges*, as he calls it (a
deliberately grandiose word, elsewhere employed by Petronius
only in verse except for the equally grandiose 114.6). While the
porter extracts them, Giton has protected himself from the dog
by throwing to it the food which Encolpius (60.7) and Ascyltos
had taken for him. They ask the porter to let them out, but he
replies that no guest of this house ever leaves by the same door
as he entered (so the watchdog not only keeps out intruders but

---

[64] There seems to be a curious parallel to this in *CIL* 6.9709 = *ILS* 7509,
the otherwise perfectly orthodox epitaph of a money-changer which unex-
pectedly ends *hic in IIII stabul(is) agitauit numq(uam)*, 'he never spent his
time in the stables of the four circus-factions'.

also keeps visitors in); this makes the trio feel that they are shut inside a novel type of labyrinth.

Now the symbolism of this chapter becomes plain. The labyrinth will recall its constructor Daedalus, a name which has several times emerged in significant contexts, particularly 52.2, where there is a muddled recollection of the story of Pasiphae and the bull. Giton is Ariadne or Daedalus himself, who showed Ariadne how to find the way through the labyrinth (Verg. *Aen.* 6.28). The labyrinth is associated in Vergil's narrative with the underworld by its appearance on the temple-doors made by Daedalus at Cumae, in the vicinity of which Aeneas descends to the underworld; it suggests the difficulty of emerging again (*Aen.* 6.128), and in fact Aeneas does finally emerge by a different exit. The *gurges* is how the Styx is referred to at *Aen.* 6.296; the porter is Charon; Giton's stratagem is throwing a sop to Cerberus (ibid. 417 sqq.); the dog has the function of Cerberus in preventing egress (not in Vergil but in other authors cited by Leary, *CQ* 50 (2000), 313). The implication of all this is plain. All the luxury in Trimalchio's house is just a way of disguising the fact that its inhabitants and guests are experiencing a kind of living death; now we appreciate to the full the proximity of the banquet and the grave which has been kept in our consciousness by continual occurrence of the theme of death in the *Cena* (note especially the Sibyl in 48.8). This profound symbolism may have been suggested to Petronius by the kind of funeral monuments investigated by Dunbabin, or by references to the νεκυία (Book XI) of the Odyssey in Plato's *Protagoras*, as I proposed (*AJP* 108 (1987), 408), or, very likely, by both. In any case the extra resonance given by the Vergilian intertextual allusions is a masterstroke.

Encolpius and Ascyltos now want nothing more than a warm bath. They find Trimalchio in a small bath like a cold-water cistern. This is very unexpected in view of the luxury of the rest of his house, and appears to have some relationship to Seneca's description of the villa of Scipio at Liternum (*Ep.* 86.4 *balneolum angustum*, a narrow little bath). The point seems to be that Trimalchio has bought and expanded his house (77.4), not built it from the ground up; its small bath shows that it had belonged to a traditionalist family. Whereas for exercise he goes to the public baths (27–8), he otherwise likes to bathe in private, *sine turba lauari* (according to Heinsius' emendation at 73.2 he boasts about this), and can achieve this by having a small bath which leaves little room for anyone else. Seneca asks (§5) 'Who would nowadays tolerate bathing so?', remarks on the luxury of baths of freedmen (§7), and criticizes the blazing temperatures now fashionable (§10 *temperatura . . . similis incendio*, cf. Petron. 72.3 *sic calet tamquam furnus*, 'it is as hot as a furnace'). Petronius apparently is answering the question put by Seneca in §5 by pointing to the trait of 'inverted snobbery' (the phrase from Walsh's note; I have also used it above, p. 78, in connection with 71.12).

Around the bath the other guests are running with linked hands and screeching loudly, or picking up rings (with their teeth?) while their hands are tied behind their backs, or kneeling and bending back to touch their toes. The point of this is obscure. Sometimes it has been related to the athletic exercises of the spirits in Elysium (*Aen.* 6.642 sqq.), which would be most inappropriate. More suitable would be a reference to acrobats in Roman funeral processions, but our only authority for such seems to be the obscure note of Festus (334b M) on *Simpludiarea funera* (references to actors and dancers are a different matter, though of course they belong to the same order of being).

After the bath the guests, somewhat sobered, are brought back into another dining-room, where more food and drink are laid out. The bath has marked the end of the elaborate symmetrical scheme which Bodel 45 has laid out for the main part of the *Cena* (this scheme invites a few minor reservations, but substantially stands up); now it is as if the whole *Cena*, which began in the baths (26.10–28), is going to start all over again, *de una die duas facere*, 'to make two days out of one', as Habinnas puts it (72.4; the phrase was perhaps suggested by Herodotus 2.133.5). Trimalchio invites them to carouse until dawn to celebrate the first beard-clipping of one of his slaves (as his own may have been celebrated; 29.8). As he is speaking a cock crows, which Trimalchio takes to be a bad omen[65]

---

[65] Grondona 58 compares Ter. *Ph.* 708 *gallina cecinit* ('a cock crowed'), which according to Donatus is an omen of the death of a husband before his wife.

predicting either a fire or a death in the neighbourhood; he has wine poured under the table (a libation to the spirit of the neighbour who will die) and on to the lamp (to make it blaze up, a symbol of continuing life), transfers his ring to his right hand, and gives orders for the cock to be fetched. Daedalus then cuts it up and cooks it, another link between death and eating. This cock-crow looks not only back (since the *bucinus*, on which see below, n. 69, recalls the probably mechanical *bucinator* which in 26.9 tolled out the hours of Trimalchio's life), as in Bodel's scheme all the episodes since ch. 47 have done, but also foreshadows what is to come; we are commencing what is to be the coda of the *Cena* leading up to the mock funeral.

Trimalchio, with his fellow-feeling for slaves (which he tries to disguise), realizes that those in attendance have not yet dined, and replaces them with another shift, among which is a handsome boy whom he begins to kiss. Fortunata, like Scintilla previously, becomes annoyed at this and starts to abuse him, over-confident in the control which in a sober state he allows her to exercise over him (37.2–7, 52.9–11). In response to this Trimalchio hurls a cup in her face, a feature of the brawls which are often described as breaking out at symposia (e.g. Lucil. 223–7 M; see Nisbet–Hubbard on Horace, *Odes* 1.27.1). He himself bursts into a torrent of abuse, finally instructing Habinnas not to place her statue on his tomb. After this 'thunderbolt' Habinnas tries to soothe him. In this we again seem to catch a hint of imperial pretensions; the prohibition of the statue is like *damnatio memoriae*, obliteration from the official record, and 'thunderbolt', though it can be used quite generally in a metaphorical sense (cf. *fulminatus* 80.7), is often a metaphor for imperial punishments implying a flattering comparison of the emperor to Jupiter (see my note on Juv. 8.92 and J. R. Fears, *Princeps a Dis Electus* (Rome 1977), index p. 349 s.v. Thunderbolt). Scintilla too tries to soothe Trimalchio, but again he delivers a long speech which is a mixture of abuse, maudlin self-pity, and boasting about what he has achieved in life (autobiographical information given here has been discussed in (i) above); it is like a funeral eulogy, *laudatio funebris*, delivered by the corpse itself (in his previous speech *pius fortis fidelis* 'loyal,

strong, trustworthy' 71.12 also recalled the lapidary style; cf.
CLE 488.2 *acri homini adque alacri forti fido adque uenusto*).
One may remark, first, that he slips into his old slave-outlook
by referring to Habinnas' *peculium* (and also to his own at 76.7;
cf. p. 78 above); second, that when he recalls the presence of his
guests, as at 34.7 he inadvertently insults them ('Please,
friends, enjoy yourselves, for I too was once like you, but
because of my talent I have reached this status' 75.8; this leads
into his boasting).

The final stage of his bragging autobiography comes with his
retirement, urged on him by an astrologer (superstition again);
Trimalchio's report of this man's intimate knowledge of him
shows how the astrologer played on his insecurity ('You are
unlucky in your friends, nobody ever repays you properly . . .
you nurture a viper in your bosom'). Trimalchio of course is
picking out the parts of the consultation which correspond to
his present mood; in a moment (77.4) he calls Fortunata a
viper. He then reports the astrologer's prophecy about his
length of life. He would still, he says, like to extend his estates
to Apulia (he had expressed a similar wish at 48.3; even Pliny,
Ep. 3.19.2, speaks of *ipsa pulchritudo iungendi*, the actual
amenity of linking the properties in question); however, pend-
ing that he has built his magnificent house. The lesson of his
career is that one is valued in proportion to one's wealth, that's
how yours truly (*amicus uester*) changed from frog to prince
(obviously a reference to a folk-tale; also yet another reference
to social mobility; and perhaps even a pun on his name 'King').

Then, with an abrupt mood-swing, he gives orders for the
shroud, which (like the tomb) he has prepared in advance for
himself, the funeral perfumes, and a sample of the wine for
washing his bones to be brought out; this goes beyond the
common practice of erecting one's tomb while still alive (as e.g.
in my *Musa Lapidaria* 175, which, like Trimalchio's tomb,
71.7, is to be a garden tomb, *cepotaphium*, and 199A, where the
tomb is spoken of as the eternal home, *aeterna domus* (67; cf.
Petron. 71. 7)). Of the two robes that are fetched one is a *toga
praetexta*, the robe in which he was to appear on his tomb.[66]

[66] The *praetextae* here and in 71.9 seem not to be attributes of his sevirate
(there appears to be no other evidence that sevirs were allowed to wear this).
He would have been allowed to wear it at the games which he would have

The guests are invited to test the quality of the cloth, as they had had to be assured of the weight of the jewellery (67.7–8). They are also anointed with the nard,[67] and Trimalchio expresses the hope that it may delight him as much in death as it does in life, thus implying (like Hermeros in 57.7, who has been manifesting pride in his achievements as Trimalchio here does) a continuum between life and death (see above, p. 96), at least in his hopes.

Now Trimalchio goes farther as his theatricality finally overwhelms him and takes control; he orders wine to be poured into a bowl and asks his guests to imagine that they are celebrating the commemoration of the dead in his honour, again to Encolpius' disgust. Finally he summons the horn-players (his favourite *acroama*: 53.12), which to Encolpius is a *nouum acroama*, a party-diversion of novel (and hence objectionable; see above, n. 5) type; then he stretches himself out on the couch, and tells them to imagine that he is dead and to play a nice funeral tune, which they do, particularly the slave of the undertaker Julius Proculus who is one of the guests (38.14–16; presumably he borrows an instrument and joins in); for such funeral music see Blümner 490–1, Marquardt 351–2. Petronius

given on entrance into the sevirate (cf. Mommsen, *Röm. Staatsrecht* 1 (ed. 3, Leipzig 1887) 422, quoting *CIL* 9.4208), and perhaps a distribution of largesse at a public meal counted as equivalent. Of course he might have usurped this as much as the gold ring (see above, n. 23). For the privilege of being cremated in the *praetexta* see Livy 34.7.3, where he is talking about lowly municipal officials.

[67] The crowing of the cock (74.1) and the pouring of the nard, both leading up to a mock death, have been compared with two episodes in the Gospel of Mark ch. 14 which lead up to the crucifixion of Jesus. This Gospel was perhaps being composed in Rome in the circle of St Peter around the very time when Petronius was writing, but it is usually put a little later (see below, pp. 211–12), and there is little indication that the author was using pre-existing writings. Moreover the purport of the first episode is very different (in Mark the crowing of the cock is nothing more than a time-marker), so I do not think that there is any significance in the comparison. Nor do I think that there is any force in the comparison made between Petron. 131.4 and John 9: 6 by Setaioli; see below, p. 196, on that passage. Ramelli 76 elaborates the parallel between 77.7—78.4 and Mark 14: 3–9 (see also John 12: 3–7) where a woman brings a jar of nard and pours it on Christ's head; His reaction is that 'she is come beforehand to anoint my body to the burying'. This seems to me to be the strongest parallel between Petronius and the Gospels, but I still cannot see it as compelling.

has here taken a hint from Sen. *Ep*. 12.8,[68] where Seneca describes how Pacuvius (known as the stand-in governor of Syria in AD 19) used to mimic this festival of the dead with wine and have himself carried from *cena* to bedroom in funeral procession with funeral music (which shows the link between feasting and death that we have remarked in Petronius). The difference is that Pacuvius did this from a bad conscience, continually expecting condign punishment from Tiberius for his malpractices.

The noise is so loud that it wakens the whole neighbourhood, and the fire-brigade breaks in, thinking that the house is on fire. The cock-crow at 74.2 had been taken to foretell a fire or a death; now in a way we have both. This cock-crow was there called a trumpet-blast;[69] though one must note that funeral-trumpets are always called *tubae*, not the military and pastoral *bucinae*, the foreshadowing of the horn-players here is clear (for the distinction between all these instruments see my note on Juv. 14.199); cf. my remarks above on 26.9 (pp. 72–3).

The upshot is that amid the tumult the trio give the slip to Agamemnon and run off as if from a real fire. The diction here clearly indicates the oppressive feelings which they have been experiencing, prevented as they have been in 72–3 from getting out and having been forced into the situation, as it seems, of reliving the experience of the *Cena*, and also indicates the sense of relief in escaping. The end of Horace's *Cena Nasidieni* showed the same sense of escape with the same verb *fugimus* (93), but note the difference; in Horace the flight shows the contempt of the guests for the host, but in Petronius it is

[68] Smith 211, stating that there is no verbal similarity between Seneca and Petronius, argues that Petronius could equally well have been prompted by personal knowledge; but *cum uino . . . sibi parentauerat* ('when he had performed the funeral rites for himself with wine') in Seneca and the mention of wine and *parentalia* in Petron. 78.4 may count as a verbal similarity, even if dictated by the ritual (Blümner 510 n. 4).

[69] The word *bucinus* (not found elsewhere in a context) there is usually taken to mean *bucinator*, trumpeter, but it is much more likely to be the vulgar masculine for the neuter *bucinum*, trumpet-blast (like *fatus* etc.); and in fact Caper, *GLK* 7.99.16, declares this to be the meaning of the word. It is necessarily used because neither *tuba* nor *cornu* forms a noun meaning 'blast'. Deonna–Renard fig. 7 (cf. Grondona 61) show a bronze of a cock blowing a trumpet. In the army a trumpet gave the sign for ending dinner (Tac. *Ann.* 15.30.1).

Trimalchio who has dominated and Encolpius and company, having failed to get away earlier, are running away in defeat. We are also to think of the end of Plato's *Symposion*, where revellers, κωμασταί, burst in and break up the party.

(vii) Overview of the *Cena*

As we look back over the *Cena* as a whole certain features become apparent. The most striking is that it can be read on either of two levels, which is in fact true of Petronius overall. One can treat it just as glorious comedy, which is indeed how it has very often been read, but if one looks more closely at the recurring themes and symbols to which attention has been drawn in the preceding sections, with a great debt to Cameron (1970), it becomes apparent that a deeper meaning is being conveyed (the significance of such themes and symbols in the *Satyrica* overall will be discussed in Ch. VIII (iii)). I do not doubt that Petronius himself intended these two options to be available to his readers, and this raises the often-discussed question whether Petronius is to be regarded as amoral, immoral, or moralistic. So long as morality was interpreted as based largely on strict Christian views of sexual morality, the omnipresence of sex in the novel imposed the second answer; if the patriarch Photius thought Achilles Tatius immoral, what would he have thought of Petronius? A judgement is also implied by the excision of all pederastic episodes in the compilation of the O-excerpts (Ch. II n. 56). In modern times, one may recall that when Franz Bücheler, the great editor of Petronius, began his career at the University of Freiburg i. B., he was attacked in the local newspaper for lecturing on such a filthy author. Though Greek and Roman religion imposed no code of sexual morality, even ancient readers would have had to consider as immoral some of the sexual episodes in Petronius—that is if they had felt obliged to submit them to moral evaluation. Of course intelligent readers would have known better than to apply this irrelevant criterion to creative literature and thereby hamstring one of the great sources of humour and comedy. Petronius may be bawdy, but he can hardly be called pornographic (ch. 140 is the most extreme in this respect); his sexual episodes are notably decorous in language (see Ch. II n. 16 and VIII (ii)) and generally restrained in detail. When Nodot produced his forged supplements in 1688, he felt compelled to spice up the author in this regard.

Nowadays most people would probably opt to class Petronius as amoral, a perfectly sensible judgement but not, I think, the whole truth. Of course one could not call him a moralist in the sense that he explicitly issues moral judgements; had he wanted to do so, he would not have chosen the technique of a first-person narrative from the mouth of a rascal. This technique enables him to detach himself from conveying moral judgements on the events narrated, though his narrator can look back with humour and irony. Yet a deeper reading reveals a coherent interpretation of contemporary life and society to which one can justly apply the epithet 'moralistic'. Life as presented by him in the *Cena* resembles nothing so much as a dance of the damned; in the midst of all Trimalchio's extravagance death keeps intruding, and it becomes a dominant theme in the climax of the episode.

Another impression that we constantly receive is a sense of unreality. Things, especially foods, are often not what they seem, and this effect is regularly achieved by trickery and deceit. In the rest of the novel this trickery and deceit is palpable in the narrative; in the *Cena*, where its presence is less self-evident, it is conveyed largely by symbolism. One notes too that the sense of unreality is enhanced by occurrence of the terminology of theatre and spectacle at 33.5 *scaena*, 54.3 *catastropha*, 50.1 *automatum*, 36.8, 68.3–4 *ludus*, a feature which will become strikingly prominent in the rest of the work (see below, p. 162); it has been remarked that Trimalchio, like Quartilla, puts on a show. One naturally links this with the fact that, from the emperor down, the Neronian age was notoriously stage-struck (see Ch. VIII (i)). This, and the fact that, as has already been pointed out, Trimalchio in some of his more bizarre and extravagant follies is merely carrying farther things which can be demonstrated to have taken place in historical reality, show that Petronius' novel must be understood to have relevance to contemporary life and society. From a historical point of view the early empire shows the beginnings of a growing dominance of

literary culture, which indeed is what is criticized in ch. 1 and
which becomes very apparent in the late empire, when high
office could be won by the ability to write flowery prose rather
than practical experience. Throughout the novel Petronius
mocks those whose pretensions make them lose sight of reality;
I have remarked how 47.6 *dum nolunt sibi uerum dicere* is based
on a moralizing phrase by Seneca and can be extended beyond
its immediate context, and more will be said about this in
Ch. VIII (iii).

It is always dangerous to bring the novel into too close a
relationship to the little that we know about the character of its
author, but with all reservations we will note how Tacitus
remarks on his *simplicitas* (a word significant in 132.15; see
below, p. 200), which in the Loeb translation given in Ch. I is
rendered 'native simplicity', but might better be represented
by 'frankness'; the context there concerns his absence of
dissimulation and pretension. His death too was arranged to
be *fortuitae similis*, as if spontaneous, free from the posturing of
Seneca's (so at least Tacitus presents it). The novel shows an
author conscious of the unnaturalness of contemporary life;
Tacitus shows us a man living by night, that is, one who did
not choose to exert himself to free himself from this unnaturalness. In talking about such *lucifugae* Seneca (*Ep.* 122.3) draws
the parallel that such a way of life offers with death. One can
remark in dandies of many ages a sense of the artificiality of the
society to which they conform. Hegel in his *Philosophy of
History* calls the comic frame of mind 'a hale condition of
soul which, fully aware of itself, can suffer the dissolution of its
aims and realizations'.

On the literary art of the *Cena*, one point, already in some
cases remarked in passing, deserves stress. That is the care
taken to introduce in advance hints which eventually lead up to
a point but the significance of which can be grasped only with
hindsight once that point has been reached. Such hints are the
clock in 26.9, the introduction of the dog (29.1; at this stage still
painted), the slaves who prefigure characteristics of their owner
(30.7–11), the various linkages between feasting and death
which lead up to the mock funeral in 78, the way in which
reminiscences of Horace and Plato are gradually introduced
and the choice of the names Agamemnon and Menelaus in

order to link to Plato's reference to Homer, and more. Petronius seems to have written quite rapidly (the sheer size of his work suggests this, and another indication will be discussed on p. 217 below), but such careful preparation shows that speed did not drive out refined literary artistry. Quintilian 10.1.20–1 shows that the Romans were well acquainted with such anticipatory placing of subject matter and the need to look back in order to appreciate it.

V

Eumolpus replaces Ascyltos

(i) 79–82, Another Quarrel

Having escaped from the *Cena*, the trio again (cf. chs. 6–8) find themselves in the difficulty, this time compounded by the dark and their drunkenness, that they do not know their way around Puteoli. After lacerating their feet (they would be wearing open sandals; cf. 138.4) on sharp stones and potsherds for almost an hour, they finally find one of the chalk-marks with which Giton (Ariadne again! Cf. 72.7) had blazed a trail to the inn where they are staying. But their troubles are not over; the old concierge has been imbibing with the lodgers and is now dead drunk. They might have been shut out all night, but a courier[1] turns up, breaks down the door and lets them in.

Encolpius and Giton go to bed and enjoy superlative love-making which evokes an ecstatic poem from Encolpius; then an immediate let-down, 'I congratulated' [see above, p. 34] 'myself for no reason' (this very clearly shows Encolpius the narrator looking back on Encolpius the actor). For when Encolpius falls into a drunken sleep, Ascyltos transfers Giton to his own bed and 'wallows[2] with a brother not his own' (*fratre non suo*). Giton, says Encolpius the narrator, either remained unconscious or pretended to be so; the second alternative is a dash of realism (of course Giton can hardly have been unaware of changing beds), the first is one of Encolpius' attempts to

---

[1] The manuscripts say that he is one of Trimalchio's couriers, but Delz is probably right to delete *Trimalchionis*. It is no doubt due to recollection of the *cursores* of Trimalchio (28.8, 29.8).

[2] Adams 193–4, on the basis of a verbal resemblance to Cic. *Har. Resp.* 59 (Clodius and Clodia), suggests that the phrase *uolutare cum sorore | fratre* was originally applied to non-sexual play, which I cannot believe. Rather Petronius reminds his readers of the Ciceronian phrase with a significant alteration of sex, what we now call *oppositio in imitando*. Cf. Herodas 5.30 with Headlam (the Callimachus there referred to being *Iamb.* 1.42).

exculpate Giton. This will be followed up in the story of the
Pergamene boy (85–7). All this is cast in the vocabulary of law:
Encolpius has rights (*ius*) over Giton, Ascyltos' contravention
of these rights is *iniuria* (cf. 81.6, 83.4, 91.6, 94.2). This quasi-
legal atmosphere is taken up in 80.6.

When Encolpius awakes, he gropes around the bed to find it
empty; now he is Ariadne finding Theseus gone (Ovid, *Her.*
10.9–12, an image taken up in 80.8)! 'If you can believe
lovers', he begins; of course notoriously you cannot. A similar
phrase is used with a similar implication in Ovid, *Am.* 1.3.16,
and here it can be taken as a hint at what modern narratol-
ogists call the 'unreliable narrator'. 'I wondered', he proceeds,
'whether to transfix both with my sword' (see Ch. III n. 16)
'and prolong their sleep into death', a grand phrase betraying
his posturing; Eumolpus later describes this happening to the
drunken Trojans, 89.63 (for other prose phrases paralleled in
his verse see Ch. IV n. 1), and comparable expressions are
found at Livy 41.4.4, Sen. *Ep.* 66.43. In similar circumstances
Hippothous does actually murder one of the lovers in Xen.
Eph. 3.2 (the whole of this chapter has some resemblance to
the narrative of Petronius, 79–115; it is adduced again in
Ch. VI n. 25). I have raised the question ((1962) 97) whether
Petronius here had in mind the death of the son-in-law of
Claudius in AD 46 or 47, who *in concubitu dilecti adulescentuli
confossus est* ('he was run through while lying with a beloved
youth'; Suet. 29).

But Encolpius characteristically decides to follow a safer plan
(violence does not come readily to his timid character); he
wakens them (cuffing Giton as Ascyltos had lashed the pair of
them in 11.4) and announces to Ascyltos that he is divorced and
must seek other habitation (the formulae used here and in 94.6
are customary if not legal; see my notes on Juvenal 6.146).
Ascyltos accepts this, as he had at 10.6, and they amicably part
what they call their *manubiae* (cf. the spurious fr. 12); this,
which means 'spoils of war to be divided up', is a military
metaphor (by now somewhat faded; see *OLD* s.v. 2), and it is
taken up just below. This division is executed *optima fide*—
honour among thieves!

We have seen that losing the way is a recurrent theme; now
division of property (10.4 and 7) and Ascyltos looking for

another apartment (10.6) as the result of *iniuria* (10.4) also repeat themselves. These particular repetitions are remarked by Hubbard 204, 207; there will be more on the general topic in Ch. VIII (iii).

After that division Ascyltos suggests that they divide Giton too (a division at which Ascyltos had hinted in 11.4), which Encolpius thinks to be a joke until Ascyltos draws his sword and says 'You shall not enjoy this booty [*praeda*] on which you are sitting alone; with this very sword I must cut off my share.' Here we have first the military metaphor continued; they see themselves as having taken from others by force everything, even apparently Giton, that they possess. Secondly, Ascyltos is equating Encolpius with an Incubo, an ogre with buried treasure in his jealous possession (with *incumbis* cf. *Incubo* 38.8). Thirdly, we are to understand that Ascyltos is just posturing (as he was when at 9.5 he drew his sword in threatening Giton), but that the naive Encolpius takes him seriously. Fourthly, we have to do with a parody of the Judgment of Solomon, or, if not Solomon, some other wise king of folklore (see Stith Thompson J 1171.1, and note 1171.2, division of a bride or a slave between competitors). Such a story is shown to have been known at Rome by a Pompeian wall-painting.[3] One will note the similarity in the removal of the boy from one bed to the other (cf. 1 Kings 3: 20), and moreover Ascyltos is no doubt hoping that, like the real mother in the Bible, Encolpius will surrender Giton rather than have him dismembered. Observe too how well *(fratre) non suo* in 79.9 (quoted above) would fit the point of blood-relationship in the Bible story, and that the man who was charged with and finally, after much negotiation with Jewish leaders, evaded the task of converting the Temple into a shrine to Caligula was P. Petronius, no doubt a relative of the author though we cannot establish the precise relationship; it is a reasonable

---

[3] On this and the painting see Lucas in *Festschr. O. Hirschfeld* (Berlin 1903) 257; Engelmann, *Hermes* 39 (1904), 146; Radin, *CJ* 13 (1917), 173; A. Rumpf, *Malerei und Zeichnung* (*Handbuch der Archaeologie* in Müller's *Handbuch* 6.4.1, Munich 1953) 174–5; Frey, *Revue Biblique* 42 (1933), 375 and pl. 22 after p. 382; Cèbe 365 and pl. 18.16; Gutmann, *Antike Kunst* 15 (1972), 122. For the reference in Pap. Ox. 41.2944 see E. G. Turner, *The Papyrologist at Work* (Durham N.C. 1973) 8.

hypothesis that he acquired some knowledge about the builder of the Temple.

So Encolpius too draws his sword and they square off. Giton embraces their knees in supplication and beseeches them not to display a *Thebanum par* in a *humilis taberna*. *Thebanum* will direct us to Eteocles and Polynices (who like Encolpius and Ascyltos were *fratres*), with Giton as Jocasta (!), but *par* (two matched gladiators) and *humilis taberna* direct us to quite a different sphere of life, and the ludicrous incongruity of the tragic allusion is explicitly underlined; it is a counterpart to that to Lucretia and Tarquin in 9.5. Giton describes their relationship as an 'illustrious friendship', which is meant to point the tragic allusion. He continues the histrionics by declaring that he is the guilty party and it is he should be executed. Here he is casting himself again as Jocasta as she appears in Seneca's *Phoenissae*[4] 405 (Antigone speaks to her) *nudum inter enses pectus infestos tene* ('Keep your bared breast between the drawn swords') and 443 *in me arma et ignes uertite* ('Turn your weapons and torches against me'); compare also 456 *si placuit scelus* ('If crime is resolved on') with Petron. 80.4 *si utque facinore opus est* ('If crime is inevitable'). This raises an interesting point, because it is widely and probably correctly held that this play was left incomplete by Seneca at his death; the question how then Petronius knew its text will be discussed below (p. 216). Of course Nisus (Verg. *Aen.* 9.427), whose friendship with Euryalus was truly 'illustrious', echoes behind Seneca; on all this see Conte 79–80.

Ascyltos and Encolpius restrain themselves, and the former proposes that Giton should go with whichever he likes. Encolpius, who thinks that his long-standing connection with Giton has turned into a blood-relationship (because they are *fratres*), readily accepts Giton as *iudex*; this one would do in an *actio communi diuidundo*, a law-suit for dividing common property (in view of *optima fide* 79.12 note that this procedure belongs to the class of *iudicia bonae fidei*, suits in which the judge could decide according to the principles of good faith, for which see A. Berger, *Encyclopedic Dictionary of Roman Law* (1953) 520). So he is shattered when Giton by his verdict

---

[4] In Euripides' play of that name she arrives too late to intervene.

(*pronuntiatio*; see *OLD* s.v. 2) immediately chooses Ascyltos; in fact, having lost the case (*damnatus*), he would have committed suicide (so he says) if he had not grudged this triumph to his enemy (*inimicus*, cf. 92.12, 98.9; previously they have been *amici*, 79.11, 80.4 and 9, 97.9). Ascyltos departs with his prize (*praemium*) and leaves Encolpius, formerly his fellow-soldier (note how the military metaphor continues) alone in a strange foreign place (which will again recall Ariadne; Ovid, *Her.* 10.121 *spiritus infelix peregrinas ibit in auras*, 'the unhappy breath of my life will depart into foreign air'). The whole episode is rounded off with a little poem on untrustworthy friends, to which the manuscripts have appended another which does not belong here but is notable because it comments on the unreality of dramatic performances and the return of the actors to real life when they end. This is a theme which has wide implications for the characterization in the novel; it is a pity that we do not have the poem in its original context.[5]

So Encolpius collects his baggage; in this context, though apparently not at 10.4, this continues the military imagery (see *OLD*, *sarcina* 1b, and add particularly Sall. *Iug.* 97.4). Then he goes off to find another isolated lodging near the shore. Why the latter specification? The answer usually given is that he is posing as Achilles sulking by the shore about his lost Briseis (*Il.* 1.348 sqq.); I have to admit that I am not sure that the resemblance is compelling. Laird 223 thinks rather that a parallel is being drawn with heroines, such as Ariadne, abandoned on the sea-shore; the sex-reversal implied would be very much in the style of Petronius, but the points of contact are vague and general. I can only suggest that the location is preparation for the embarkation in 99, as the introduction of the barber in 94.8 seems to be motivated partly as preparation for his role on board ship (see below); in such matters Petronius does not appear to worry about details (we might ask how the sailor in 99.5 knows to look for Eumolpus in Encolpius' lodgings).

Encolpius shuts himself up for three days and finally bursts out into a rhetorical denunciation,[6] the autobiographical part of

---

[5] Conte 82 and Walsh (1990) 183 think that we do in fact have it in its original context.

[6] For such declamations in the Greek novel see Hägg (1971) 262

which has been discussed above (p. 43). It starts with the *ergo*
which shows that what is uttered is the continuation of an
unspoken train of thought (cf. 83.4; see *OLD* s.v. 4, and e.g.
McKeown on Ovid, *Am.* 2.7.1); 'well then, could the earth not
have opened and swallowed me up?', a topos which goes back
to *Il.* 4.182; the word *ruina* perhaps has specific reference to the
episode mentioned in 9.8 if that referred to the collapse of an
amphitheatre in an earthquake. He reviews his life, all of which
seems to lead up to his present situation of poverty and
abandonment; the words *solus* and *solitudo* occur four times
in ch. 81 (he still feels his abandonment at 83.4), and we must
consider how such a situation would affect a weak character like
Encolpius, who most of the time is reacting to others. He then
expresses his indignation that this has been brought on him by
the dissolute Ascyltos and the equally dissolute Giton, who
assumed a *stola* (a married woman's dress) when a freeborn lad
would have assumed a *toga uirilis* (for the exact interpretation
of this see above, p. 41) and was 'talked into effeminacy by his
mother' (Sullivan).[7] This tirade of moral indignation (from the
mouth of Encolpius!) has echoes of Cicero's invective against
Antony, who allegedly forthwith turned his *toga uirilis* into the
toga muliebris of a whore, but was 'married' by Curio, thus in
effect gaining a *stola*; *Phil.* 2.44. Petronius here did not need to
create his favourite sexual reversal; he found it ready-made in
Cicero. Now, defaulting on his obligations[8] and fleeing to
another jurisdiction (i.e. that of Ascyltos), Giton has sold
everything at the price of one night with Ascyltos. For such
flight (*exilii causa solum uertere*, voluntary exile to avoid legal
difficulties) see *TLL* 5.1487.52, and for the factual background
in the law of debt see my note on Juv. 11.49. Encolpius tortures
himself with the thought of the two lovers enjoying each other
in bed and mocking him, which perhaps means that he has now

(Chariton), 273 (Xenophon of Ephesus), 283 (Achilles Tatius); in Helio-
dorus e.g. 1.8.2, 2.4.1–2, 5.6, 6.7.3–4. A few examples are mentioned by
Conte 11 n. 10. In many of the Greek instances Tyche is blamed; see
Hunter 1062–3. Heinze 514 compares in particular Chariton 3.6.6.

[7] This has been compared with Callimachus, *Iambus* III, in which a mother
set up her son with a rich man.

[8] The verb *conturbare* is used in a similar metaphor by Cic., *Pro Plancio* 68;
in the *Philippic* he had employed *decoxisse*, to go bankrupt, in a literal sense.

become Medea abandoned in a foreign land for Creusa (Ovid, *Her.* 12.173–7).

Finally he resolves to seek sanguinary revenge and girds on his sword, *gladio latus cingor*, 'I gird my side with my sword'. Here a stylistically interesting point. Petronius in his prose does not elsewhere employ such 'middle' voices outside the perfect participle (as at 60.8), a limitation which he shares with a number of other authors, but here Encolpius is assimilating himself to another hero, Aeneas, who in *Aen.* 2.664 sqq. reacts to the capture of Troy thus:

> 'hoc erat, alma parens, quod me per tela, per ignis
> eripis, ut mediis hostem in penetralibus . . .
> .   .   .   . cernam?
> 670   .   . numquam omnes hodie moriemur inulti.'
> hinc ferro accingor rursus.

'Was this, protective mother, why you rescued me through weapons and fire, so that I might see the enemy in the middle of my house? No way shall we all die unavenged today.' After this I again gird on my sword.

Note how we here have the recapitulatory frame discussed above (p. 48) as leading up to apparently imminent disaster. Though the grammatical construction in Vergil is not the same as that in Petronius, the epic colour in the latter is unmistakable. The self-irony is accentuated by Encolpius' reference to his *militia* (82.1), for which he builds up his strength with a hearty meal, in this suggesting simultaneously a gladiator about to fight (remember that he has apparently fought in the arena) and the advice of Odysseus (*Il.* 19.160). Then he sallies out, but a real soldier, noting the ridiculous figure which he cuts in his slippers and ironically addressing him as *commilito*, comrade, disarms him (for *despoliare* so used in a military context see Caes. *BG* 2.31.4) and sends him back to his lodgings, a letdown after the epic build-up, but one for which on calm reflection Encolpius is grateful.

(ii) 83–90, In the Picture-Gallery

After a gap in the text, Encolpius drops in to an art gallery, which, like many such in the ancient world (see my note on

Juv. 9.22–4), is a temple, and sees there many works of the
greatest classical painters (which, if rational criteria are to be
applied, must be assumed to be copies). The subjects—the rape
of Ganymede, Hylas trying to repel the nymph, Apollo mourning Hyacinth—are pederastic (or, in the case of Hylas, have
pederastic undertones) and are understood by him to echo his
own situation. This invites him to reflect 'So love touches even
the gods. Jupiter at least did no harm to anyone in carrying off
Ganymede' (Ganymede's relatives might have disputed this
point), 'the nymph would have subdued her passion if she had
believed that Hercules would seek an injunction' (for the
humorously applied legal phrase cf. 13.4; it follows up the
legal terms of 80–1), 'Apollo gave life as a flower to the dead
Hyacinthus. None, unlike me, had trouble from a treacherous
rival'. His logic, however, is rather muddled. In the first case
Jupiter corresponds to Ascyltos, in the second and third
Hercules and Apollo to himself. Moreover in all three cases
the boy did not depart voluntarily, whereas Giton did (though
later in ch. 91.8 he claims that he did not); Encolpius is in the
familiar situation of looking for excuses for him. This tirade, in
which Encolpius characteristically sets himself against mythological models, is described as 'quarrelling with the winds', a
phrase which Conte 21 takes to underline its theatrical character; however, rather than adducing Otto *uentus* 2 (Laird 226
also compares passages of this type from the lament of Ariadne
in Catullus 64) he should have referred to Otto *aer* 3.

This passage may distantly recall Aeneas' contemplation of
the temple doors in Carthage (rapt attention is indicated by the
same verb *haerere*. Petron. 89.1 and Vergil *Aen.* 1.495), but it is
much more closely linked with the Greek novel, and particularly the beginning of that of Achilles Tatius (discussed by
S. Bartsch, *Decoding the Ancient Novel* (Princeton 1989) 40,
and Zimmermann, *Poetica* 31 (1999), 66); he of course wrote
much later than Petronius, which raises a methodological
question discussed in Ch. II (i). In Achilles the narrator, as
he contemplates the temple dedications, sees a picture of the
rape of Europa in which Cupid is escorting the bull, and, as a
lover himself, reflects 'Look how that imp dominates over sky
and land and sea' (Loeb translation). At this Clitophon, who is
standing beside the narrator, declares that he can bear witness

to the truth of this remark, and proceeds to narrate the subject of the novel, his adventures with Leucippe. A little later, when Clitophon has fallen in love with Leucippe at first sight, a song of the love of Apollo for Daphne sets him to reflect 'Look, even Apollo is in love' (1.5.7); cf. *ergo amor etiam deos tangit* ('So then love touches even the gods') Petron. 83.4; Heinze 514 compares also Chariton 3.3.5–6. This motif is one of the many derived by the novel from comedy (Ter. *Eun.* 586 sqq., also compared by Heinze); this and the novel instances are of course in heterosexual contexts. The resemblance will become yet stronger when in 83.7 we find Eumolpus coming into the gallery and standing by Encolpius' side, *constitit ad latus*, a notion regularly conveyed in the Greek instances below by παρεστώς (see Schissel von Fleschenburg, *Philol.* 72 (1913), 103, an over-schematic treatment of the motif). All this will be discussed further in a moment.

Eumolpus, not yet named, is described as an old man whose countenance hinted at something great, despite his shabby attire. This is a build-up (lasting through ch. 84) to a let-down, which comes in ch. 85, just as his name Eumolpus (see Ch. II n. 42; unfortunately we cannot tell exactly when it was introduced) is let down in ch. 89. Encolpius at first sight identifies him as one of the brand of literary men who cannot obtain patronage. How could he know this? As actor at this moment he cannot; this is Encolpius the narrator reading back from the knowledge which he is about to acquire in 84.2–3 (see above, p. 38).

Eumolpus boastfully introduces himself as no mean poet; his evidence for this consists of the garlands which he has won in competitions[9] without the benefit of the influence which can bestow them even on the undeserving. Could this be an allusion to the Neronia of AD 60, when the garland for Latin poetry was awarded to Nero without his participation, and to all the other prizes won by Nero? He explains his poverty by his opposition to vice (strange opposition, as the next chapter will show!), and his lack of patronage by the urge of the rich to disparage everything but wealth (which will recall the attitude of Echion in ch. 46).

[9] For the proliferation of poetic contests at this time see A. Hardie, *Statius and the Silvae* (Liverpool 1983) ch. 2.

The text now becomes very scrappy (but one should note that 84.5 indicates that Encolpius has told Eumolpus something about Ascyltos); when it resumes in coherent form Eumolpus is recounting a story about his youth. When he was taken to Asia as assistant to a quaestor, he lodged at Pergamum with a family. The handsome son attracted him, but he gained the trust of the parents by expressing puritanical attitudes, so that he began to escort the boy to the gymnasium, supervise his studies, and instruct him not to admit any sexual predator into the house. One holiday evening their enjoyment kept them from going to bed, and they continued to recline on the couches in the dining-room. About midnight, realizing that the boy was still awake, Eumolpus whispered a vow to Venus that if he could kiss the boy without his feeling it, he would give him a pair of doves next day. Hearing this the boy began to snore, Eumolpus got his kiss, and next day gave the present. Modern readers need to realize that such gifts from *erastes* to *eromenos* were a regular item in pederastic courting (see Dover 92, Teodorsson on Plut. *Quaest. Symp.* 1.5.622f). Next night Eumolpus went a step farther: 'if I can caress him without his feeling it, I shall give him two fighting cocks'; same result. On the third night the vow was a thoroughbred pony in return for full intercourse, with the stipulation that the boy, who of course hears this, feels nothing; this indicates an implicit contract between them, just as in ch. 140 Philomela and Eumolpus understand each other. Full pederastic intercourse without the realization of the boy might seem an impossibility to modern readers, but it has to be remembered that in ancient practice such intercourse would often be intercrural rather than anal (Dover 98). Eumolpus gains his wish, but next day, unable to find a pony and fearing that suspicion might be aroused by such a large gift, he returns home empty-handed, to be greeted by the boy with 'Where's my pony?' This both discloses the complicity of the boy and violates the etiquette that an *eromenos* may receive but not request expensive gifts (see Kay on Mart. 11.58, who quotes Ar. *Plut.* 157 for the gift of a horse; cf. also Ach. Tat. 1.8.11–1.14).

The boy's disappointment cuts off Eumolpus for a few days, but then one night (*similis casus*, a similar occasion, in 87.1, by taking up *forte*, by chance, in 85.4, marks this as Act II) he tries to reconcile the boy, whose only answer is 'Go to sleep or I'll tell Daddy'. However he puts up only a feeble resistance when Eumolpus assaults him (Eumolpus speaks of this in the terms which can represent a reprobate as an attractive dare-devil; *improbitas*, with which cf. *improba manu* 86.1 and also Ovid, *AA* 1.665, 676, *nequitia*, both meaning 'wickedness'). In fact he is rather pleased (his enjoyment suggests that they have now passed to anal intercourse), though he scolds Eumolpus for letting him down before his schoolfellows, to whom he had boasted of Eumolpus' wealth (a revealing detail). Now the initiative passes to the boy. 'If you like, do it again', he says, with a euphemism still common today (perhaps meant also at 45.8, misinterpreted by Adams 204); so Eumolpus does, and then drops off to sleep. But the boy wakens him and asks 'Would you like anything?'; somewhat wearily Eumolpus complies and goes off to sleep again. In less than an hour (*interposita minus hora*, contrasted with the interval of a few days, *interpositis paucis diebus*, in 87.1) the boy prods him again and says 'Why don't we do it?', thus matching Eumolpus' three initial assaults on him with three of his own, at which Eumolpus blazes out in rage (*uehementer excandui*; the same verb and adverb had been applied in 85.2 to his faked anger at pederasts!) and turns the tables by the retort, 'Go to sleep, or I'll tell Daddy'. This is the technique of humour which we find in the *Frogs* of Aristophanes 1471 sqq., when Dionysus uses Euripides' own words as a justification for rejecting him. One may compare also how Ovid, having been accused by Corinna of seducing her maid Cypassis, ends up by using the blackmail of threatened confession to exact more lovemaking (*Am*. 2.8).

Many features of this hilarious story require comment; first of all, the generic. Such scabrous stories were known as Milesian tales; a collection of them was compiled by a man called Aristides, which was translated into Latin by Sisenna (his fragments are in Bücheler's Petronius, ed. maior p. 342), and Apuleius at the beginning of his *Metamorphoses* relates that work to this genre.[10] Ionians were often regarded as living dissolute lives (see Trenkner 8, and for short stories set there

---

[10] The evidence about the nature of the work of Aristides has recently been surveyed by Harrison, *GCN* 9 (1998), 61; see also *Der Neue Pauly* s.v. *Milesische Geschichten*.

Bürger, *Hermes* 27 (1892), 356 n. 2); hence the link with Miletus, which is about 120 English miles south of Pergamum. Secondly, the subtext is a reversal of the narrative of Alcibiades in Plato's *Symposion*, a work still fresh in our minds from the *Cena*. This has been remarked by Cameron (1969) 369 and worked out in detail by McGlathery in D. H. J. Larmour and others (eds.), *Rethinking Sexuality* (Princeton 1998), 204.

Eumolpus' original outbursts against pederasty came when mention of it was made at dinner, *in conuiuio* (which is ἐν συμποσίῳ!), and these made the mother regard him as 'one of the philosophers'. He takes on the traditional educative relationship with the young boy, gives him instruction (*praecipere*, cf. Socrates as the *praeceptor* of Alcibiades in 128.7), and escorts him to the gymnasium, as Alcibiades contrived to have Socrates accompany him (217b–c). Alcibiades, plotting to seduce Socrates, invited him to dinner, kept him talking until late, and persuaded him to stay the night; so they rested on adjacent couches in the dining-room with nobody else present (217c–d). If we bear in mind that Alcibiades was an orphan, that helps to account for the rather surprising absence of the parents in Petronius. Finally Alcibiades nudged Socrates, enquired if he was awake, and offered himself to him (218b–d). In all this we are involved in a series of reversals. Plato himself is reversing the usual situation. Petronius first reverses Plato, then with a twist at the end, when the boy, like Alcibiades, takes the initiative in seduction, returns to him ; but not quite, for the boy represents the desire as belonging to Eumolpus, not to himself, which is how it is supposed to be in a regular pederastic relationship. By all these reversals Petronius brings home to us the distance between the ideal pederastic relationship as envisaged by Plato and those shown in his novel.

Thirdly, one may note the elaborate symmetries in the construction; attention has been drawn to these in my summary.

Fourthly, there is the function of the story in the plot; it is unfortunate that we do not know exactly how it was introduced, but it certainly has close relevance to Encolpius' loss of Giton and was probably meant to comfort him by showing the venality of such *eromenoi*. Note in particular how the boy pretends (85.6) to be unaware of his molestation, in relation to Giton, who may or may not have noticed (79.9). It also leads up to the coming attraction of Eumolpus to Giton, and it brings the literary approach of Encolpius (83.4–6) down to earth by presenting a non-idealized picture of a sexual relationship.

After a gap Encolpius is found seeking information from Eumolpus about the paintings. Here we return to what was clearly an established format for such discussions, usually with an authoritative older man as expounder (see Elsner, *PCPS* 39 (1993), 35–8, and Zimmermann (above, p. 134) 64; *opus pandere*, to expound the work, in 89.1 corresponds to ἐξηγεῖσθαι and the like). The most relevant occurrences, apart from Achilles Tatius, are in the *Tabula* of Cebes (a work perhaps more or less contemporary with Petronius), where it is used for philosophical instruction; the *Imagines* of Philostratus II, in which the narrator is lodging in a suburb of Naples facing the sea, and he explains the paintings in a portico (cf. Petron. 90.1) to the son of his host; and the *Heracles* of Lucian, in which a Celt explains to the narrator, who is contemplating an image of the god as an old man as represented by the Celts, the reasons behind this, which the narrator sees as a consolation for his own advanced years. The nature of these compositions is excellently analysed by Bartsch (above, p. 134) 14 sqq.

When we see that Lucian's *Heracles* is called a προλαλία (a discourse preliminary to a declamation) and that Philostratus refers to his work as an ἐπίδειξις (a display speech), it becomes clear that this motif has made its way into the novel from rhetorical ecphrastic exercises. A few remarks here on the technique of Philostratus will be helpful in advance. His 'interpretation' of the paintings can be as basic as identification of their subject, but what he concentrates on is drawing out the sentiment; compare how Encolpius can see even the minds of the subjects in the paintings, 83.2. The paintings themselves and Philostratus' interpretations show strong links to literary treatments of their subjects. The pictures often show progression of action and different scenes (e.g. in book I nos. 12, 17, 18, 26, 28), and sound is spoken of as if represented in them, not just inferred from depiction of the mouth but integral to the action (e.g. again in book I.4.3, 18.1, 28.6 (a prayer))).

Encolpius also enquires the reason for the present decline in

artistic achievement (*desidia*; cf. Pliny, *NH* 14.3, and especially
35.5 *artes desidia perdidit*, 'laziness has ruined the arts'); this is
a matter which he had previously remarked to Agamemnon in
2.9. Eumolpus answers that the reason is avarice, a vice from
which the ensuing narrative shows him to have been just as free
as Agamemnon was of cadging meals. Avarice of course is a
convenient scapegoat in moralistic explanations of many kinds
of decline (e.g. in natural history, Pliny *NH* 2.118, 14.4; in
rhetoric, Sen. *Contr.* 1 pr. 7). In the old days beneficial (this is
emphasized by Pliny 2 loc. cit.) research in botany, astronomy,
and philosophy flourished with great rivalry. This is an
adaptation of Sall. *Cat.* 1.5 *magnum inter mortalis certamen
fuit* ('there was great rivalry among men'), a passage which
exalts *uirtus* (so Petron. 88.2) and criticizes *desidia* (2.5) which
makes many men *dediti uentri atque somno*, devoted to their
belly and sleep (2.8); compare with this Petron. 88.6 *nos uino
scortisque demersi* ('we, besotted with wine and whores'), and
notice that Agamemnon had warned the ambitious against
drunkenness in 5.6. There were brilliant sculptors too, such
as Lysippus, who died in poverty while concentrating on the
outline of just one statue. Here Eumolpus is adjusting the facts
to suit his own situation; Walsh (1970) 96 and Elsner loc. cit. 39
point out that Lysippus in fact died a rich man (Pliny, *NH*
34.37). Nowadays we do not even learn what has previously
been ascertained in logic, astronomy, or philosophy; complaints similar to this will be found in Pliny, *NH* 14.2, Sen.
NQ 7.32 (on philosophy, with use of rhetorical devices like
those of Eumolpus), and a passage of Galen quoted by Fuchs,
HSCP 63 (1958), 384–5 n. 62. No one now prays for eloquence, nor even for the traditional requests, a sound mind and
sound health (cf. 61.1), but for wealth. No wonder then that
painting has declined. It is of course clear that after this string
of slanted and rhetorical commonplaces we cannot take Eumolpus seriously as an art critic.

But, says Eumolpus, coming in chiastic order to the second
point of Encolpius' consultation in 88.1, 'I see that you are
absorbed in that painting which shows the capture of Troy, so I
shall try to expound the work in verse'; his exposition confines
itself purely to the story behind the picture. The poem itself
can be understood in two ways. Eumolpus may have written it

long ago and have been awaiting a captive audience. More likely, since Eumolpus clearly improvises at 93.2 and 109.8, it is an improvisation; this accomplishment was much admired at this time, and is said by the Vacca life to have been demonstrated by Lucan in his *Orpheus* (see A. Hardie [above, n. 9] 76).

The poem in fact makes little pretence to be describing a picture, even if we think of a composite picture with a series of scenes, like some of those in Philostratus and the so-called *Tabulae Iliacae*, or the paintings of series of Homeric scenes at Pompeii (Maiuri 156; Horsfall, *JHS* 99 (1979), 42–4). The whole poem is narrative and temporally arranged, not static and descriptive; see the very beginning, 'Now the tenth summer was continuing the siege of Troy'. Moreover no picture could show sounds like those described in 24–5 (the mutterings of the Greeks inside the Horse); the Greeks are not even visible, unlike those represented as making sounds by Philostratus. Lessing, *Laocoon* ch. 5, remarks how Petronius in 29 sqq. compared with Vergil stresses the sound of the serpents. The poem is spoken in the persona of a Trojan, and is accordingly framed like the narrative of the fall of Troy from the mouth of Aeneas in *Aeneid* 2; naturally there are reminiscences (e.g. 11 *o patria* ~ *Aen.* 2.241; the arrival of the serpents 29–31 ~ *Aeneid* 2.203 sqq.; their 'binding' (43 ~ *Aen.* 2.217) of Laocoon's sons with their coils). However its verse form is not that of epic, but of drama, the iambic trimeters employed by Seneca; some scholars have erroneously referred to the metre as senarii, as if that word meant trimeters written in Latin. Particular points of contact are the invariable spondee in the fifth foot and the fondness for ending with a disyllable, often a word which is repeated in the vicinity. But there are also points of difference: first, Petronius is not so concerned as Seneca is to show awareness of Porson's Bridge (so that when Seneca ends a line with a trisyllable, he usually elides before it, whereas Petronius more often does not), and secondly an anapaestic third foot, as in Petronius 49, is allowed by Seneca only when preceded by word-boundary. These facts can be interpreted in two ways: (1) Petronius had not noticed all the refinements of Senecan verse-technique, or found them unappealing; (2) more likely, he presents Eumolpus as technically unable to handle them.

Placed in a dramatic context, the nearest analogue to the poem would be a messenger's speech. With regard to the style, there are a few mannerisms of Seneca, e.g. the introduction of new events with *iam* (1, 15, 54) and *ecce* (29); with the latter one may compare Sen. *Ag.* 528 (a messenger speech) *ecce alia clades* ('behold, another disaster'), but, although Eumolpus in 119.3 *ecce aliae clades* seems to refer to this, 89.29 is not compelling as a specific reminiscence, first because *ecce alius* is a common combination, secondly because of Vergil's introduction of the serpents (*Aen.* 2.203) with *ecce autem*. Lines 27, 53, and 65 closely resemble Seneca's fondness for paradoxical phrasing, and we also have an oxymoron in 51. There are a few, but only a few, seeming verbal reminiscences of Seneca; with 1–2 cf. *Tro.* 75–6 *et Sigeis trepidus campis | decumas secuit messor aristas* ('on the Sigean plain the trembling reaper has cropped his tenth harvest', Fantham), with 15 *Phaedr.* 483 *libera ac uitio carens | . . . uita* ('a life free and without vice'), with 24–5 *Ag.* 634–5 *tacitumque murmur percussit aures | ut fremuit . . . Pyrrhus* ('a subdued murmur smote the ears as Pyrrhus growled'). Two recalls of Vergil are interesting because they show *oppositio in imitando*; in Petronius Laocoon is characterized by a weak arm, *inualidam manum* (23), in Vergil (50) by powerful strength, *ualidis uiribus*, and in Petronius his spear bounces off the horse (22), while in Vergil (52) it sticks in it. The motive seems to be to accentuate the hostility of destiny beyond *Aen.* 2.54, since the reason for his 'weak arm' is that destiny retards it (21); the same appears to be the motive for representing the building of the horse as due to an oracle of Delian Apollo (4), though Apollo is a steadfast champion of the Trojans.

Petronius suggests to us by this poem's reception how it is to be evaluated; its author is stoned by those within earshot. Petronius has written it very carefully; he has avoided making it so bad as to be absurd, but he has also avoided putting one spark of inspiration into it. Anyone could have thrown off mechanical stuff like this; and many may react in the same way to the stiff diction of Seneca himself, which scholars sometimes feel driven to defend by alleging that its failure to touch any emotional springs is deliberately intended to create an effect of distancing from the often horrific action. Different people will react to this differently, but to me personally

Petronius seems to be pointing to what he sees as a flaw in Seneca's artistry.

There has been a temptation to relate this poem to the *Halosis Ilii* which Nero sang to the lyre during the fire of Rome in AD 64 (Suet. 38.2, Dio Cass. 62.18.1, Tac. *Ann.* 15.39.3). That composition, however, was probably part of his hexameter *Troica*, and even the similarity of the 'title' is insignificant in view of Aesch. *Ag.* 598 etc. I think that it is unprofitable to try to see any relationship.

One final point to be observed about this poem is that in the realm of poetry it may well have balanced a demonstration of a prose *suasoria* by Agamemnon before the beginning of our text; 6.1 suggests that there was such. The correspondence in their practical demonstrations would neatly balance a corres-pondence in literary theory between 3–5 and 118.

Eumolpus, being well acquainted with this form of 'applause', takes to his heels. How does Encolpius the actor know at this point that this experience is familiar to Eumol-pus? He does not; Encolpius the narrator learns it in §5 and projects it back to here (see above, p. 38). Once out of range Encolpius, who has followed Eumolpus at a distance for fear that he too might be identified as a poet, asks him 'What are you up to with that disease of yours? I've known you less than two hours, and you've spoken more often like a poet than a human being'.[11] Eumolpus explains that he has experienced this welcome when he enters a theatre to recite; this is probably a reference to his participation in agonistic contexts (see above, n. 9; P. White, *Promised Verse* (Cambridge, Mass. 1993) 293 makes unnecessarily heavy weather over the word 'theatre'). He promises, however, to abstain for a whole day in order to keep the peace with Encolpius; in return for this Encolpius invites him to dinner and arranges for the concierge to prepare this.

---

[11] Cf. ἀνθρωπείως φράζειν Ar. *Frogs* 1058, with which Dover ad loc. compares Strato fr. 1.46 ap. Athen. 9.383b. Note that Encolpius can see unreality in another, if not in himself; for the problem of his denunciation of rhetorical unreality in ch. 1 see Ch. III (i).

(iii) 91–99, In the Inn

In the following gap Encolpius and Eumolpus, observing normal custom, go to the baths before dinner, where Eumolpus typically seizes the opportunity for recitation, as Trimalchio had at 73.3. Encolpius sees Giton with towels and strigils, passing for a slave as he often does and as he had done in the baths before Trimalchio's dinner (26.10); yet another instance of repetitive motifs. Giton looks very unhappy, but cheers up when he sees Encolpius. 'Pity me, brother', he says; 'I can speak freely when no weapons' [such as Ascyltos' sword, 80.1] 'are around. Rescue me from a sanguinary brigand' [cf. 84.5, spoken by Encolpius] 'and punish your repentant judge' [i.e. Giton himself, who in 80.6 had judged the dispute between Encolpius and Ascyltos in favour of the latter; cf. 91.7]. 'It will be sufficient consolation to me to have died by your will.' This last utterance is again histrionic posturing; it puts Giton in the position of Lausus dying at the hand of Aeneas (*Aen.* 10.829; other instances of the motif collected by Casali on Ovid (?), *Her.* 9.70). Encolpius abducts Giton through a back door to his lodgings, embraces him, and mingles reproaches with expressions of affection. When Giton is reassured that he is still loved, he characteristically becomes haughty, pretends to wipe away tears, and suggests that Encolpius might with equal justice be accused of abandoning him; caught between two armed men, he had had no real choice but to take refuge with the stronger. Encolpius kisses 'his chest full of intelligence', which probably means that he will take anything from Giton. The reconciliation is sealed by a hug.

By now it is evening, the meal (90.7) has been served, and Eumolpus returns. Seeing Giton serving the wine to Encolpius, he at once expresses his admiration in comparing him to Ganymede serving wine to Jupiter; the reader will recall here the picture of Ganymede at 83.4, and the insight into Eumolpus' predilections given in the episode of the Pergamene boy. After more compliments to Giton, Eumolpus reports that he had almost received a beating (like the stoning of 90.1) for his attempts at recitation in the baths and had been ejected. As he wandered around naked, he had encountered another naked man (Ascyltos of course), who was shouting out for Giton,

since Giton had ceased to look after his clothes when he left
with Encolpius and they had been stolen (a frequent hazard at
Rome in the absence of lockers, so that it was usual to depute a
slave to look after the clothes (30.7–11)). Ascyltos is surrounded by a large crowd admiring his huge genitals, so huge
that the man seems their appendage instead of the other way
around; this brings with it an implicit comparison to Priapus
(cf. *Priapea* 37.8–9 *fer opem, Priape, parti | cuius tu, pater, ipse
pars uideris*; 'Priapus, bring help to the part of which you,
father, seem yourself to be a part'). A disreputable *eques* throws
his cloak around him and takes him home, for immoral
purposes of course, *ut tam magna fortuna solus uteretur* ('so
that he alone might enjoy such great good fortune'), a delicate
euphemism when one compares *inguinum pondus tam grande*
(such enormous genitals) just above; Ascyltos had had a similar
experience at 8.2–4.

Eumolpus too had some difficulty in recovering his clothes
after his abandonment by Encolpius; 'so much more profit-
able', says he, 'is it to stimulate balls than brains.' In all this
Eumolpus and Ascyltos have been appearing in perfect sym-
metry; this is Petronius' way of forewarning us of the coming
replacement of Ascyltos in the plot by Eumolpus. Encolpius is
by now very uneasy about Eumolpus, and pretends to know
nothing about the events which he has narrated; we must
remember that Eumolpus so far has not been in a position to
identify the wine-server with Giton.

So they sit down to the meal, the modesty of which evokes a
poem from Eumolpus to the effect that exotic food, unlike that
now served up, is attractive just because it is exotic. Encolpius
scolds him for breaking his promise (90.6) to refrain from
poetry today, which gives Giton the chance to take Eumolpus'
part, thus matching his handsomeness with his sensitivity
(*uerecundia*, a quality which Encolpius had alleged in him at
25.3 to deter Quartilla from his 'marriage'). Eumolpus greatly
appreciates this; 'happy your mother, who bore a son like you;
may your goodness bring you prosperity.' This is again in the
heroic mode; it presents Giton first as Dido coming to the aid
of the distressed Trojans (*Aen.* 1.606; see Austin's note there,
and add Xen. *Eph.* 1.2.7 for congratulation of parents), then as
Ascanius (*Aen.* 9.641; in his commentary J. Dingel remarks

how often the phrase *macte uirtute esto* is found with sardonic
undertones). We may, however, doubt the feelings of Giton's
mother if we recall what was said of her at 81.5 (not that
Eumolpus knows about this). 'One doesn't often find intelligence' (which Encolpius had admired, 91.1) 'coupled with
handsomeness. I shall be your lover, and fill volumes of verse
with your praises. I shall follow you as tutor and bodyguard'—
at which point the reader will recall that these are exactly the
functions which he fulfilled with the Pergamene boy (85.3)!
'Don't be concerned with Encolpius, he loves someone else'
(this he says because Encolpius has told him about a beloved
boy but not disclosed that Giton is this boy).

Giton, aware of Encolpius' murderous reaction to all this,
goes out, and Encolpius declares that he is 'divorcing' Eumolpus (*ocius foras exi*, 'leave the house at once'; see above on
79.11) on grounds of incompatibility (*non conueniat*; for the
verb applied to spousal relations see Afran. 53, Mart. 8.35.3,
Suet. *Tib.* 7.2, and also Prop. 3.25.8); the same grounds applied
in the 'divorce' from Ascyltos (10.4). Eumolpus at once leaves
the room, but quickly shuts the door behind him and locks it,
then runs off to look for Giton. Encolpius, who had contemplated suicide at 80.7, is so desperate that he decides to hang
himself; one may compare Chaereas' attempt at suicide by
hanging, Chariton 5.10.6 sqq., and that of Soraechus in
Iamblichus, pp. 197, 216 Stephens–Winkler. So he inserts
his neck into a noose made from his belt; he hangs this from
the frame of the bed which he has set upright against the wall.
In the nick of time Eumolpus and Giton return and 'recall him
from a fatal turning-point to the light of day'.[12] Giton in a
torrent of self-reproach claims that he himself would have
committed suicide if he had been able to find Ascyltos' sword
in his lodgings, and that he would have thrown himself off a
cliff if he had not encountered Encolpius again. So between
them the two have run through three standard forms of suicide
in the ancient world, ξίφος, ἀγχόνη, κρημνός (see Trenkner 62–3,
and for the novel in particular S. MacAlister, *Dreams and
Suicides* (London 1996) 66, adding Apul. *Met.* 4.26); the

---

[12] This combines the common *reuocare* (see *OLD* 11) *a morte* (to recall from
death) with a metaphor from recalling participants in a race after a false start
(ibid. 2a).

strength of the motif of suicide in the Greek novel is shown by
its persistence in Arabic stories, though suicide is totally alien
to Islamic beliefs and tradition (G. E. von Grunebaum, *Medieval Islam* (ed. 2, Chicago 1953) 307–8). Giton now seizes a
razor from Eumolpus' hired help, who is a barber (we later find
out that his name is Corax); we have not heard of him before,
and it is a surprise that someone so poor as Eumolpus has a
servant. It seems that Petronius here overrode probability for
the sake of the following comic point and in order to lay the
ground for the coming scene on the ship of Lichas, in which the
barber's trade has a role in the plot (I have suggested on p. 181
that *locum . . . proximum litori* at 81.1 has a similar preparatory
function).

Anyway Giton cuts, or seems to cut, his throat and falls in
front of them. Encolpius tries to do the same, but finds that the
razor is blunt; it was intended only for the training of
apprentice barbers (this is knowledge which Encolpius the
narrator must have subsequently gained; see above, p. 38).
That throws a new light on Giton's collapse, because of course
he knew perfectly well that he was not dead; and that was why
Eumolpus and his servant had not tried to interrupt this death-
scene from a farce, *mimica mors*. This phrase underlines the
histrionic character of what has been going on, and it is taken
up by the next sentence, 'While this play was being staged
between us lovers'; both of these two are naturally later
interpretations by the narrator Encolpius. The whole episode
has a remarkable parallel in Ach. Tat. 3.20.7, where a stage
sword with retractable blade is used to perform a fake murder;
note also the feigned death in a mime in D. L. Page, *Greek
Literary Papyri* (Loeb) 350 sqq.

The lodging-house keeper[13] arrives half-drunk with the next
course of the meal, wonders what is going on, and voices his
suspicion that they intend to abscond without paying their
bill. At this Eumolpus starts brawling with him, and all the
household staff and the drunken lodgers join in. Encolpius
grasps the opportunity to shut out Eumolpus, who by means

---

[13] The Latin word is *deuersitor*, and Rowell, *CP* 52 (1957), 222, thinks that
it means one of the lodgers who is helping out; this is certainly in agreement
with the usual sense of the word (cf. 79.6) but here seems to me to require
reading much into the narrative.

of a lamp-stand defends himself against all comers, including
apparently tenants of the apartments above the inn, which is
to be envisaged as occupying the ground floor of an apartment
block (98.5; Rowell [n. 13] 224). Giton and Encolpius watch
all this through a hole in the door, and Encolpius ironically
applauds (*fauebam*) Eumolpus. Giton wants to let him in; this
makes Encolpius lose patience with him (which he elsewhere
does only in furious reaction to infidelity at 79.11) and cuff
him. Encolpius continues to watch the assault on Eumolpus
with enjoyment and (again ironically) suggests that he get a
lawyer (*aduocationem commendabam*). The manager of the
block arrives, denounces both people planning to abscond
and drunk lodgers, but then recognizes Eumolpus and tells
the servants to desist from attacking him. This is rare
appreciation for Eumolpus (*o poetarum disertissime*, 'most
eloquent of poets'), but it turns out that the manager wants
a quid pro quo; his *contubernalis* (sexual partner) is spurning
him, and he wants Eumolpus to write abusive (i.e. iambic)
verses against her and shame her into respect—a utilitarian
view of poetry!

While they are talking privately, a town-crier with a municipal slave enters and in the due form[14] of proclamation for a
runaway slave describes Giton and offers a reward for his
recovery while Ascyltos stands by in a multicoloured garment
(presumably given to him by the *eques* to replace his stolen
clothes), holding a copy of the description and the reward on a
silver tray (*lanx*).[15] Encolpius tells Giton to get under the bed,

[14] For such notices and descriptions see Misener, *CP* 19 (1924), 102,
H. Bellen, *Studien zur Sklavenflucht* (Wiesbaden 1971) 7 n. 26, C. G.
Bruns, *Fontes Iuris Romani Antiqui* (ed. 7, Tubingen 1909) 361, Gow–Page
on Meleager, *AP* 5.177, *Hellenistic Epigrams* (Cambridge 1965) p. 628, with
parallels from papyri and inscriptions. There is a parody in Apul. *Met.* 6.8.

[15] This is often (e.g. by F. Wieacker, *Röm. Rechtsgeschichte* (Munich 1988)
245 n. 42 with bibliography) related to the ancient *quaesitio per lancem et
licium* established in the Twelve Tables, according to which one searched for
stolen goods carrying a plate and wearing only a loin-cloth (so that evidence
could not be planted). However, this procedure seems to have been abolished
by the lex Aebutia of the 2nd cent. BC (Gell. 16.10.8); Gaius 3.192 speaks of
the procedure, which he explicitly calls ridiculous, in the present tense, but he
appears to do this sometimes simply in elucidating the text of obsolete laws
(see my note on Juv. 1.55). Gell. 11.18.10, immediately after mention of the
procedure *per lancem et licium*, states *sed nunc a lege illa decemuirali discessum*

insert his hands and feet into the straps supporting the mattress, and thus escape those searching for him as Ulysses had escaped the Cyclops by hanging beneath the ram. This is an interesting case in which grammar determines literary understanding. The reference to Ulysses has a subjunctive verb (*ut olim Ulixes †pro ariete† adhaesisset*), which means that it is presented as part of what Encolpius said; this indicates that we have to do with heroic posturing at the time of the action, not with a comparison later introduced by Encolpius the narrator.

While Giton does this, Encolpius arranges the blankets so that it looks as if he is sleeping in bed. But this turns out to be pointless; when Ascyltos arrives at the door he is not content just to look in, but gets the municipal slave to break the lock. Encolpius falls at his feet and to divert suspicion asks him to reveal Giton's whereabouts; he even pretends to fear that Ascyltos has really come to kill him, which Ascyltos denies, claiming only to be looking for his runaway slave. The municipal slave uses a cane to probe under the bed, but Giton lifts himself above it and holds his breath.

There is now a gap, in which Ascyltos and the slave leave; this is the last appearance of Ascyltos in our surviving text. Eumolpus bursts in; not until just now has he been able to identify the boy with Encolpius as Giton, and he threatens to reveal this and get the reward. Encolpius embraces his knees in supplication (as he had Ascyltos' knees in 97.9), but proceeds to allege that Giton has run off in the hubbub. He is on the point of convincing Eumolpus when Giton, unable to hold his breath any longer, sneezes. It is likely that we should here see a reflection of the popular adultery-mimes, which often involved concealment of the adulterer (in a similar situation in Apul. *Met.* 9.24 there is betrayal by a

---

est ('But now that decemviral law has been abandoned'), but he is thinking of the law of theft in the Twelve Tables generally. One must note also that Ascyltos is fully clothed, and that a search for a runaway slave is not the same thing as one for a stolen object. Ulpian, *Dig.* 11.4.3, states that Marcus Aurelius gave the right *scrutari cubilia atque uestigia occultantium* ('to search the beds and tracks of those concealing the runaways') to pursuers of runaway slaves; this must have been a contested point. See in general Plaut. *Merc.* 661–6 and *RE*, *quaestio* 789.

sneeze). In that case Ascyltos and Eumolpus share the role of
the deceived husband.

In response to the sneeze Eumolpus says 'Gesundheit', lifts
the mattress to reveal Giton and abuses Encolpius for trying
to hoodwink him. However Giton soothes him, dresses the
wound which he had sustained on his eyebrow (95.6), and says
'We are under your protection' (*custodia*; this is what Eumolpus had offered to Giton in 94.2). 'I wish that hostile flames
would envelop me alone or the stormy sea assail me, for I am
the cause of all these crimes. If I should perish, the hostility of
you two could be reconciled.' Here Giton is repeating his
histrionics of self-reproach from 80.4, but this time he is
posing as the Sabine women who caused discord between
their fathers (he addresses Eumolpus as *pater*) and husbands
(Livy 1.13.3 *nos causa belli, nos uolnerum ac caedium uiris ac
parentibus sumus; melius peribimus quam sine alteris uestrum
uiduae aut orbae uiuemus*, 'We are the cause of war, of wounds
and slaughter to our fathers and husbands; it will be better for
us to die than to live as orphans or widows without one group
or the other of you'); for Giton as 'wife' see 81.5. There is also
a recall of Verg. *Aen.* 2.600 *iam flammae tulerint inimicus et
hauserit ensis*, 'The flames will soon have carried them off and
the sword of the enemy will have drained their blood' (the
adjective is not so appropriate in Petronius' combination
inimicus ignis). This recall is not contextual but purely
verbal, intended in a general way to underline the literary
undertones of the situation. Thirdly, Giton's self-reproach for
getting Encolpius into trouble is meant to mirror Encolpius'
self-reproach for allowing Giton to reduce him to desperation
on a previous occasion (81.3).

Encolpius tearfully requests that Eumolpus be reconciled
with him too, in highly poetical style (*ast ubi aratro domefacta
tellus nitet*, 'But when the earth shines, tamed by the plough');
for the literary affinities of this see Courtney (1962) 100, but
note that I now regard the second Einsiedeln eclogue, which
has a phrase very like this, as much later than Petronius (*REL*
65 (1987), 156), so that I now take the alternative of supposing
a common model. In any case Encolpius calculates that a poetic
allusion will be effective to sway the poet Eumolpus. Eumolpus
agrees to reconciliation, and as he is telling them to pack up, a

sailor knocks on the door and informs them that the ship is about to cast off; when Eumolpus had arranged passage (this is referred to at 101.3) is uncertain. So Eumolpus tells his servant to carry his luggage, Encolpius and Giton do the same with theirs, and they all board ship.

VI

The Voyage

(i) The *Odyssey* and the Wrath of Priapus

The embarkation of the trio initiates a sequence of events, stretching virtually to the end of our text, which are closely related to the plot of the *Odyssey* (see a brief outline in Courtney (1991) 45). A poem so much of which is devoted to the wanderings of the hero, many of them outside the confines of the familiar Greek world, is naturally suited to provide themes to a genre like the novel in which wandering abroad is prominent; moreover the central theme of the work consists of the attempts (finally successful) of Odysseus to overcome obstacles, to be restored to his identity and his home, and to be reunited with Penelope, a situation in which the heroes of the novels often find themselves. One may note too that on the way to this reunion Odysseus is unfaithful, as novel-heroes sometimes are, with Circe and Calypso. Much of the account of the wandering is in the first-person narrative of Books 9–12, and it is in these books that we encounter monstrous and fantastic creatures—the Laestrygonians, Polyphemus, the Sirens, Scylla and Charybdis. Fantastic travelogues of Baron Munchausen character are often recounted by a narrator in his own person (see Ch. II (iii)), sometimes (as with the good Baron) to show that the narrator is a liar, sometimes (as with Odysseus) to display his character and the resourcefulness with which he copes with difficulties; see how Odysseus surmounts the threats posed by e.g. Polyphemus and Circe. Note how in his first-person narrative Apuleius compares the wanderings of his Lucius to those of Odysseus (*Met.* 9.13). Heliodorus also at 2.21 makes Calasiris imply the same comparison by his allusion to *Od.* 9.39, and at 2.19.1 the suggestion of disguise as beggars is accompanied by an allusion to Odysseus as beggar (*Od.* 17.222), not to mention the apparition of Odysseus to Calasiris

(5.22); moreover, Theagenes (5.5.2) can, like Odysseus, be recognized by a scar on his knee resulting from hunting. After their long separation Chaereas and Callirhoe go to bed (Chariton 8.1.17) with the line (*Od.* 23.296), regarded by some ancient critics as the *telos* of the poem, which describes the reunion of Odysseus and Penelope. Encolpius seems to be referred to as *maior Ithacus*, a greater Ulysses, in fr. 37 B = 31 M = *AL* 469 R, discussed above (pp. 45–6).

One may discern an Odyssean narrative pattern in Ach. Tat. 5.23 sqq. There Thersandros, who had been thought lost at sea, returns to find Clitophon, to all appearances a suitor of his wife Melite, dining with her in his house. He assaults and imprisons Clitophon, but Melite finds an opportunity to go to bed with the latter. Melite claims to Thersandros that she was just offering hospitality to Clitophon, shipwrecked like himself. Moreover Thersandros is abetted by his slave Sosthenes, who has some of the function of the Odyssean Melanthios. The Odyssean pattern, however, is stood on its head. Melite is no chaste Penelope, Thersandros no cautious and self-controlled Odysseus; in fact he is like the Odyssean suitors, whereas Clitophon, who makes no resistance when attacked, is like Odysseus himself. These reversals seem to me to bear a strong resemblance to the way in which Petronius uses the *Odyssey*.

Apart from the Cicones and the Lotus-Eaters, all of Odysseus' wanderings are caused by the wrath of Poseidon at Odysseus' blinding of his son Polyphemus. It has long been discussed whether the wanderings and misfortunes of Encolpius were motivated similarly, by the wrath of—Priapus (a deity much more appropriate to this anti-hero)! It is certainly true that Priapus is strikingly prominent in the novel. In Ch. II (v) the scanty information which we have about the beginning of the *Satyrica* has been reviewed; no deductions were there drawn about the origin of the wrath of Priapus, and none could be on the evidence of frs. 1 and 4 in itself. From the episode of 16–27 it becomes clear that Encolpius and his companions have violated a ritual of Priapus, but in our text at any rate the tribulations which they suffer are not represented as punishment for this; it might, however, be noted that Juvenal 6.315 refers to celebrants of the ritual of the Bona Dea (the violation of which by Clodius must surely be in our mind as we read Petronius) as *Priapi maenades*, by contrast to the normal *Bacchi maenades*. Whereas Poseidon repeatedly intervenes personally in the action, Priapus does so only at 104.1, where in a dream he reveals to Lichas the presence of Encolpius on the ship; a similar dream about Giton is sent by a statue of Neptune (= Poseidon!) to Tryphaena, which could well be a deliberate reminder of the *Odyssey*.

In 133.3 after repeated sexual failures Encolpius prays for salvation to Priapus. His words need careful interpretation:

> 6   non sanguine tristi
> perfusus uenio, non templis impius hostis
> admoui dextram, sed inops et rebus egenis
> attritus facinus non toto corpore feci.

I do not come stained with grim blood, I have not laid my hands on temples as a wicked enemy, but reduced to helplessness and in sore straits I have committed a crime with part of my body.

Here *non toto corpore* clearly implies 'but only with my penis'. What then is the *facinus*? Is Encolpius referring exclusively to his present circumstances and regarding his impotence as a crime against the pre-eminently phallic god? That might seem to be favoured by 6–7, since Encolpius does seem to have committed murder in the past (see above, p. 48). What then about *inops et rebus egenis*? If this refers to material deprivation, it is inconsistent with his present situation of material prosperity (125); we should then have to interpret the phrase as referring back to the starting-point of the novel, and presumably of the wrath of Priapus, at Marseilles, where, it will be recalled, the scapegoat was chosen *ex pauperibus*. We would consequently infer that Encolpius actually did something there to arouse the wrath of Priapus, and in fact C. Cichorius (*Röm. Studien* (Leipzig 1922) 438), on the basis of *Hellespontiaco parem Priapo* in the allusion by Sidonius (fr. 4; see above, p. 44), suggested that Encolpius impersonated Priapus in order to take advantage of such characters (imaginary of course) as are represented in the *Priapea* as using the phallus of Priapus statues as a dildo, and that he thus aroused the wrath of Priapus.

All this goes well beyond safe deduction. *Inops* can perfectly

well refer to helplessness in general; can *rebus egenis*? Some of
the passages listed in *TLL* 5.231.39 and by Austin on Verg.
Aen. 6.91 show that it can. The probable conclusion therefore
is that this passage refers strictly to the present situation and
tells us nothing about any 'crime' committed by Encolpius and
his penis in the past and provoking the start of the wrath of
Priapus. Yet it still does imply that at least Encolpius regards
Priapus as responsible for his present predicament, a fact to be
elaborated in a moment. We shall understand the following
promise to give offerings to Priapus 'when Fortune smiles' on
Encolpius to mean 'when I recover my virility'.

The final two references to Priapus come in 136–7, when
Encolpius kills the sacred goose of the god, and in 139.2, when
Encolpius alleges that he is persecuted by *grauis ira Priapi*, the
heavy wrath of Priapus, over land and ocean as various
mythological heroes were persecuted by various other gods
(including Odysseus by Poseidon). This latter reference
appears to be a reflection on his sexual failures; to Circe and
her maid he had not revealed what he sees as this fundamental
cause, but had used witchcraft as an excuse (128.2, 138.7; to a
woman named after the archetypal witch Circe!), an excuse
which they swallow and treat (129.10, 131.1–7); Ovid had
thought of this same excuse in a poem which underlies much
of the narrative of Petronius (*Am*. 3.7.35; see below,
pp. 194 sqq.). Contrary to my earlier opinion (1962.96,
1991.44) I now think that 140.11 (another attack of impotence)
me numen inimicum ibi quoque inuenit ('there too the [OR a]
hostile deity found me') does specifically mean Priapus, as
133.2 *numen auersum* (the adverse deity; *numina uersu* the mss.)
certainly does; the room for ambiguity is provided by the fact
that *numen* fundamentally means divine power in general and
not necessarily a specific deity. Thus 139.2.1 *numen et im-
placabile fatum* could be more general, though three lines later
gemini numinis (two deities) means specifically Apollo and
Poseidon, and Priapus is referred to as *numen* in 133.3.2.

The upshot of this discussion is that there is enough to make
it probable that the wrath of Priapus was indeed an objective
motivating force in the wanderings and tribulations of Encolpius, and that Encolpius is not just subjectively interpreting
things that way because of a bad conscience. Petronius' choice

of this god permits fusion of the erotic strand and that of epic-style wandering. One may note that in the 'Vergilian' Priapeum 'Quid hoc noui est?' (OCT *Appendix Vergiliana* p. 151) a man blames Priapus for rewarding his offerings to the god with impotence; see especially 14–15 *uale, nefande destitutor inguinum,* | *uale, Priape* ('Farewell, you who vilely leave virility in the lurch, farewell, Priapus'). This poem is one of those in which a penis is directly addressed (see below, p. 198, on 132.9).

The detailed allusions to the *Odyssey* will be best elucidated as they occur in the narrative. Remember that one has already cropped up in 97–8, and that it has been pointed out above, p. 149, that it is represented as present to the minds of the characters at the time of action. It follows, first, that the author Petronius has placed his character Encolpius in a series of Odyssean events, and second, that Encolpius in a metatextual way recognizes the allusions and himself interprets his adventures (especially from ch. 127 on) as an Odyssey; the difference is that to Encolpius these events are melodramatic, to Petronius they are farcical. It may also be remarked here that for the most part these allusions occur in the same sequence as the events in the *Odyssey*: the Cyclops (*Od.* IX) in 97 and 101, the arrival at the land of the Laestrygonians and Aeaea (X) in 116, Circe (X) in 126 sqq., the Sirens (XII) in 127.5, the cattle of Helios (XII) in 136–7. Out of order are the recognition scene (105.10) and the reference to an utterance of Odysseus in 132.12, both of which come from much later episodes of the *Odyssey*.

Finally it is worth while to examine the occurrence of the 'wrath of a god' theme in Chariton. In 8.1.2–3 it is revealed that the wanderings of Chaereas have been due to the wrath of Aphrodite (caused by his inappropriate jealousy), who now takes pity on him (Chariton himself came from the city of the goddess, Aphrodisias). Callirhoe at 7.5.3 expresses a suspicion that her misfortunes may be due to the same source (2.2.6 is rather different). The author himself at 2.2.8 states the involvement of Aphrodite, but in a benign way. In all this 'it is difficult to see anything systematic in her . . . behaviour' (Reardon (1991) 107 n. 7); see further Baier, *WJA* 23 (1999), 110. The 'wrath of a god' theme also appears in Xenophon of Ephesus; see in general Sandy *ANRW* 2.34.2.1558.

A notable modern adaptation of the story-pattern of the *Odyssey* deserves a mention here, namely the *Ulysses* of James Joyce. It is hard to say whether he adopted this pattern in awareness of Petronius, but he certainly knew Petronius, since apart from other scattered references he explicitly refers to the story of the Widow of Ephesus; see Killeen, *Comparative Literature* 9 (1957), 193 sqq., esp. 199–210. He also seems to make use of the werewolf story of 61–2; see R. J. Schork, *Latin and Roman Culture in Joyce* (Gainesville 1997) 204. However, Joyce's use of the *Odyssey* had its roots in his childhood reading of Charles Lamb's *Adventures of Ulysses*.

(ii) 100.1–110.5, Lichas and Tryphaena Encountered Again

When the narrative resumes, Encolpius is uneasily soliloquizing about Eumolpus' attraction to Giton; Eumolpus has now (100.1; already at 92.3) replaced Ascyltos (83.6) as *hospes* (acquaintance), a turn of events foreshadowed at 92.4. All nature's best gifts are for communal use, he says;[1] love cannot be an exception; it is really a compliment to one's possessions if they arouse envy. All this is expressed in high-flown language, incorporating apparently bits of a poetic quotation from an unknown source. Now comes the let-down; one rival will not be a problem, for, being an old man, if he tries to molest Giton, he will betray himself by his panting (which recalls his panting at the demands of the Pergamene

[1] A common sentiment; cf. e.g. Sen. *Ep.* 73.6, Dio Chrys. 40.15, Menander fr. 416a.4 and 737, Bömer on Ovid, *Met.* 6.349. Note especially Sen. *Ep.* 44.2 *omnibus lucet* ('the daylight is for everyone'). Sutphen in Otto, *Nachträge* 213–14, quotes what looks like the only other occurrence of *sol omnibus lucet* from a letter by Alcuin, but his quotation is both incomplete and given with a false reference to Migne's *Patrologia*. The phrase is better read in Duemmler's edition, *Monumenta Germaniae Historica, Epistulae IV Karolini Aevi II* no. 42 p. 86.16, where we have *unus sol omnibus lucet, non tamen propter oculorum distantiam aequaliter ab omnibus uidetur*. Here the addition of *unus* (omitted by Sutphen) somewhat alters the sense and brings it nearer to a phrase of Alcimus Avitus, *sol omnibus unus | seruit*, quoted by Chatillon, *Revue du moyen age latin* 20 (1964), 23 (he refers to Petronius on p. 17). One could not conclude on this basis that Alcuin had read Petronius. I am grateful to Professor M. L. Colker for guiding my steps in researching this matter.

boy, 87.8)! So, trying but failing to convince himself, Encolpius settles down to go to sleep.

Now, however, a turn of events which seems like an intervention of malignant Fortune. Not much has been heard of this goddess in the plot so far (unimportant references at 13.1 and 4, 82.6, plus one, not to be taken seriously, from Trimalchio at 55.1–3), but henceforward she becomes more important. The enhanced role of Tyche in the literature of the fourth century BC and the Hellenistic age is well-known, and she is prominent in the novels also; for the 'another trial from Tyche' theme, a complaint which often provides the occasion for emotional declamation, see e.g. Ach. Tat. 5.2.3, 6.3.1 and above, Ch. V n. 6; for Chariton see Baier, *WJA* 23 (1999), 105, and the index of Goold's Loeb edition p. 419 s.v. Fortune, and in general Rohde 281 and the preceding discussion, Schmeling in *Ars Narrandi, scritti . . . L. Pepe* (1996) 79, Sandy *ANRW* 2.34.2.1557.

The turn of events in this case is that Encolpius and Giton hear a man (the text is somewhat dubious here, but this is probably what is meant) on the deck above them groan 'So he has mocked me, has he?' The voice sounds familiar; then a woman in angry tones says 'If some god should put Giton in my hands, what a fine reception I would give him.' The two are thunderstruck, but Encolpius collects himself enough to pull the sleeping Eumolpus' clothes and enquire about the ship's owner and passengers. Eumolpus is annoyed, but informs them that the owner is Lichas and Tryphaena a passenger; the reader will already know (see above, pp. 46–7) that they have been victims of the roguery of Encolpius and Giton and would clearly welcome revenge. Encolpius bares his throat for Fortune, whose complete triumph over him he sees in this, to slit it; Giton faints. Eumolpus, unaware of all this, is bewildered, having acted in all innocence. Lichas, he says, is executing a perfectly normal contract to deliver some goods for sale; this is the Cyclops and pirate captain whom they fear. Eumolpus of course means 'pirate captain' ironically, but novel-readers will be reminded of the real pirates in them; this is significant for the way in which Petronius deflates the high drama of pirates, kidnappings, trials etc. to low-life characters and petty criminality. As for Tryphaena, she is just a woman of leisure going from one playground to another. Giton explains that these are the very people whom he and Encolpius are trying to avoid, so Eumolpus opens a discussion as to what they are to do. 'Imagine', he says, 'that we are in the Cyclops' cave and have to find a way out.' His ironical reference to the Cyclops a moment ago now turns out to have a practical relevance to the situation, 'practical' in the sense that when these characters encounter a problem their way of coping with it is to seek a solution from a literary parallel. One can hardly agree with Laird's remark (246) 'Eumolpus appears to have a firm grasp of the difference between life and literature'.

Various answers are canvassed: (1) they might engineer[2] a shipwreck; (2) they might pretend that one of them is ill and ask the steersman to put in to shore; (3) they might slide down the tow-rope into the lifeboat and cut themselves loose. All these solutions pose problems, so Eumolpus suggests that he roll them up in two leather bales, declare that they were his slaves and have jumped overboard fearing punishment, and then have them carried off in harbour as luggage. Encolpius admits that a trick like this worked once; what he has in mind is the story that a man called Antius escaped from the proscription of the second triumvirate in this way (Appian *BC* 4.40). The allusive 'once' may be compared with 'always' in 127.7 (see below, p. 192). But he rejects this plan too on the amusing grounds that they will not be able to defecate and are liable to betray themselves by snoring or sneezing (cf. 98.4); a rare touch for him of the down to earth. He himself suggests that Eumolpus, with the ink which as a literary man he carries, should disguise them by dyeing them as negro slaves; Giton argues that this too will not work, and proposes that they just cover their heads, leap overboard, and drown themselves, thus adding a fourth method of suicide to those listed in 94.8–11 (see Ogilvie on Livy 4.12.11).

Finally Eumolpus comes up with a practical solution. His servant, as they know from 94.12 sqq., is a barber. He will shave their heads and eyebrows[3] and Eumolpus himself with

---

[2] If the manuscript reading *naufragium ponimus* is correct, it will have to be understood to mean 'stage a shipwreck', as Watt suggests, *C et M* 37 (1986), 181; cf. *mimicum naufragium* (shipwreck in a farce) Sen. *De Ira* 2.2.5.

[3] Cicero, *Q. Rosc.* 20, uses the shaving of the eyebrows in a freedman to cast

his ink will paint tattoo marks as if they were recovered runaway slaves.[4] This plan is forthwith carried out; in the light of the Odyssean motifs it will correspond to the disguise of Odysseus by Athena at *Od.* 13.429 sqq. A seasick passenger leaning over the side witnesses the operation and curses them for cutting their hair on board ship, because this was regarded as a very bad omen in that those in danger of shipwreck (cf. 104.5) or actually shipwrecked regularly vowed to cut off and dedicate their hair if rescued (see my note on Juv. 12.81); it would follow that cutting the hair during a voyage would portend shipwreck, which in fact eventually happens in the narrative of Petronius (so we have foreshadowing here). In dream symbolism cutting of the hair is indeed taken to symbolize this (Artemidorus 1.22). The trio ignore this cursing and go to sleep.

After a gap Lichas and Tryphaena are found discussing with Eumolpus their matching dreams (examined on p. 154 above); for corresponding dreams in the novels see Achilles 4.1, Heliodorus 8.11 (and also 9.25.1 combined with 10.3.1), Longus 1.7–8. Eumolpus invokes the 'divine' Epicurus (so he had been called by the Epicurean Lucretius 3.15; even *deus* 5.8), who derided the attribution of such dreams to the literal gods; this of course does not imply that Eumolpus is a serious Epicurean. Fr. 30 B = 43 M = *AL* 651, which ascribes dreams to the preoccupations of the preceding day, very likely stood in the following gap (Courtney (1991) 63–5).[5] 'In actual fact of

an imputation of villainy. Cf. also Apul. *Met.* 9.12 *frontes litterati et capillum semirasi* ('with writing on their foreheads and their hair half-shaved').

[4] For the tattooing see C. P. Jones, *JRS* 77 (1987), 139. The shaving of the head was a regular accompaniment to make the mark stand out; see Headlam on Herodas 5.79, where we also have the word ἐπίγραμμα (mark) which Encolpius uses just below. This is perhaps a subtle reminder of the passage of Herodas, since Eumolpus (103.2) and Lichas (106.1) use the Latin *inscriptio*. At the least it is linguistic affectation by Encolpius.

[5] This is denied by Deufert, *Hermes* 124 (1996), 82–5, on the grounds that the dreams of Lichas and Tryphaena belong to the type of wish-fulfilment and that in the poem there is no idea of wish-fulfilment. In the light of Reeve's attractive emendation, adduced by Deufert, of *inuenit* 11 to *inuidet*, I would now concede the last point, but not that this would make the poem incompatible with the context. Against this, this is one of the last places in the world to apply logic like Deufert's, since all Eumolpus' efforts are devoted to obfuscating the issue (*causam confundere* 107.7). Moreover, to say that the dreams are wish-fulfilment is over-simple, since they are sent by the divine

course the dreams are reliable, as Eumolpus very well knows, and Lichas can in the sequel contradict Epicurean doctrine (106.3 *deos immortales rerum humanarum agere curam, puto, intellexisti, o Tryphaena*)', ibid. 14; 'I imagine that you, Tryphaena, have understood that the gods are concerned with the affairs of men'.

Lichas, however, is clearly unconvinced and orders a search of the ship, feeling that the operations of the 'divine' should not be ignored; what is divine to him is very different from the 'divinity' of Epicurus on which Eumolpus has opportunistically called. The passenger who had witnessed the shaving of Encolpius and Giton informs Lichas of this; Lichas orders the production of the culprits so that the ship may be purified by their execution. Eumolpus, trying to avert discovery, says that he gave orders for the shaving with no intention of creating a bad omen, since he was himself literally going to be 'in the same boat',[6] but so that their tattoos might jump to the eye; they are being punished for their dissipation.[7] Lichas is content with forty lashes for each as an adequate expiation. Encolpius endures three lashes with the fortitude of the Spartan youths who were hardened by whipping (this is of course the subsequent narrator Encolpius, still posturing even if there is a touch of self-irony). But one blow is enough to make Giton cry out, and his voice is recognized by Tryphaena and her maids; in fact his beauty had already softened the hearts of the sailors who were whipping him (there is a similar motif in Heliodorus 5.7.3). As Tryphaena runs to Giton, Lichas rushes to Encolpius. His way of identifying him is not by his countenance or hands. This last item might seem surprising, and indeed I once wrongly proposed to emend it, but it is a subtle allusion to the recognition-scene between Eurycleia and Odysseus, also alluded to in another recognition-scene in Heliodorus 5.5.2 and in Petronius explicitly referred to in the next sentence; in *Od.* 19.359 Penelope remarks to Eurycleia that the disguised stranger's hands and feet are just like those of Odysseus as they

intervention of Priapus (and Poseidon), of whose role in the plot of the novel I am now more convinced than I was in 1991 (see (i) above).

[6] He is alluding to a figurative, proverbial use of this expression; see Otto no. 1206, to which *Nachträge* 61 adds Amm. Marc. 30.10.2.

[7] Fr. 32 B = 34 M = *AL* 472 perhaps came here.

presumably are after 20 years (cf. 4.149). But Lichas adopts a much more Priapic means of recognition by handling Encolpius' genitals; in a wider sense this is an indication to the reader that sex and identity are the same thing for the characters created by the author.

Tryphaena's heart is softened by the wretched state of Encolpius and Giton, since she thinks that they really have been enslaved and punished. But Lichas realizes that it is all just a disguise and that they have been duped by tricks from a farce, *mimicis artibus*. This word *mimicus* has occurred in 19.1 (*mimico risu*, play-house laughter) and 94.15 (*mimicam mortem*), and the laying of a plan against the legacy-hunters of Croton will be described as composing a farce plot, *mimum componere* (117.4; see below, p. 179). In this particular case we have to remember that mime-actors regularly had shaven heads (Stöcker 15 n. 1). The use of mime in Petronius as a paradigm of deceit struck John of Salisbury (Walsh (1970) 24 n. 6). The word *fabula*, play-acting, is also applied to the doings of the characters (95.1, just after one of the above references), and we encounter other theatrical terminology (e.g. *catastropha* 54.3, *scaena* 33.5, 117.2 and 10, *tragoedia* 108.11, 140.6). Remember too the comparison to mime-actors in the misplaced 80.9 and the theatricality shown in the Quartilla episode (see above, p. 69 and n. 26), but bear in mind that such references in the *Cena*, in which Trimalchio is consciously staging a spectacle, are on a different level. In some of the Greek novels also (not Xenophon of Ephesus or Longus) the action is often referred to in dramatic terms (see Walden, *HSCP* 5 (1894), 1 and F. Conca and others, *Lessico dei Romanzieri Greci* (Hildesheim 1983–97) s.v. δρᾶμα; for Chariton in particular Ruiz-Montero 1018 and Hunter 1063–4, for Achilles Tatius the German translation by K. Plepelits (Stuttgart 1980), index s.v. Theater). The difference of course is that in the Greek novels such terminology is applied for what we would now call 'dramatic' effect in the tragic style (see for instance Ach. Tat. 8.2.3 after 8.1.5), not comic purposes often involving deception (there is the exception that ὑπόκρισις 'charade' at Heliod. 6.12.1 does indicate deception); it is significant that the word μῖμος and its derivatives never occur in the novels.

Lichas in the end, by arguing that the gods have deliberately

put Encolpius and Giton in the way of punishment (which
Epicurean gods would not do), overcomes Tryphaena's inclination to pity. In the following gap a regular trial must have
been set up, since after it we find Eumolpus delivering a speech
for the defence. Such trials are a standard set-piece in the
novels (Chariton 5–6, Achilles 7–8, Longus 2.15–17) and offer
a splendid opportunity for rhetorical display (*deprecatio* 107.7,
a plea for mitigation; *declamatio* 107.12). There was once
another one in Petronius (81.3, discussed above, p. 48), but
the occasion and setting of this one constitute a clear debasement of formal court-room proceedings. Eumolpus even
argues that the companions could not have accidentally
'fallen into the net',[8] but deliberately embarked on the ship
hoping for a reconciliation with himself as intermediary; the
penalty of their shameful aspect is enough in free-born men
(Eumolpus does not actually know if they are free-born; see
above, pp. 41–2). But Lichas angrily refutes Eumolpus point
by point. Eumolpus replies that he can see that the real
sticking-point is the shaving of their heads by night; this is
what makes Lichas believe their presence on ship accidental,
not deliberate. This statement is not exactly accurate, but is
made to give Eumolpus the chance of a feeble diversionary
explanation, that they wanted to do this before embarkation,
but the arrival of a fair wind required sail to be set earlier than
expected, so they had had the operation performed on board
ship, unaware of nautical superstitions and conventions. Lichas
brusquely dismisses both the explanation and Eumolpus and
demands what his reasons for shaving were from Encolpius
himself, who is tongue-tied and has to submit to having the ink
wiped off his face with a wet sponge.

Eumolpus protests that he will not allow violence against
'free-born' men; he even offers physical resistance, aided by his
barber-servant and a few ineffectual passengers. Encolpius too
threatens Tryphaena if she should assault Giton. The whole
ship's complement takes sides,[9] that of Eumolpus having the

---

[8] After the Cyclopean references, this phrase is perhaps due to recollection
of Eur. *Cyclops* 196.

[9] *turbam diducit in partes* ('[Tryphaena] causes the ship's complement to
take sides'), cf. the *Bellum Ciuile* 124.265–6 *regia caeli | in partes diducta ruit*
('The whole kingdom of heaven was divided and rushed to take sides'), an

advantage of being armed with the barber's implements (a new kind of quarter-master, this). A brawl breaks out, with one side fighting for revenge, the other for life, *illis pro ultione, nobis pro uita pugnantibus* (108.9); this is a recall of Sall. *Iug.* 94.5 (in much more momentous circumstances) *pro gloria atque imperio his, illis pro salute certantibus* ('One side fighting for glory and supremacy, the other for survival'). One may in a way compare how the great trial in Chariton (6.2.2) is introduced by a Homeric battle-reference, 'the prize, however, was not a wild olive wreath, not apples, not a pine wreath, but rather supreme beauty' (Loeb translation; cf. *Iliad* 22.159–61), though not in the same mocking tone as is conveyed in Petronius. So 'many' (an exaggeration, of course; §12 shows similar inflation) on both sides fall (not dead, however; see below, p. 174), others retreat with cuts. One may recall, despite obvious differences, the fight on board ship against the pirates at Ach. Tat. 3.20; the passengers there are armed with the stage-props of the Homeristes, and, naturally enough, there is a real slaughter.

Then Giton applies a razor, knowing full well that it is the blunt razor which he had used in 94.12, to his genitals and threatens to cut off the source of all the trouble; Tryphaena stops him by promising pardon. Encolpius similarly threatens to slit his own throat, but with less assurance than Giton; presumably he inferred from Giton's confidence at the time that Giton knew he had the blunt razor, and therefore that he himself did not. Things are at this impasse when Tryphaena is persuaded to bring about an armistice; formal promises of immunity are given, and equipped like a herald with an olive-branch (this described in Vergilian terms, *Aen.* 8.116; a striking shift of tone) taken from the figure-head she starts the negotiations, with the prose flowing into verse as remarked above (p. 22).

That puts an end to the fighting, and Eumolpus draws up the terms of a treaty in proper diplomatic form. It begins with the 'So help you God' formula, *ex tui animi sententia*,[10] and stipulates that Tryphaena will let bygones be bygones (μὴ

indication of the mock-epic tone of this passage; cf. Ch. IV n. 1. Stöcker 5 n. 1 compares the partisanship which appears in the novel trials.

[10] See *OLD sententia* 1c, *TLL animus* 95.8, and Wilkins on the punning Cic., *De Or.* 2.260.

μνησικακεῖν); then, with a sudden let-down, it lays down that
she shall be fined for breach of contract if she exacts sexual
services from Giton without his consent; Lichas too will not
abuse Encolpius by word or look, nor (again a let-down)
investigate where he sleeps, on pain of a fine. All lay aside
their 'weapons', embrace each other and enjoy a meal which the
conflict had postponed. A calm permits them to fish and catch
the birds sitting on the yard-arm. Eumolpus cracks jokes
against the bald and tattooed (Stöcker 15 recalls that Eury-
machus ridicules the baldness of the disguised Odysseus, *Od.*
18.355), and improvises a poem (or two poems) on baldness,
ending with the ominous phrase 'So that you may realize that
death is coming more swiftly than you expect, let me tell you
that a part of your *caput* has already been lost'; here *caput*
means firstly 'head', secondly 'existence', thirdly (Hendry,
PSN 23 (1993), 7–8) 'civic status', which Encolpius and
Giton have given up by impersonating slaves. This is a foreshadowing of a death which turns out to be that of Lichas in the
coming storm, not that of Encolpius. In view of our 'calm
before the storm' we might be tempted to interpret the
preceding mention of a calm also as foreshadowing a storm,
but I cannot find that the Romans had a corresponding
conception (the nearest approach seems to be Sen. *Ep.* 74.4).
At any rate we here have a slackening of the tension before the
coming storm tightens it again.

A maid of Tryphaena takes Giton into the cabin and fits him
with a wig of her mistress (remember that he would previously
have been a *puer capillatus*, a long-haired boy) and false eyebrows. Encolpius is pleased that Giton has recovered his
beauty, but depressed at his own appearance; the same maid,
however, provides him with a blond wig, about which he is
rather vain. Stöcker loc. cit. points out that in Homer Athena,
having previously made Odysseus bald (13.399, 431), makes his
hair grow again (23.157); that of Encolpius has literally grown
again by 126.2, when it is admired.

(iii) 110.6–112.8, the Widow of Ephesus

Everyone is now cheerful (*hilaritas* has been remarked in 109.5
as a result of the meal), and Eumolpus seeks to keep this up by

the conversation with jokes against female fickleness, obviously
directed against Tryphaena. Women, he says, fall in love easily,
forget even their children, and however chaste they may be
they can be driven to distraction by love of a foreigner; all this
is clearly a reference to Helen, hinted at also in the phrase
tragoedias ueteres et nomina saeculis nota ('tragedies of old and
names familiar to the centuries'). He will recount a story not
from those ancient times but one that took place within his own
memory. So everyone gives him their full attention (this has
often been compared with Verg. *Aen.* 2.1) as he begins his
famous story of the Widow of Ephesus,[11] which, like that of the
Pergamene boy, has as its central theme the shallowness of
what is often taken for love.

A few preliminaries about this. First, like the story of the
Pergamene boy, where we previously encountered Eumolpus'
talents as a raconteur, it is generally accepted that this is a
'Milesian Tale', even though we know very little about the
collections of stories so entitled; as the crow flies Ephesus is
about 30 English miles north of Miletus. Secondly, its setting is
(*a*) in a *cena* marked by *hilaritas*, like the stories told in 61–3
(note especially *hilaria* 61.4); see Sandy 471: (*b*) as a means of
whiling away the time on a journey (since the ship is

---

[11] The literature on this is huge. Two full-scale treatments with bibli-
ographies are O. Pecere, *Petronio, la novella della matrona de Efeso* (Padua
1975), and G. Huber, *Das Motif der 'Witwe von Ephesus'* (Tübingen 1990).
Important is O. Weinreich, *Fabel, Aretalogie, Novelle*, Sitzb. Heidelberg.
Akad. 1930–1, abhl. 7, 53; see also Sedgwick appendix B, Stith Thompson K
2213.1, and E. Lefèvre, *Abhl. Akad. der Wissenschaften und der Literatur in
Mainz, Geistes- und Sozialwiss. Klasse* 1997.5 (*Studien zur Struktur der
'Milesischen' Novelle*) 15, who in fact doubts whether the fable (see p. 167)
really is by Phaedrus. One might remark also the discussion by M. Bakhtin,
The Dialogic Imagination (Eng. tr. Austin 1981) 221–3, which goes rather
beyond the facts; it is elaborated by McGlathery, *Arethusa* 31 (1998), 313.
Note that Petronius nowhere uses the term 'widow', which would imply too
close a bond between her and her deceased husband. It is true that she does
express deep love for him (112.7), but the beginning of the story is phrased in
such a way that the impression is conveyed, without any explicit statement,
that solicitude for reputation motivates her no less than love; note the words
spectaculum (she is a showpiece), *in conspectu* (in full view). The word which
introduces the story, *matrona*, indicates social rather than marital status, and,
like *pudicitia*, conveys an air of Roman moral values. The same designation
appears at 111.5 and 112.1, in the latter case as in the first sentence linked with
the chastity which she is about to abandon! Elsewhere she is just 'the woman'.

becalmed), like stories often told on the road (cf. pp. 180–1 below); and indeed one may in a way compare the coming recital of the poem on the Civil War on the journey to Croton (Sandy 474). One may note how Menelaus in Ach. Tat. 2.34 tells his life-story on board ship, this being followed by the storm at the beginning of book 3. Thirdly, the story had been told before Petronius in Latin by Phaedrus, appendix 13 (Postgate OCT) = 15 (Perry, Loeb, and Guaglianone) = 543 (Perry, *Aesopica*). It seems to be generally agreed that Petronius did not take the story from Phaedrus, but that both derived it from a common source, perhaps even the original collection of Milesian tales by Aristides or the translation of this by Sisenna. I myself can see no firm grounds for this; it seems to me that all the divergences can be quite comfortably explained as adjustments by Petronius to the bare account of Phaedrus in order to make it more amoral and sardonic.[12] One significant difference is that Phaedrus does not localize the story; in Petronius Eumolpus is to be presumed to have heard it during his sojourn at Pergamum, and his insistence on its topicality is a means regularly used by storytellers to buttress veracity. This point, for which see my note on Juv.15.27, actually reinforces my contention of direct derivation from Phaedrus because it is put in language framed on another passage of Phaedrus, 3.10.7–8 (after reference to Hippolytus and Cassandra) *sed, fabulosam ne uetustatem eleues,* | *narrabo tibi memoria quod factum est mea* ('But, lest you make light of my ancient examples, as being mythical, I will tell you of something that happened within my own memory' Perry); Stöcker 57-8 fails to notice this. Of course Phaedrus did not invent the story; it is based on themes which are part of the repertoire of folk-tale shared by many cultures. In fact, as a fable it is not easy to derive a moral from it; one can hardly count 31 *sic turpitudo laudis obsedit locum* ('Thus infamy usurped the place of fair fame') as such.

[12] One point sometimes used to urge that Petronius is closer to a common source than Phaedrus is that Phaedrus speaks of *custodes*, sentries, in the plural, which would cause a problem with the mechanics of the story if they were all on duty at the same time; of course Phaedrus does not mean this, but that there was a roster of sentries, only one of whom would be on duty at any particular time. In his own interest the soldier always volunteers for the (literally) 'graveyard' shift.

On the death of the husband of a woman of Ephesus[13] famous for her chastity, she was not content with conventional mourning but escorted him into the tomb and insisted on guarding the body and lamenting day and night (Weinreich [above, n. 11] compares an anecdote in Aelian, *NA* 8.22). The body was laid out *Graeco more*, in Greek fashion, which might just mean the opposite of the *Romanus mos* of cremation (Tac. *Ann.* 16.6.2) or, as Pecere [above, n. 11] 52 explains, placed on a stone slab, not in a sarcophagus as in Phaedrus; in the latter case Petronius will have made this adjustment so that the soldier can grasp the situation (111.8) and does not have to lift a heavy stone lid in order to move the body (112.8). This is the method of sepulture referred to by Lucr. 3.892 *summo gelidi cubat aequore saxi* ('lies on the upper surface of a cold slab') and indicated in the Gospels after the Crucifixion. After five days the exemplary woman too was given up for dead, *complorata singularis exempli femina*; the language is that of an epitaph (see *CIL* 6.21732, 8.26150, Pliny, *Ep.* 8.5.1). She was accompanied by a faithful maidservant who put her tears at the disposal of her mistress[14] and fed the lamp[15] often kept alight as a symbol in tombs (see my note on *Musa Lapidaria* 186.11). The whole city saw all this as a unique pattern of chastity (the third occurrence of this word since 110.6).

Meanwhile the governor[16] ordered the crucifixion of some

---

[13] She is referred to both in Petronius and Phaedrus with the traditional storyteller's *quaedam*, a certain woman.

[14] This is also a funereal concept; see *CLE* 213.7 *lacrimam accommoda*, and Donatus on Ter. *Andr.* 109, both quoted by Pecere 59–60.

[15] Petronius leaves the purpose of the lamp to be inferred; in Phaedrus too we are to deduce that the lamplight directed the soldier, in need of a drink of water, to the tomb, but it is given the weak explanation that the widow, who in Phaedrus has not devoted herself to death, had sat up late that night. The soldier's thirst too is a weaker motive than the one Petronius assigns, his curiosity, which later becomes a critical theme in the *Metamorphoses* of Apuleius; it is appropriate that this curiosity is followed by his first impression that he sees a ghost.

[16] He is referred to as *imperator prouinciae*, commander of the province (just *imperator* in 113.2), not a formally correct term; it might represent στρατηγός or ἡγεμών, both of them terms applied to provincial governors, but is more likely to reproduce the typically vague references to the authorities in such stories (Pecere 65 quotes *rex urbis*, 'king of the city', in Phaedrus 1.14.6 and other parallels). If so, it indicates great stylistic sensitivity in Petronius.

brigands next door to the tomb[17] and posted a sentry to ensure
that no relative should remove any of the bodies for burial; it
was usual to leave the bodies of the crucified to decompose or
be consumed by carrion birds (hence *crucis offla, coruorum
cibaria*, 'gallows-meat, crows' dinner' 58.2). This soldier then
is in an analogous position to the widow; each is guarding a
body or bodies (cf.111.2), like the centurion who maintained
watch after the death of Jesus (Mark 15:44). One may incidentally remark that the crucifixion of Jesus is not in all respects
(e.g. the removal of the body from the cross) typical because of
the imminence of the Sabbath.

In the evening the soldier remarked the lamp in the tomb
and the lamentation, and being curious went to look. At first he
thinks that he is seeing a ghost, this with a good parallel in
Chariton 1.9.4. But after sizing up the situation he brought his
packed meal into the tomb (this is preparation for the role of
food in the sequel) and began to urge the woman not to persist
in superfluous and useless mourning; all come to the same end
and the same final home (*domicilium*, cf. *domus* 71.7). In doing
this he uses the language and topics of consolation-literature, as
Eumolpus in fact indicates by his summary 'the other things by
which scarred minds are restored to health'; of course it is not
factually plausible that a common soldier should know these,
but we must remember that the story is being told by the
literary man Eumolpus, and just as he himself sees his life in
terms of literary situations, so he projects the same on to
others. But the author Petronius has a share in this as well as
the narrator Eumolpus; the incongruity is highly amusing, and
can also be understood to be showing the triteness of such
precepts. To illustrate some of them, for *dolore nihil profuturo*
(pointless grief) some examples are collected in my *Fragmentary Latin Poets* (1993) pp. 90, 326, and others from Seneca by
Pecere 77–8; for *superuacuo* see Sen. *Ep.* 99.4 and 6, *Cons.*

---

[17] I do not grasp the tone of the word *casula* to indicate the tomb. The root
form *casa* is found in this sense on *CIL* 6.15526; the diminutive on *CLE*
1583.5 = *CIL* 6.9659 does actually signify modesty. It has been suggested,
possibly rightly, that it is intended to foreshadow the cosy domesticity with
which the soldier and woman 'set up house', or that it is to convey a contrast
to the power of the governor. Rhythm, which influences the choice of some
diminutives (Müller (1983) 454), is not a factor here.

Polyb. 5.1, 18.4; for 'all come to the same end and the same home' *CLE* 995, quoted by Nisbet–Hibbard on Hor. *Odes* 1.28.15 with *CLE* 1097.2 (see too *CLE* 965.9).

The woman remains obdurate and rejects the food which he, refusing to 'retreat' (the first occurrence of the military terminology suitably applied to his actions in the sequel), tries to press on her (presumably the maid has told him about her fasting);[18] she is referred to by the diminutive *muliercula* 'poor little woman' as he sees her. But the odour of the wine is too much for the maid to resist (women of that station are traditionally represented as prone to tippling; see Plaut. *Curc.* 96 sqq.). So she holds out her conquered hand, which is both a term for military submission (Ovid, *Am.* 1.2.20, and generally Otto no. 1040) appropriate to the soldier victor, and a request for the sustenance to be put into it. Refreshed with drink and food (the normal order, as Pecere 92 points out, would be 'food and drink', as in 113.6!), she too begins to 'overcome the resistance' (again military terminology, *expugnare pertinaciam*)[19] of her mistress, like the soldier using the consolatory topic *quid proderit?* ('What good will it do?'), which is essentially the same as *nihil profuturo*, and couching the sentence in the rhetorical form of an anaphoric rising tricolon. Hammering home the word *uiuere*, to live, and its cognates, she reinforces her argument by quoting the words of Anna to Dido (we are reminded of Chariton's frequent direct quotations from Homer) exhorting her to abandon her devotion to her late husband (*Aen.* 4.34; the alert reader will recall that Dido has just sworn that her dead husband would keep her love in her tomb, and also, in view of 110.6, that Aeneas was a foreigner, *peregrinus*); this situational parallel from literature works in exactly the same way as the soldier's knowledge of the topics of consolation treatises, and also foreshadows that the widow will succumb to a new love despite a vow of fidelity to the old. The quotation is altered in one word; it now reads *id*

---

[18] Pecere 88 aptly quotes Lucian *De Luctu* 24 for exhortations to the mourning to eat; see also R. Kassel, *Untersuchungen zur gr. und röm. Konsolationsliteratur* (Munich 1958) 92, with occurrences of Hom. *Il.* 19.225 and 24.602 in treatises of consolation, including Sen. *Ep.* 63.2.

[19] At one time Fraenkel objected to the combination *expugnare coepit*, 'began to take by storm', but it is found in *Bell. Afr.* 87.4. For *expugnare pertinaciam* see Livy 37.56.9 (not a military context).

cinerem aut manes credis sentire sepultos? ('Do you think that the ashes and buried remains *feel* this?') instead of *curare* ('are concerned about'), which some manuscripts of Petronius have interpolated from Vergil. This means that we no longer envisage the sentient dead as indifferent, but implicitly deny sensation to them, a doubt often expressed in funereal contexts (see Pecere 95–9 and my note on *Musa Lapidaria* 199A.39). The quotation alerts us to another allusion to Dido in the preceding words 'if you breathe forth your uncondemned life before the fates demand it'; see *Aen.* 4.698–9 'Proserpina had not yet condemned her head to Orcus' (Pecere 100). 'The very corpse here', concludes the maid, 'reminds you to live', a reprise of the 'skeleton-moral' of 34.8–10; as there, we have to recall the common secondary sense of *uiuo*, 'live an enjoyable life' (cf. 34.10.3 and my note on *Musa Lapidaria* 61), not a living death.

The emphasis on life is reinforced by Eumolpus' sarcastic comment 'No one listens unwillingly (*inuitus*) when he is compelled to eat or live (*uiuere*)', with the almost oxymoronic combination of 'unwillingly' and 'compelled'. So the widow allows her obstinacy to be broken down (*pertinacia* again; *pertinaciam frangere* in a military context, Livy 38.15.10). The phrasing implies that she avoids explicit assent; Justin 12.8.6 (the defeated Porus) *neque cibum sumere uoluerit . . . aegreque sit ab eo obtentum ut uellet uiuere* ('He refused to take food . . . and was with difficulty persuaded to consent to live') has been compared. So she eats as greedily as the previously 'defeated' maid. 'You know', says Eumolpus, 'what temptation usually follows repletion', i.e. sex; cf. the proverb *sine Cerere et Libero friget Venus* [Ter. *Eun.* 732 with Barsby's note = Otto 1868; 'Without Ceres and Bacchus Venus is cold'], and see R. B. Onians, *Origins of European Thought* (edn. 2, Cambridge 1953) 225. The soldier now applies his blandishments to 'attacking' the woman's chastity, backed up by the maid, who again plays the part of Anna by quoting *Aen.* 4.38 'will you fight against even a love that pleases you?' The woman herself finds the soldier 'quite attractive and articulate' (at which point we will reflect on the purpose for which he is now using his eloquence!). So he is 'victorious' and they are 'united in matrimony', a wonderfully sardonic use of a common euphemism,[20] not just that night but the following two also, with the doors of the tomb now shut (like the doors of the room in which Encolpius and Giton get together, 91.4), whereas they had been open when the soldier saw the light. This, according to Bücheler's inevitable emendation, was to create the impression that the chaste wife had expired over her husband's body.[21] In this context J. Griffin, *Latin Poets and Roman Life* (London 1985) 161–2, reminds us that prostitutes often carried on their business in cemeteries; another nail in the coffin of the matron's 'chastity'!

When the parents of one of the crucified saw that the sentry was abandoning his post, they took down and buried the body. In the morning the soldier, seeing the empty cross, communicated to the widow his intention to commit suicide in order to escape punishment. One may compare the reaction of the jailer in Acts of the Apostles 16: 27, but also think of the soldier as now taking over the role of Dido, who killed herself with a sword after neglecting her duties (*Aen.* 4.86–9) for love; this role-reversal, which was also a feature of the story of the Pergamene boy, indicates the turning-point at which the woman now becomes the dominant partner. The soldier requested that she share the tomb between himself[22] and her husband; here the triangular nature of this relationship (as of others in Petronius) becomes prominent. She, being as compassionate as she was chaste (this hardly suggests a high degree of compassion, and sabotages any notion that her rescue of the soldier may have been for purely altruistic motives), is unwilling to see the simultaneous decease of the two men[23] dearest to

[20] See 26.3, Pecere 122, Adams 159–60. The phrase also suggests how the woman excuses herself in her own mind, like Dido (*coniugium uocat, hoc praetexit nomine culpam*; 'She calls it marriage and with this name veils her lapse').

[21] Some scholars keep the manuscript reading *putasset*, understand *ut* as consecutive, not final, and translate 'would have thought', but to convey this sense Latinity would require *putaturus fuerit* (R. Kühner and C. Stegmann, *Grammatik der lat. Sprache, Satzlehre* (ed. 3, Leverkusen 1955) 2.409).

[22] He too refers to his relationship with an emollient term, *familiaris*, friend, taken up in 113.8; cf. Pecere 133 n.264.

[23] *duorum mihi carissimorum hominum duo funera*, 'the two bodies of the two men dearest to me'. Eumolpus is thinking of the line (655 Ribbeck) of Accius quoted by Cicero, *Or.* 156, *uideo sepulcra dua duorum corporum* ('I see two tombs of two bodies').

her (triangular again). Therefore she decides to 'expend' (with a pun in the Latin which might be rendered in English by 'suspend'; cf. *pendentem* 112.5) a corpse rather than see a living man perish. So, now dominant, she persuades him to live. She 'orders' him to take the corpse from the slab and fix it to the cross; next day the populace, which had previously so admired her chastity, wonders how the dead man got on the cross. This last phrase is paralleled by 137.2 *ibis in crucem* ('You will mount the cross'), and refers to the fact that the victim had to lie down on the cross before it was erected; there is nothing to suggest that we should see any relationship to the imprecation *i in malam crucem* ('Go to Hell'). Greek often uses the word *anabainein*, to mount, in this context (see e.g. Lampe, *Patristic Greek Lexicon* s.v. A 1 b), and Chariton 4.3.5 has *epibainein*.

The artistry of this story is beyond all praise, but I shall just briefly draw out one implication of some of my comments. We saw earlier how Hermeros in describing Fortunata simultaneously revealed himself. In this story we can see how Petronius makes characteristics of his fictional creation Eumolpus come through, but what is even more striking is how, through the mouth of Eumolpus, by scrupulous selection of vocabulary and phraseology he is able to make the feelings and state of mind of the characters emerge. To do this by implication, without explicit factual intervention of the author and his narrator, is a mark of the greatest subtlety and mastery in a writer of fiction; one may contrast Petronius in this respect with a second-rate novelist such as C. P. Snow, who has to tell us what his characters are feeling.

(iv) 113–115, the Shipwreck

The sailors laugh at the story, Tryphaena blushes and reclines her head on Giton's shoulder, but Lichas is not amused, remembering the fickleness of his own wife (so we presume: see above, p. 46) Hedyle; Eumolpus, though informed in 101.6, has incautiously stirred up an old grievance. However, the words of the treaty forbid holding a grudge (*nec . . . permittebant meminisse*, μὴ μνησικακεῖν; 109.1–4) and cheerfulness (*hilaritas*) continues to prevail. Encolpius is furious at Tryphaena's fondling of Giton and the way in which they both ignore him, but as usual he finds an excuse for Giton, inferring that he did not wish to reopen old wounds.

The narrative now becomes very scrappy. When a more continuous text resumes, a storm blows up. This is described in the high-flown language and conventions of a *poetica tempestas* (Juv. 12.23, with my note; cf. Lucian, *Quomodo historia conscribenda* 45), particularly that opposing winds blow simultaneously, thick clouds black out the sky, and the helmsman is helpless.[24] The ancestry of such poetic storms goes back to the *Odyssey* (books 5 and 12). In the novel this is a set theme, providing much scope for rhetorical ἔκφρασις.

Lichas implores Encolpius to placate Isis, the protectress of mariners, by restoring to her figurehead the vestments and sistrum which he had stolen (these were already in his mind at 113.3 *expilatum . . . nauigium*, the plundered ship), but the wind blows him overboard and he is drowned, like the steersman and sailors in *Od.* 12.413–19 and the steersman at *Aen.* 1.115. This is the only fatality in the extant parts of the *Satyrica*, though there seems to have been a murder in a lost part; the comic novel must not become too tragic (note the emphasis on the fact that nobody was killed in the fight, *sine morte* 108.9). Tryphaena and her retinue escape in the lifeboat. Encolpius and Giton apparently (there is a gap in the text here) remain on board. Encolpius with the revealing phrase *si uere Encolpion dilexisti* ('If you truly loved Encolpius') laments their coming separation in death, Giton strips, slips inside Encolpius' tunic and ties them together with the belt, saying that whether they survive or perish they will be together; this has close parallels in the novel shipwrecks (Courtney (1962) 98).[25] The ship breaks up and bits of it wash ashore, including

---

[24] 114.1–3 *nubes . . . obruere tenebris diem . . . spissae repente tenebrae lucem represserant* ('Clouds overwhelmed the daylight with darkness . . . thick darkness had suddenly suppressed the light'); cf. Juv. 12.18, Verg. *Aen.* 1.88 *eripiunt subito nubes caelumque diemque* ('Suddenly clouds blot out heaven and daylight'). For 'suddenly' in these descriptions see Tarrant on Sen. *Ag.* 470 (add Sen. *Contr.* 7.1.4), remarking two instances in the novels; see also Stephens–Winkler 164–7 (Antonius Diogenes?), with the opposing winds (as in Ach. Tat. 3.1–2) and clouds too. For the helmsman see Juv. 12.31–2; Verg. *Aen.* 3.201 (cf. generally 194–9); Ovid, *Met.* 11.492–3, *Tr.* 1.2.31, 1.4.12; Ach. Tat. 3.3.1, Heliod. 1.22.4, 5.27.

[25] In the narrative of Xen. Eph. 3.2.12–13 there cited Hippothous supports

that which carries the two. From the captain's cabin in another they hear what sounds like the cries of an animal wanting to escape. It turns out to be Eumolpus, who had evidently gone below and in his concentration ignored the storm, reciting a poem as he writes it down in a huge notebook; this is a foreshadowing of his coming recitation of the lengthy *Bellum Ciuile*. They pull him out and bid him to be of good cheer (*bonam habere mentem*), but he, not having even noticed the storm, is just annoyed at the interruption, and they have to drag the 'lunatic' ashore as he continues to bellow; 'lunatic' (*phreneticus*) both puns on the preceding *bonam mentem* (as if it meant 'be of sound mind') and alludes to the 'poets are mad' topic. A famous passage about this comes at the end of Horace's *Ars Poetica*, which states that it is dangerous to rescue mad poets from peril, for then they will fasten on to auditors and suck their blood with incessant recitation; as Conte 58 suggests, following F. M. Fröhlke, *Struktur und Wirklichkeit* (Frankfurt and Berne 1977) 57, Petronius surely had this passage in mind. But he had something else in mind too, as pointed out by Cucchiarelli, *Antike und Abendland* 44 (1998), 130 n. 11 and 137 n. 35. For there was another poet who composed during a storm, namely Ovid (*Tr.* 1.11); he too excuses his imperfections (35 sqq.), comments on the helplessness of the steersman (21; see n. 24), and admits that his activity might be called *insania* (11). Ovid also remarks his own incessant urge to poetry: *sponte sua carmen numeros ueniebat ad aptos | et quod temptabam scribere uersus erat* (*Tr.* 4.10.25–6; 'Unbidden poetry would come to rhythms which fitted, and whatever I tried to write was verse'). Surely Petronius is here making good-humoured fun of Ovid.

The three take refuge for the night in a fisherman's hut and make a poor meal out of the provisions spoiled by the salt water (this is a recall of *Aen.* 1.177). Next morning they see a corpse being carried to shore by the tide. This evokes from Encolpius a diatribe on mortality which reflects the words of Alcyone as

Hyperanthes as he swims for as long as he can, but the latter is finally drowned and buried by the former, who inscribes an epitaph for him on the tomb.

she sees the corpse of Ceyx washed to shore after a storm
(Ovid, *Met.* 11.719–21):

> qui foret ignorans, quia naufragus, omine mota est,
> et, tamquam ignoto lacrimam daret, 'heu miser' inquit
> 'quisquis es, et si qua est coniunx tibi'.

Unaware who it was, she was affected by the omen, because it was a
shipwrecked man, and, as if she were shedding tears for a stranger,
she said 'Poor fellow, whoever you are, and unhappy your wife, if you
have one'.

It ends with an amusingly ambivalent sentence *en homo
quemadmodum natat!*, the surface meaning of which is 'see
how mankind is at sea' metaphorically (see *OLD*, *natare* 5a;
naufragium, shipwreck, in §16 below incorporates a similar
metaphor, see *OLD* s.v. 1b and add Sen. *Cons. Polyb.* 9.6); in
the context, however, it also implies the let-down 'look how the
man floats'. The ambivalence has been suggested to Petronius
by the spectator of another shipwreck in Plaut. *Rud.* 154
homunculi quanti estis! eiecti ut natant! ('Puny men, how
worthless you are! How they swim after being thrown overboard'). Then when Encolpius sees the face of the corpse he
recognizes Lichas (as Alcyone recognizes Ceyx), which provokes more impassioned declamation on the futility of human
aspirations couched in the conventional formulae *ubi nunc est,
nempe, ite nunc et* (for this last see my note on Juv. 12.57); note
too the rhetorical *occupationes* with *at enim* and *tamen*, 115.17–
18. The ideas expressed have analogies in the *Rudens*, Propertius 3.7, and other moralizing passages (Courtney (1962)
98–9;[26] Sullivan's Senecan parallels (198–202) show little
verbal resemblance). One aspiration which he deplores is that
for *opes fraudibus captas* (wealth won by deceit), which is highly
ironical from the mouth of Encolpius and is meant to mock the
frequent hollowness of such moralizing declamation, as well as
to foreshadow the coming deception of the legacy-hunters of
Croton. Finally, with clear recalls of Seneca, he refutes the idea

---

[26] Note that the passage there quoted from Seneca (?), *De Remediis
Fortuitorum* 5.2, is imitated by Min. Fel. *Oct.* 11.4 (Newman, *AJP* 109
(1988), 96), which goes a long way to establish its genuinely Senecan
paternity.

that death at sea is particularly horrible because of lack of burial.

So they bury Lichas, and as the text breaks off Eumolpus is composing an epitaph for him. But the next chapter begins *hoc peracto libenter officio* ('when we had gladly performed this duty'), which shows the insubstantiality of the tears shed over Lichas in 115.

VII
Croton

(i) 116–117, Laying the Plot for Legacy-Hunting

Having decided in which direction to go (this takes up 115.7), they quickly ascend a mountain; this combines allusions to Vergil (*Aen*. 1.419) and the *Odyssey* of Homer (10.148, Odysseus' arrival at Aeaea, the model of the scene in the *Aeneid*; 10.97, the same line, arrival at the city of the Laestrygonians). From this height they see a hill-town (Carthage too is on an *arx* in Vergil); Croton, as this turns out to be, was not actually on a hill, but on a plain surrounded by hills, but topographical accuracy is less important to Petronius than literary resonance. They learn from a farm-supervisor, just as Odysseus' three scouts do from the daughter of the king of the Laestrygonians, what it is: Croton, 'once the leading city of Italy'. 'Once' means 'in the days of Pythagoras', who migrated there and established his philosophical sect there. They enquire what sort of men inhabit this celebrated place (*qui homines inhabitarent nobile solum* = οἵ τινες ἀνέρες εἶεν ἐπὶ χθονὶ σῖτον ἔδοντες *Od*. 10.101) and what are their pursuits after the destruction of their prosperity by long wars; this too is a reminiscence of *Aen*. 1.307 'to explore' (the same verb in Petronius) 'the unfamiliar places and who occupies them, men or animals' (the animals in the case of Petronius will in a moment turn out to be birds of prey). The informant replies that commerce, culture, and morals are all absent from the town, and the only way to make a living is by lying; the whole town is divided between legacy-hunters and those whom they hunt. This is a theme which had made its home particularly in satire since Horace, *Satires* 2.5, in which the legacy-hunter is Ulysses. In Croton only the childless and unmarried are honoured; the town is like one afflicted with the plague, where there are only fields covered by corpses being torn to pieces and the carrion crows which tear them (this last a common metaphor; see e.g. Horace 56, Sen. *De Ben.* 4.20.3, Otto no. 1946). This metaphor of eating corpses will become literal fact at the end of our text, at which point we may recall that the Laestrygonians were cannibals.

Eumolpus[1] might have been expected to be deterred by the aforementioned lack of culture (far from it!), and to recoil from legacy-hunting, which he had criticized in 88.8. However, he gets an idea, which at first Encolpius thinks to be only poetic licence. But he takes it more seriously when Eumolpus says that if they had better stage-trappings, clothes, and props to give plausibility to deception (*mendacium* taking up the *mentiri* which the farm-manager had suggested), he would quickly bring them to prosperity. Encolpius offers the use of property which he had evidently salvaged from the wreck (114.14), a garment and the spoils from the villa of Lycurgus which they had robbed (see above, p. 48). This garment is described as *rapinae comes*, and whatever exactly that means it is probably the vestment which had been stolen from Isis (114.5). In providing costumes Encolpius is performing the function of the *choragus* (producer) in the Roman theatre.

So Eumolpus says 'Let's compose a mime' (taking up the imagery of *scaena*, 'stage-trappings'; for the theatrical vocabulary see above, p. 162) 'and, if this form of trade is to your liking, make me director' (*dominus* sc. *gregis*); the word *negotiatio* is suggested by the farm-manager's statement that they cannot make a living as *negotiatores* (116.4). The others accept this and swear an oath like that of free men selling themselves as gladiators, putting them body and soul in his power (see my note on Juv. 11.8); such *auctorati* had to swear to accept servile punishments like slave gladiators, so this marks their transition to acceptance of the role of slaves. Next they learn their lines (*condiscimus*; cf. the converse *condoceo* at Plaut. *Poen.* 580–1). Eumolpus has lost his son, in misery has gone abroad, has lost a

---

[1] Because of abbreviation the narrative presents problems in this area. V. Tandoi, *Scritti di Filologia* (Pisa 1992) 1.62, revives Bücheler's idea that Giton or Encolpius had originally suggested that they pose as begging priests of Cybele (their shaven heads would fit this). This suits some details, e.g. the mention of the mother of the gods at 117.3, *diuinatio* (prophecy) at 117.1 (cf. Apul. *Met.* 9.8.6), but still seems to me rather hard to fit into the wording of what is preserved.

large sum of money in the shipwreck (this event can be
verified), though it was not the financial loss that troubled
him (a good ploy this) but the lack of a retinue to establish his
dignity; still he has huge properties and investments in Africa
(this also plausible; for large estates there cf. 48.3 and see
Pliny, *NH* 18.35). To make him a more attractive bait to
legacy-hunters, he is to pretend to be in poor health, talk
continually about finance and keep reviewing his accounts, and
renew his will every month. To keep up the role-playing
(*scaena* again), when he summons one of the companions he
is to do so by the wrong name, as if confusing him with one of
the many not with him; shades of Trimalchio (see above,
p. 102, on 47.11–13), but also of the traditional character-
type of the *ostentator pecuni⟨ae glori⟩osus* (the man who boastfully shows off his money; *Ad Herenn.* 4.50.63 according to
Kayser's emendation).

All this reminds me strongly of Heliodorus 6.11-2, where
Charicleia and Calasiris disguise themselves as beggars in the
hope of finding it easier to procure food, and make their way
towards the village of Bessa; their harmless deception, as
remarked above (p. 162), is characterized by the theatrical
term ὑπόκρισις, play-acting.

With all this settled, and a pious prayer (!) for success in their
enterprise, they set off. But Giton, who is not used to carrying
heavy loads, is not up to the weight of the luggage. Eumolpus'
servant, who has previously acted as porter in 99.6, also puts
down his load, objecting that he is not a beast of burden but a
free man who has hired himself out to Eumolpus; he underlines
his discontent by frequent farting. Only now (at least in our
text) do we find that his name is Corax; perhaps this was
suggested to Petronius by the metaphor of carrion birds
applied to the legacy-hunters (as a slave-name it is found at
Plaut. *Capt.* 657, but does not occur in Solin's list of slave-
names of the city of Rome). All this is a complex of literary
allusion to:
(1) the beginning of the *Frogs* of Aristophanes, in which
Xanthias, riding a donkey, carries the luggage and objects to
doing so, threatening to fart;
(2) the ninth Bucolic of Vergil, in which Lycidas and Moeris
converse on a journey; both of them quote brief specimens

from the poetry of Menalcas, one of them from an uncompleted poem. Finally Lycidas encourages Moeris to recite more and offers to relieve him of his burden (*fascis*, cf. Petron. 117.12) to help him do so;

(3) the model of this Bucolic in Theocritus 7, in which again travellers relieve the tedium of a journey by having two of them recite substantial specimens of their poetry. For imitation of the model of a model see below, p. 203, on 135.8, and Reed, *CP* 92 (1997), 262 n. 5; one may also compare how Propertius in referring to Vergil's poetry (2.34.69–70) alludes not to the version of Vergil himself, who represents the presents as sent to a boy (*Buc.* 2.40, 3.70), but to that of Theocritus, who makes them gifts to a girl (3.10, 34–6). These reminiscences of Theocritus and Vergil, which I have pointed out in *AJP* 109 (1988), 349, will be further discussed in relation to the end of the next chapter of Petronius.

(ii) 118, the Literary Theory of Eumolpus

After a gap Eumolpus is found expounding his literary theories. Poetry according to him has tripped up many who think it easy (here we hear echoes of Hor. *Sat.* 1.4.40 sqq.) and have taken refuge in it from forensic rhetoric and the strain of composing *controuersiae* with scintillating epigrams (*sententiolae*, a contemptuous diminutive); possibly this is a hit at the Piso whose conspiracy was used as a pretext for compelling Petronius to suicide and whose rhetorical and poetic achievements are lauded in the anonymous *Laus Pisonis*. But the nobler spirit does not love such frivolity.[2] Moreover the

---

[2] Like Müller in his latest edition, I adopt the emendation *uanitatem*. The manuscript tradition has *sanitatem*, which would mean that the nobler spirit does not love sobriety and rationality, an allusion to the Democritean theory of the madness of poets (see e.g. Brink on Hor. *AP* 296). This can be supported by §6 *praecipitandus est liber spiritus ut potius furentis animi uaticinatio appareat quam religiosae orationis sub testibus fides* ('The unfettered inspiration must be sent soaring . . . so that it gives the impression of prophetic ravings rather than the accuracy of a solemn speech before witnesses', Sullivan). However, this does not fit the train of thought in the immediate context at all well (see R. Häussler, *Das historische Epos* 2 (Heidelberg 1978) 124 n. 45); *uanitatem* can be compared with 1.2 *sententiarum uanissimo strepitu*, the empty rattle of epigrams. *Praecipitandus est liber*

mind needs to be soaked in a flood of literature (the same metaphor in 4.5 and 5.21); just below it emerges that the point of such immersion is the very classical idea that a poet should develop his conceptions within a framework of generically standardized *loci*. Diction must be choice, *sententiae* must not stand out but be integrated; the mention of this feature links poetry with rhetoric, a link suggested also in 2.8.

Failure awaits whoever embarks on the vast task (cf. Lucan 1.68 *immensumque aperitur opus*, 'A vast task opens up') of writing about the Civil War without being replete with literature (the same metaphor again; cf. 5.21–2 *flumine largo | plenus*, 'filled with an abundant stream'); this section is introduced by *ecce* ('let me point out'), which marks a transition and suggests something which is before the eyes, i.e. contemporary. For (*enim*; this implies that the following specifications indicate the use to which literary culture is to be put) it is not a matter of versifying history, but unrestrained[3] inspiration must rush headlong through mysterious utterances[4] and interventions of the gods and something else which is unfortunately lost in a hopeless corruption but at least seems to include fiction (*fabulosum*); μῦθοι are appropriate to poetry as opposed to history (Lucian, *Quomodo Historia conscribenda* 8 and 10). The result should not resemble testimony in a court case but the madness of a raving prophet (who could say that Eumolpus fails to live up to this advice?). For example, the following specimen, even if it hasn't received final polish; and

spiritus was characteristically a favourite quotation of Coleridge, but he had to leave out the preceding words!

[3] This is another link with 5.13 *mittat habenas | liber*, 'Let him relax the reins without constraint'.

[4] Others take *ambages* to mean 'digressions' (and admittedly there are many 'amplified episodes' in Eumolpus' *Bellum Ciuile*), but at Verg. *Georg.* 2.46 the word means 'beating about the bush' rather than specifically 'digressions'. I take Petronius' point to be that poetry cannot be tied down to one precise meaning as history can. D. C. Feeney, *The Gods in Epic* (Oxford 1991) 263, takes it on similar lines to mean 'oblique representations', comparing *obliquis figurationibus* in a passage perhaps due to Suetonius (A. Rostagni, *Suetonio, De Poetis* (Turin 1956) 13). For *liber spiritus* compare ἐλευθερία in Lucian's contrast between history and poetry, *Quomodo historia conscribenda* 8; see Brink on Hor. *AP* 9–10 and note *Aetna* 91 *debita carminibus libertas ista*, 'That freedom is owed to poetry', as opposed to *uerum*, the truth which is the business of the didactic poet.

here Eumolpus begins to recite his own poem on the Civil War, which he was composing during the shipwreck (there too he admits its incompleteness, and his behaviour is that of a madman; 115.4–5). At this point the full connection with Vergil (the quotation from an uncompleted poem) and Theocritus becomes apparent; but in the light of what I say above (p. 175) we will also remember that Ovid carried on board ship his unfinished *Metamorphoses*, which he describes in almost the same terms, *his summam . . . abesse manum* (*Tr.* 1.7.28; 'it lacks the final polish').

It is inconceivable, though it has been conceived, that the second half of this chapter is written without reference to Petronius' contemporary Lucan. Specific reference has been sought at the beginning also, for Lucan was a highly successful declaimer; however, he did not turn from rhetoric to poetry, for according to the Vacca life he was simultaneously debarred by Nero from both. At first sight Dio Cass. 62.29.4 seems to date this ban to AD 65, but he has grouped this with the banishment of Cornutus almost certainly out of chronological order; though Rose makes this dating fundamental to his reconstruction, the ban was surely earlier (see Griffin 157). F. Ahl, *Lucan* (Ithaca 1976) 352, puts the ban in mid-64; Tac., *Ann.* 15.49 implies that it was earlier than the beginning of 65. The mention of *sententiae* (§5; the later mention in §6 is part of a deep corruption) at the transition from generalities to specifics does suit Lucan, as he was famed for these (Quintil. 10.1.90). So does the emphasis on avoiding concentration on historical fact (Lucan was accused of such concentration; *Lucanus historicus an poeta* ('Is Lucan a historian or a poet?)' Serv. *Aen.* 1.382, Berne scholia on Lucan 1.1, Iordanes, *Getica* 43) and on introducing interventions of the gods, *deorum ministeria* (Lucan's great innovation of course was to expel such). The insistence on absorption in literature might not seem to fit him, since Lucan does draw much from his poetic predecessors, but it becomes clear that Eumolpus has in mind particularly conventional literary apparatus such as divine intervention. One cannot doubt that all this relates to Lucan, but his name is not mentioned because he is contemporary (perhaps even still alive, depending on the view taken of literary chronology), and the fictitious narrative needs to keep its distance from real life; we are just given the hint that Eumolpus' poem has not received its final polish, which of course is true of Lucan too, whether we date Petronius' composition of this part before or after Lucan's death.

How seriously all this is to be taken will be considered after the *Bellum Ciuile* has been discussed.

(iii) 119.1–124.1, the *Bellum Ciuile*

I begin by laying out the structure of the poem:

(1) The causes of the war: (*a*) moral degeneration 1–60; comparatively little space is given to this in Lucan; (*b*) 61–6 historical causes, on which Lucan expands. So the relative proportions have been reversed by Eumolpus, in accordance with the precepts of ch. 118.

(2) An episode (67–121) between personified Fortuna and Dis, the upshot of which is that Rome has had prosperity for too long and is now overwhelmed by it. Though Lucan emphasizes Stoic *fatum*, he does mention Fortuna at 1.84, 160. We can observe a growing taste, which reaches its height in Statius (see Dewar on *Th.* 9.32), for personified abstractions; most of the supernatural figures in this poem are of this type, not the traditional epic gods of Vergil etc. The meeting of the gods takes place in the Phlegraean fields, which carries with it associations of the gigantomachy, a frequent symbol for violent conflict; see Connors 121–4.

(3) Prodigies (122–43); as in Lucan 1.522–83, these are based on Verg. *Georg.* 1.466–88, transferred from Caesar's death to his approach. 136 explicitly contradicts Lucan in one detail; see Connors 119–20.

(4) The crossing of the Alps 144–208; this is only briefly indicated by Lucan 1.183, following Verg. *Aen.* 6.830. In fact Caesar's army was at Ravenna when he embarked on his invasion of Italy. Eumolpus models himself on Livy's (21.35–7) dramatic account of the crossing by Hannibal, who was a favourite figure of the declaimers (Juv. 10.167); he seems to be pointing to an opportunity missed by Lucan. Caesar's view of Italy from the Alps (154) is particularly Hannibalic. This passage includes a speech by Caesar which,

despite *furentes* 168, is noticeably less aggressive than Lucan 1.299–351.

(5) 209–44 The flight from Rome, corresponding to Lucan 1.469–522. This is motivated by a personified *Fama*; the idea is taken up from unpersonified *fama* in Lucan (1.469), but given a Vergilian aura from *Aen.* 4.173 sqq.

Three supernatural episodes:

(6) 245–63 Personifications of evil come as those of good depart.

(7) 264–70 The gods take sides. The resulting lack of equilibrium in the sky is surely a parody of Lucan's admonition to Nero to consider carefully his position there (1.57).

(8) 271–fin. Discordia emerges and prophesies the coming disaster, an episode perhaps modelled on that in Ennius, *Annals* 7, which leaves its reflection in *Aen.* 7; with the last line of his poem (*factum est in terris quicquid Discordia iussit*: 'All Discord's commands were achieved on earth') Eumolpus recalls this (cf. *Aen.* 7.545 *en perfecta tibi bello discordia tristi*, Allecto's words to Juno; 'See, discord has been achieved for you through grim war'). He also leaves it open for himself to continue the poem.

Overall Eumolpus' poem shows divine and supernatural action predominating over strictly human events; in avoiding one extreme he has rushed to the other. The personifications come and go quickly, there is none of the cohesion and consistency of Lucan.

Lucan himself was able to publish only Books 1–3 of his poem, though 4–6 seem to have been almost ready for publication; 7–10 appear to have been left in a less finished state. Eumolpus has many recalls of Lucan, mostly of the three published books but occasionally also of the later books. To take two important instances, the opening is modelled not only on 1.110 *quae mare, quae terras, quae totum possidet orbem* (sc. *Romae fortuna*; 'The fortune of Rome, which possesses land, sea, the whole world') and 160 *opes nimias mundo fortuna subacto | intulit* ('Fortune imported excessive wealth after the subjection of the world') but also on 7.423–4:

> haud multum terrae spatium restabat Eoae
> ut tibi nox, tibi tota dies, tibi curreret aether

Only a little of the Eastern earth remained to prevent night and day from beginning to end and all the sky from revolving for Rome.

Likewise the penultimate line is modelled on 7.473 *primaque Thessaliam Romano sanguine tinxit* (sc. *lancea*; 'The first lance stained Thessaly with Roman blood'). Most of the prominent recalls, like these, of the later books come from the highlight of the poem, Book 7; otherwise only 21 ~ Lucan 10.133–4, 25 ~ Lucan 5.30, 64 ~ Lucan 10.338–9 seem at all plausible. How did Petronius know unpublished parts of Lucan's poem? The answer must be, from recitations or the circulation of drafts; it was quite common to recite or circulate work still lacking final polish in the hope of eliciting criticism and suggestions (see further below, pp. 216–17). No doubt Lucan had recited drafted portions of his later books before Nero's ban (which, I have suggested, was earlier than AD 65); a similar assumption was made in relation to Seneca's *Phoenissae* on p. 130 above, and chronological conclusions are drawn on p. 217 below.

How is all this to be understood? The possibilities are:
(1) Eumolpus' statements in 118 are to be taken seriously as representing the views of Petronius himself, and the poem is a serious specimen intended to show how in the eyes of Petronius Lucan should have done it.
(2) Eumolpus' statements in 118 are to be taken seriously, but the poem shows his inability to match his ideals in practice. A variation of this would be that 118.1–5 are to be taken seriously, but not the following remarks applying specifically to historical epic; this, however, is discouraged by the remarks about the need for absorption in literature in both parts.
(3) Neither is to be taken seriously.

(3) seems unlikely, as it is hard to dismiss the views expressed in 118 as trivial; phrases like *Horati curiosa felicitas* ('Horace's studied felicity') have not struck many as nonsense. One has to remember that because of the nature of his material Petronius has no respectable characters to expound any opinions which he might happen to agree with himself. (1) is a view often held, e.g. by Dryden in his *Examen Poeticum*:

> Petronius, the greatest wit perhaps of all the Romans, yet when his envy prevailed upon his judgment to fall on Lucan, he fell himself in his attempt; he performed worse in his Essay of the Civil War than

the author of the Pharsalia, and, avoiding his errors, has made greater of his own.

Following Sochatoff, *TAPA* 93 (1962), 451, scholars some-times quote a remark of Voltaire which seems to point in the same direction, but if that is read in its original context its purport is quite different. However, it is hard to believe that Petronius, whose taste Dryden begins by praising ('wit' of course intended in the seventeenth-century sense), could have been blind to the poor quality of the poem; and if the *Halosis Troiae* is not to be taken seriously, then the *Bellum Ciuile* hardly can.

(2) seems much the most likely solution; it fits in with the pattern which I detected above (p. 57), particularly if, as was suggested on p. 143, the theoretical discussions of Agamemnon and Eumolpus were balanced by a practical prose demon-stration on the part of Agamemnon like that in verse which here follows from Eumolpus. It also fits the emphasis which I have been laying on the primacy of characterization in Petro-nius, and it is supported by the incongruity of moralizing coming from the mouth of Eumolpus and the presumed circumstances of composition during the shipwreck (115.1–5). Eumolpus' poetry never gets any respect from Encolpius (only from Bargates, 96.6–7!), and it would be hard to claim that Petronius took the opposite view of it. He has allowed Encolpius this time to listen without protest because there is nothing else to do while they walk, but after the conclusion Encolpius does show a critical reaction, describing the poem as having been 'poured out with immense volubility', which one can hardly consider praise. The 'lack of final polish' in Eumolpus' mouth is an excuse for imperfections, but it is also a signal to the reader that there are such (and, as remarked above, a link to Lucan). Yet characterization alone would not account for Petronius' introduction of this sizeable poem. He must feel that the poetry of Lucan raises issues which need consideration, such as those already mentioned; compare what I say above (pp. 61–2) about his discussion of rhetoric.

As a raconteur Eumolpus is a success because then he is talking about 'real' life and his own experiences, but as a poet he is a pompous ass who likes to show how it should be done but fails miserably; there is an excellent characterization of him by Beck (1979), some of whose wording is here reproduced. In 118 he advocates the classical style of such poets as Vergil, but in his composition he follows the mannerist style of Lucan. He aspires to grand poetry, whereas his real talent, such as it is, is for witty epigram. Classical aesthetic theory traps him in mediocrity, and one of the central themes in Petronius is pretentious mediocrity (cf. 132.16), which in the case of Eumolpus makes him imagine that he can write better than Lucan but fail in practice.

It is worth while to comment on some features of the poem which associate it with the style of Lucan. First, there is the same fondness for paradox and oxymoron (e.g. 45–6, which distantly resemble Lucan 1.128, 9.299; 224, which equally distantly resembles Lucan 1.504; 29); for *sententiae* (e.g. 33, taken over by Martial 13.62.2; 57, 66), which, consistently with 118.5, are well integrated; and for exaggerations and startling and novel expressions (e.g. 36–8, 187–91). The poverty of vocabulary which often makes Lucan repeat a word within a short space (e.g. *carina* five times in 9.32–48) is apparent in Eumolpus too; some instances are *quaero* five times within 7–27; *annus* 20 and 23, *iaceo* 192 and 195, *maerentia* 225 and 229, *relinquo* 225 and 227, *os* 272 and 275, all in the same position in the line; *insolitus* 180 and 184, *ruptus* 197 and 199, *Pontus* 239 (the kingdom of Pontus) and 241 (the Black Sea). One notes too repetition of phraseology: *perfundere sanguine* 64 and 214 (not to mention 96 *p. cruore*), *sanguine tinguere* 160 and 294 (also, as remarked above, in Lucan 7.473), *arma* and *strues* in association 62 and 195. *Potestas* (43, 48, 80; 79 is probably corrupt) three times ends the line, *putares* twice (129, 190). Similar features have been remarked in Eumolpus' Senecan poem (89). 'Parody' would be too strong a word to apply to this; 'mimicry' might be better.

What does all this say about Petronius' opinion of Lucan? It would of course be extremely interesting from an historical viewpoint to know the answer to this, but we simply should not ask the question. Because we have the author Petronius creating an 'unreliable narrator' (to use a term of modern narratology), Encolpius, who reports the poetic activity of a disreputable poet Eumolpus, the possible permutations are too many to enable us to get back to views of the author. Here, as throughout the novel in general, Petronius withholds himself, and leaves the reader to make what he will of what is put before him. It will follow that divergent interpretations and a degree of subjectivity in our response are not a matter for surprise; a scholar's attempt to reach less slippery ground can be based only on teasing out themes which underly the whole work, an enterprise which will be attempted at the end of this book.

(iv) 124.2–125.4, Resumption of Legacy-Hunting

At last (a hint here of the tedium of Eumolpus' poem) they arrive at Croton and lodge at an inn. Next day, as they seek to rent a fine house, they meet a crowd of legacy-hunters who enquire *quod genus hominum aut unde ueniremus* ('what sort of people we were and where we came from'); this recalls the Homeric τίς πόθεν εἰς ἀνδρῶν (as e.g. Arete enquires of Odysseus after his shipwreck, *Od.* 7.238). They spin their concocted tale, and are at once believed and showered with gifts.

'While this was happening over a long period at Croton' is the beginning of ch. 125. Why say 'at Croton'? F. Jones (*Latom.* 46 (1987), 818 n. 37) noticed the oddity of this, and suggested that either the word is spurious or that it marks the opening of a new book; the latter seems very probable to me (see above, p. 13). All goes so well that Eumolpus becomes hybristically self-confident, but Encolpius, though feeling that Fortune has at last relaxed its hostility (cf. with this [Lucian], *Asinus* 47), nevertheless is aware of possible dangers; 'feeling that' is *putabam*, which might well foreshadow misfortunes after the end of our text (cf. p. 64 above on 15.8). He reflects that someone might investigate in Africa and discover their falsehood, or Corax might betray them;[5] then they will have to resume their vagrant life. 'What a hard time those who live outside the law have! They always expect whatever they deserve', a parody of Sen. *Ep.* 105.7 *dat poenas quisquis*

---

[5] Fr. 28 B = 38 M = *AL* 476 deals with the revelation of Midas' ears by his barber, and Ciaffi 105 n. 2 suggests that it might come in the gap between 125 and 126. There, however, it would return to a topic already left behind and would destroy the epigrammatic conclusion of 125.4. Collignon 366 had suggested that it might belong in 21.3.

expectat; quisquis autem meruit expectat, 'Whoever expects punishment suffers it, and everybody who deserves it expects it' (see the whole context).

(v) 126.1–139.4, Circe

When ch. 126 opens, a maidservant named Chrysis is appealing to Encolpius to embark on an amour with her mistress, a situation which to a degree repeats that of Psyche and Quartilla (16 sqq.; such thematic repetition in Petronius will be discussed in Ch. VIII (iii)). Chrysis suspects that he is a gigolo who does this for money. His humble status (remember that he is posing as Eumolpus' slave) actually is an attraction to her mistress, who belongs to the class of women (already encountered in 45.7, 69.3, 75.11) who are fascinated by low life; we will see her to be one of the *femmes fatales* who in the novels pursue the heroes (Reardon (1991) 82). The maid, as slaves do (see e.g. my note on Juv. 6.147), has identified herself with the interests of her mistress in the phrase *siue ergo nobis uendis quod peto . . . effice ut beneficium debeam⟨us⟩* ('Whether therefore you are selling what I request to *us* . . . see to it that *we* are indebted to your kindness'). This leads Encolpius to suspect that Chrysis may actually be the mistress posing as a slave; as narrator he comments on his own folly (*tam frigidum schema*, 'such a frigid ploy' 126.8), as he had done at 7.1. She, however, in amusement explains that her tastes are the opposite of those of her mistress; the latter jumps from the *orchestra*, where the local magnates sat in the theatre, over the seats of the *equites* to find lovers among the plebs, but Chrysis herself 'sits' (with a sexual pun; cf. 140.7 and Adams 165 n. 5) only in the equestrian benches. In this Petronius is amusingly reversing Ovid's denial (*Am.* 2.7.19–22) of a relationship with Corinna's maid, but there is also an extensive recall of the dialogue between the maid Milphidippa, the soldier Pyrgopolynices and the slave Palaestrio in Plautus, *Miles* 1039–58 (Courtney (1962) 99), in which the maid is acting as a go-between between her mistress and the soldier in order to trick the latter. Petronius (126.11) explicitly draws attention to the reversal of our expectations about the mistress and the maid, this time a social and not his usual sexual reversal.

So Chrysis brings together Encolpius and her mistress, who has been hiding in an adjacent grove of laurels, into the promenade of plane-trees where they have been walking. The woman's beauty seems beyond all description to Encolpius as his gaze travels over her from head to foot; this is the movement prescribed for such descriptions in rhetorical progymnasmata (see e.g. McKeown on Ovid, *Am.* 1.5.19–22, F. Navarro Antolín's commentary on Lygdamus p. 302), it had been followed by Chrysis herself in listing the attractions of Encolpius in 126.2, and is followed by e.g. Xen. Eph. 1.2.5–6 and Varro, *Sat. Men.* fr. 375, from a satire with the sub-title Περὶ Ἐγκωμίων (on Encomia), though sometimes we find the reverse order. In fact she seems to him as beautiful as a statue of the finest marble made by a master sculptor; for such a comparison cf. Ach. Tat. 5.11.5 and see Rohde 155. Encolpius in a little poem compares her beauty to that of mythological heroines beloved by Jupiter; her pleased reaction, though the poem is followed by a gap, suggests that he spoke it aloud. However, we should not press this in detail; rather, I think, we are intended to understand this poem as the subsequent writing up by the narrator Encolpius of a prose utterance of admiration, part of which indeed might have stood in the gap.

She says 'If you do not disdain an upper-class woman who has had her first experience of sex this year, I offer you a sister. I know, having enquired, that you have a brother [i.e. Giton], but why not adopt a sister too? Just condescend to acknowledge my kisses[6] as well as his.' There are several subtleties here. The beginning reminds us of her own disdain for upper-class men; the statement that until recently she has been a virgin is laughably hypocritical in the light of what Chrysis has told Encolpius; and 'sister' is an amusing euphemism, here propped up by the contrasting 'brother', but also existing in Latin to describe a Platonic relationship between men and women (Lygdamus 1.23–6, Sen. *Phaedr.* 611) and used as a term of endearment (Plaut. *Cist.* 451), in which use it can be given obscene undertones (Mart. 2.4, 10.65.14–15). After the poem's reference to Jupiter, the Roman reader might think of his relationship with Juno.

In reply Encolpius addresses her as if she were a goddess and

[6] M. Bettini, *The Portrait of the Lover* (Eng. tr., Berkeley 1999) 105 ingeniously relates this to the *ius osculi*, the right of male relatives to kiss a woman.

he her worshipper; taking up her word *fastidire*, he asks her not
to disdain the adoration of a foreigner like himself. He will even
offer a dedication at this temple of hers ('this' because they are
beside a temple of Venus, 128.4), *dono tibi fratrem meum* (a pun
suggesting both 'I consecrate my brother to you' and 'I
surrender my brother for you'). All this is a forceful reminder
of those passages of the novels in which the sudden appearance
of the beautiful heroine makes the bystanders think that they
have experienced an epiphany (see Steiner 124, Billault in
Schmeling (1996) 126).

She replies, with gentle sarcasm mocking Encolpius' readi-
ness to give up Giton, in tones as melodious as the Sirens. He
in response, unlike the original Ulysses succumbing to Siren
blandishments, enquires the name of the 'goddess', as one
might do in an epiphany (see e.g. Verg. *Aen.* 1.328–9, with
which Austin compares *Hom. Hymn* 5.93 sqq.; see also Acts of
the Apostles 9: 5). She answers that her name is Circe, though
she is not of the same divine parentage as the Homeric Circe
(*Od.* 10.138–9), not *Circa Solis filia*, Circe the daughter of the
Sun (Plaut. *Epid.* 604); fate has brought her together with
Polyaenus (i.e. Encolpius). The point of this is that the
adjective πολύαινος is a Homeric epithet for Odysseus (also
found in a dithyramb, *Poetae Melici Graeci* p. 493 Page) and
thus makes a connection with the Homeric Circe. Petronius is
reminding us particularly of *Od.* 12.184, where the Sirens, just
mentioned in Petronius, address him as πολύαιν' Ὀδυσεῦ. The
names Polyaenus and Circe, she says, always (that is both now
and in Homer) attract each other; this 'always' in a literary
allusion reminds us of the 'once' in another, this time historical
rather than literary, allusion at 102.10.

What are we to make of these names? We must assume that
Encolpius as Eumolpus' slave is going under the name Polyaenus, that Circe believes this to be his real name, and that she
chooses for herself a matching pseudonym, seeking to protect
herself from the legal penalties (Tac. *Ann.* 12.53.1) for liaisons
between free women and slaves (she is *matrona* 132.2) if
Encolpius should blurt out her real name. But there are
considerable problems with this. First, Eumolpus (probably;
140.3) and Giton (128.1 etc.) do not assume pseudonyms;
second, Proselenos and Oenothea know Circe under that

name (134.9); third, if Circe wanted to conceal her real identity
from Encolpius, she would hardly have brought him to her
house (131–2). I have no explanation to solve these problems,
but one might argue that, if the name Circe is a pseudonym, it
would have caused Petronius severe narratological problems to
refer to her by her real name in 134.9.

'Embrace me here and now', she concludes; 'there will be no
Peeping Tom' (*curiosus*; see my note on *Musa Lapidaria* 94d),
'your brother isn't here'. She throws her arms around him and
pulls him down to the ground, which, as a little poem explains,
blossoms as it did for the $\Delta\iota\grave{o}\varsigma$ $\mathring{a}\pi\acute{a}\tau\eta$, The Deception of Zeus, in
Il. 14.347 sqq.; because of the epic antecedent, the poem is
suitably couched in hexameters. Setaioli, *Prometheus* 25 (1999),
252, remarks that the flowers specified in Homer are wild
flowers, whereas here, suitably to the context, garden plants
are named, with the curious exception of galingale, which is
due to a reminiscence of the seduction of Anchises by Aphrodite as described by Theocritus.[7] Note that in Homer it is Zeus
who pulls down Hera (346), so here we have Petronius'
favourite technique of sex-reversal. Moreover, just before the
poem in which Circe's beauty is compared to that of heroines
beloved by Jupiter, Encolpius says that she was the first to
make him forget an earlier love Doris (126.18); in *Il.*
14.315 sqq. Zeus says that Hera's beauty puts his former
amours with Danae, Leto, Europa (all of them referred to in
Petronius' poem in 126.18[8]) etc. in the shade. Finally, in *Il.*
14.331 sqq. Hera fears an observer (*curiosus* in Petronius) and
Zeus assures her that there will be none.

All in vain, for Encolpius is afflicted with impotence! The
detail of this has been expurgated in our manuscripts. When
the text resumes, Circe is expostulating with Encolpius; there
is a certain resemblance to Ach. Tat. 5.27.7–8, where Melite
reproaches Clitophon for his refusal to have sex. Is she
physically repulsive? Or is the thought of Giton's reproaches
inhibiting him? Encolpius replies that he is as frustrated as she
(he addresses her as *regina*, princess, perhaps a reminder of

[7] Two other points made by Setaioli were already in my text before I read
his article.

[8] There, by contrast to here, Jupiter is now a *senex amator*, a superannuated
Casanova.

πότνια Κίρκη, august Circe, in Homer); witchcraft must be the
explanation. All this is modelled on Ovid's poem about his
impotence, *Am.* 3.7; in each it is the same *languor* (129.4)
brought on by *ueneficium*, sorcery (see McMahon 10; in Ovid
79 *Aeaea uenefica*, Aeaea of course being the island of Circe). In
each a rival lover is suggested by the offended party as a cause,
in Ovid (80) naturally another woman (in Herodas 5 also, a
poem which will again crop up in a moment, the woman accuses
her slave lover of having another mistress). Circe's opening
tricolon of indignant questions with anaphora of *numquid* is
modelled on Ovid's opening with a tricolon and anaphora of *at*.
Of course we are also meant to recall the Odyssean Circe's
invitation of Odysseus to bed (10.333), and Odysseus' fear that
acceptance of this invitation may, as Hermes has warned him
(301), make him ἀνήνωρ, unmanned (341).

In a textual gap Chrysis was evidently summoned, and she
and a mirror are consulted by Circe to make sure that there is
nothing wrong with her appearance; then she hastens into the
temple of Venus. Encolpius, abandoned, asks himself if he
really has been cheated of his pleasure or (in verse) whether he
has just awakened from a dream.

The narrative now becomes discontinuous, but clearly
Encolpius and Giton are together, and Giton is sarcastically
thanking Encolpius for his abstinence, as Socrates abstained
from Alcibiades (a reminder of the *Symposion* and its reversal
in the story of the Pergamene boy); clearly Encolpius had tried
straightaway to test his virility on him. In reply Encolpius
explains that he has been afflicted by impotence; that part of his
body which once made him an Achilles (for mention of him in
this connection cf. Prop.2.22.34) is dead and buried. Here we
see that to Encolpius life and sex, impotence and death are two
pairs of synonyms, a point to be taken up in 140.12; compare
also 20.2 *inguina mea mille iam mortibus frigida*, 'my genitals
now cold with a thousand deaths'. Note that Ovid too has the
comparison with death (16, 59-65).

When the text resumes, Chrysis delivers a letter from Circe
to Encolpius. This begins with sardonic comments (the *frigus*,
chill, which she attributes to him is like that at 20.2, and she too
implies the equation of impotence and death); then, however,
she hints a willingness to forgive, and suggests that Encolpius

will recover if he sleeps three nights apart from Giton; the conclusion is *uale si potes*, a witty ambivalence between 'farewell' and 'get well'. When he has finished the letter Chrysis tells him that such things happen to many men, especially in Croton, where witches can even bring the moon down to earth; this will confirm Encolpius in his idea or pretext (128.2; see above, p. 155) that the root of his troubles is magic. She suggests that he write back, which he does; for such interchange of a pair of letters cf. Achilles Tatius 5.18–20 and particularly Xenophon of Ephesus 2.5, where Habrocomas rejects the proposal of Manto, in whose power he is, saying 'Mistress, do whatever you wish. Treat my body as that of a slave. If you wish to kill me, I am ready, if you wish to torture me, do so . . .' In Petronius Encolpius admits that he has often erred, being human, *homo sum*; this recalls Herodas[9] 5.27 ἄνθρωπός εἰμ', ἥμαρτον ('I am human and have erred'), spoken as an excuse by the slave who is the lover of his mistress, and who is suspected of infidelity and threatened with punishment for it (see Headlam's note; *inter alia* he compares Petron 75.1). Again we must remember that Circe is under the impression that Encolpius is a slave. But, says Encolpius, before today his wrongdoing never incurred the penalty of death (this in a double sense, one being the equation of impotence and death remarked above). 'You have a defendant who pleads guilty', an amusing quotation from Cicero, *Pro Ligario* 2, a speech in which Cicero, as he has just said, is appealing to Caesar's mercy which has granted to many not acquittal from wrongdoing but pardon for their mistakes. His fault is the equivalent of the gravest crimes and deserves commensurate punishment; if she is content with just a whipping, he runs to his mistress already stripped (this foreshadowing 132 and reminiscent of Herodas; compare too the passage quoted above from Xenophon of Ephesus). She should, however, remember that it was not he but his equipment that was at fault; he was a soldier without

---

[9] Herodas was quite a popular author in Rome; see for Ovid *BICS* 16 (1969), 82–3, and *Vir Bonus Discendi Peritus*, *BICS* suppl. 51 (1988), 18, and in general my *Fragmentary Latin Poets* p. 106. For parallels to line 15 of this very poem ('I who set you among men', Headlam) in Petronius see Headlam's note and Ch. IV n. 31. At this point in Petronius Blickman, *PSN* 17 (1987), 8, sees a specific resemblance to Chariton which I cannot see.

weapons (this too from Ovid 68–71). Maybe his mind outstripped his body, perhaps in his desire for complete enjoyment he used up all the pleasure in dallying—a sentence which
shows remarkable psychological insight. At any rate, he pleads
for the opportunity to redeem himself.

When Chrysis leaves, Encolpius avoids taking the usual
bath, which might prove enervating, but dines on aphrodisiac
foods, takes just a little wine (more might dull his sexual
appetite[10]), and sleeps apart from Giton, who, he fears, might
nudge him (cf. 87.9). Next morning he goes to meet Chrysis in
the promenade with the plane-trees. She is accompanied by an
old woman, whose name we presently learn to be Proselenos,
one of those providentially appropriate names discussed on
pp. 42–3 above; she is implied to be as old as the Arcadians,
who claimed to predate the birth of the moon (προσέληνοι).
Chrysis greets Encolpius as *fastose*, 'Mister Disdainful' (taking
up 127.1). The old woman then performs various magic rituals,
some of them probably modelled on the now mutilated
Hipponax 78 West, others known as precautions against the
evil eye applied to children (Setaioli, *Prometheus* 26 (2000),
161, compares Persius 2.32–4 etc.; remember that Encolpius
has blamed his failure on witchcraft). Then she manually tests
his virility, producing a splendid erection, which similar testing
had failed to do at 20.2 (there an aphrodisiac potion proved
necessary). One may note the possibility that the same passage
of Hipponax (78.13 sqq.) served as a general model for the
narrative of 130.7–131.7.

After a gap there follows a poetic description of a grove,[11]
probably the peristyle garden in Circe's house (note that the
pine-trees are pruned; there are also plane and laurel as in the
previous grove); we may recall that the Odyssean Circe's house
is surrounded by groves. Anyway this is the rendezvous, where
Circe is found reclining on a couch. In words that echo

---

[10] For snails as aphrodisiac see Alexis 281.1–2 with Arnott's note. Wine was
sometimes regarded as aphrodisiac, sometimes, as here, sedative of sexual
desire; see C. A. Faraone, *Ancient Greek Love Magic* (Cambridge, Mass. 1995)
125–6.

[11] The phrase *dignus amore locus* 131.8.6 is reproduced by Reposianus (*AL*
253) 44, as remarked by L. Cristante in his edition (Rome 1999) of the
Concubitus Martis et Veneris; this should be added to the testimonia in
Müller's Teubner text p. xxx.

Chrysis' 'Mr Disdainful' (compare 131.3 and 10) she takes up her reproach to him in 129.6 and enquires whether 'Mr Paralytic' has recovered. One must recall that *paralysis* in such contexts does not denote what we now mean by the word, but rather 'flaccidity' (in fact modern medicine knows a condition 'flaccid paralysis'); for its application to the penis see *TLL* s.v. 309.1 and Cael. Aurel., *Tard. Pass.* 2.1.13 p. 572 Drabkin. 'Just try me', is the reply, and they fervently embrace.[12] But failure again, though again its description has been eliminated from the excerpts. Circe in rage orders Encolpius to be whipped, thus fulfilling the foreshadowing of 130.3, and spat upon by the lowliest members of her household. Finally both he and Proselenos are thrown out, Chrysis is beaten, and the whole household is overcome by apprehension; all this has a very close parallel in [Lucian], *Asinus* 56, where Lucius, having satisfied an upper-class woman with his asinine sexual vigour, returns to her in human form only to be ejected ignominiously from her house.

It will by now have become clear that the two encounters between Circe and Encolpius have followed exactly the same pattern (the following analysis anticipates a little):

(1) Chrysis brings a communication and guides Encolpius to a rendezvous in a grove, where he and Circe ardently embrace.

[(1a) mythological comparison 127.9 and perhaps 132.1, on which see n. 11]?

(2) frustration.

(3) attempts by Encolpius to understand what has happened (128.5–6 and 132.9–12).

(4) consultation of Giton (128.7–129.1–2).

(5) attempts at cure involving magic (130.7–131.7 and 133.4 sqq.).

---

[12] The title given by the manuscripts to the excerpt in 132.1 must be erroneous, and presumably derives from a comparison in a missing part of the text between this encounter and that of Endymion and Selene; that would balance the earlier reference to the Deception of Zeus. Note the reference to Endymion as a generic 'pretty lover' at Apul. *Met.* 1.12. Less probably Di Simone, *MD* 30 (1993), 104, thinks that Encolpius' inability to perform was compared wth the eternal sleep of Endymion, which Meleager, *AP* 5.165 (= LI Gow-Page), uses as a paradigm of sexual inactivity.

The thematic function in Petronius of such structural repetitions has already (pp. 128–9) been remarked and will be elaborated in Ch. VIII (iii).

Encolpius now covers up his weals so that Eumolpus and Giton will not know about his mishaps, and feigns illness. When alone, he turns his anger on his offending member in the appropriate metre of Sotadeans in which he contemplates self-castration in mock-epic, Vergilian phraseology (Vergil in Sotadeans!), but fails because of his own lack of nerve and the shrinking of his penis so that it cannot be 'beheaded' (with a parody of the legal procedure). Returning to prose (the first words of which are *erectus* (!) *igitur in cubitum*, 'rising on to my elbow') he expostulates with his penis. 'Did I deserve that when I was in heaven you should drag me down to hell?' (another equation of impotence and death). 'Explain yourself at once'. An apology requested from one's penis! For such personification see A. Richlin, *The Garden of Priapus* (edn. 2, New Haven 1992) 114–19, to which one should add Strato, *AP* 12.216; similar reproaches are found in Ovid, *Am*. 3.7.69–72. The reaction of the penis is described in Vergilian terms (for the first word in the following translation remember that the Latin word *mentula*, prick, which is in Encolpius' mind though not named in his words, is of feminine gender, cf. *eam* §7): 'She, turning away, held her eyes fixed to the ground, and her countenance is no more moved by the attempt to engage her in conversation than —'. So far these are the words in which the encounter of Dido's shade with Aeneas in the underworld (remember 'drag me down to hell' above) is described (impotence and death again). The next words in Vergil are 'if she were a hard flint or a Marpessian crag standing there'. This is quite unsuitable for the Petronian context, to which nothing could be more inappropriate than paradigms of hardness. So he takes two paradigms of softness from Vergil and continues '(than) pliant willows' (this from *Buc*. 5.16) 'or poppies with fainting neck' (this from *Aen*. 9.436, a simile describing the death of Euryalus, premature like that of Dido; impotence too is premature and associated with old age [132.10, Ovid, *Am*. 3.7.17–20] as well as death). The reader of course is expected, as he regularly is in classical literature, to know the contexts of the models and to make a mental comparison between these

and the adjusted end-product; and only when he does will he
savour this, the wittiest joke in Petronius.[13]

At the end of his denunciation, Encolpius (*nec minus ego*;
after the meeting with Dido Aeneas departs with the words *nec
minus Aeneas* 6.475) feels ashamed at having expostulated with
a member the existence of which puritans (a foreshadowing of
the coming mention of the Catos) do not even acknowledge (cf.
Cic. *De Off.* 1.126–7; Stöcker 142 n. 1 also compares [Sall.]
Epist. 2.9.2). But then he justifies himself, characteristically
appealing to literary precedents; we curse other parts of the
body when they cause us pain, Ulysses even remonstrates with
his heart (*Od.* 20.13–22), figures in tragedy revile their eyes as
if they could hear (Philoctetes in Soph. *Phil.* 1354; Oedipus,
who tears them out as Encolpius thinks of cutting off his penis,
in *OT* 1270 sqq.).

Now a remarkable poem which has caused much controversy:

Why, men like Cato, do you frown as you look on me, and condemn
a work of novel openness? The attractiveness of my refined language
smiles free of austerity [*the mention of this is motivated by that of Cato*]
and my guileless tongue reports what men do. (5) Everyone knows
about the joys of sex; who would try to prevent them? (7) Epicurus
himself, the fountain-head of truth, told philosophers to love and said
that this was the ultimate purpose of life.

What I was forced to translate 'men like Cato' is in Latin just
Catones; there were of course two famous Catos, the second of
whom as a Stoic sets up an antithesis with Epicurus. It may
come as a surprise to readers of Lucretius 4 to hear that
Epicurus advocated love, but we have preserved a fragment
of his work 'On the Ultimate Purpose of Life' which stresses
(rather incautiously seems to over-stress) physical pleasure as a
component of his ideal of Pleasure (the problems of this
fragment are discussed by Purinton, *Phronesis* 38 (1993),
281). Moreover we have to remember that Encolpius is just

[13] It may be added that it was quite a sport to apply Homeric verses in
obscene fashion (V. Buchheit, *Studien zum Corpus Priapeorum* (Munich 1962)
102), and that later Ausonius did the same with Vergil in his *Cento Nuptialis*;
for Greek erotic epic centos see Alan Cameron, *The Greek Anthology from
Meleager to Planudes* (Oxford 1993) 172.

the sort of person who would be willing to employ vulgarized
Epicureanism as an excuse for hedonism; this bears on the
question about to be raised whether we should hear the voice of
Encolpius or that of Petronius behind this poem. The main
problem depends on the word 'work', which many have taken
to imply that the author Petronius is emerging from behind the
mask of his character Encolpius and programmatically defend-
ing his novel; the other possibility is that Encolpius was
represented at the beginning of the *Satyrica* as writing down
his adventures in a book (like Apuleius in his *Metamorphoses*)
rather than recounting them verbally (like Clitophon in
Achilles Tatius). I believe that I can now settle this question.
In 65.1 Encolpius says of himself *si qua est dicenti fides* ('If you
can believe what I say'), in 126.14 *quicquid dixero minus erit*
('Whatever I say will be inadequate'); 70.8 *pudet referre quae
secuntur* ('I am ashamed to report the sequel') uses the same
verb as 132.15.4. The first of the above references is linked
with mention of Encolpius' recollection (so also 30.3, 56.10),
which looks much more like something one would say rather
than write. These passages surely prove that, like Clitophon,
Encolpius was verbally recounting his story to an auditor; in
that case the word *opus* is unsuitable, and must imply that here
we indeed have to hear the voice of the author behind that of
his character. We must also infer that this poem conveys a
message not limited to the immediate context in its import; 5–8
do not relate to the topic of impotence, and 3–4 seem to raise a
broader issue. So too does *simplicitas*, perforce translated
'openness' above but conveying much wider connotations;
Kay on Mart. 11.20.10 surveys the semantic range of the
word. In implied contrast to the *prisca simplicitas* of the
Catos, it will suggest a life-style free from voluptuousness; in
relation to Tacitus' ascription of this word (*Ann.* 16.8.1) to the
perception of Petronius' character by his contemporaries it will
suggest ingenuousness; in relation to literary qualities, it will
mean calling a spade a spade. It is striking that the next
preserved sentence after a gap is 'There is nothing falser than
the silly convictions of men and nothing sillier than pretended
austerity' (an elegant instance of the rhetorical figure *commu-
tatio*). This too might well be considered a basic theme of the
novel, as well as linking with the 'puritans' of §12 (*seuerus* in

both places) and the Catos. This sentence was presumably part of a *declamatio* (cf. 3.1) to which 133.1 looks back.

Though the above discussion has concluded that we are indeed to hear the voice of the author behind the beginning of this poem, we must remain aware that, as usual, Petronius does not come out fully from behind his characters or present us with an unambiguous picture; the reference to Epicurus, as remarked above, brings us back from the author himself to Encolpius, in conformity with the pattern detected above (p. 57).

In 133.1–2 Encolpius summons Giton and enquires whether Ascyltos, on the night when he filched away Giton (79.9), assaulted him. We need to get the chronology straight here:

(1) the event of 79.9.
(2) the enquiry about it at this stage of the action.
(3) the subsequent narration of 79.9 by Encolpius.

In stage (3) the narration expresses doubts whether Giton was aware of what was going on or not; these doubts had not been clearly formulated in Encolpius' mind in stage (1), though since then they must have been nagging at him and now demand to be cleared up in stage (2). Giton's response is to swear that no violence had been done to him, an obvious equivocation but one which satisfies Encolpius, we may presume (his actual reaction is lost), since he will always give Giton the benefit of the doubt. Attention was drawn above (p. 18) to a similar equivocation in Achilles Tatius; contrast the mutual asseverations of fidelity in Xen. Eph. 5.14. What is the point of this episode? Perhaps that Encolpius feels that his manhood will be confirmed if he can feel assured of Giton's fidelity.

After a gap Encolpius is found kneeling before a temple of Priapus and praying to the god for pardon and salvation; the detailed interpretation of this prayer has been discussed above (pp. 154–5). An old woman with dishevelled hair and dressed in mourning black enters the temple and drags him outside; this is presumably Proselenos, whose mourning dress is remarked by Oenothea at 134.7, but the indirect reference to her just as *anus* is odd. In the next preserved extract Proselenos is abusing him for his sexual failure with ı̇rce.[14] Evidently they are together in the apartment of the priestess joined to the temple, and then for some reason move outside, because in the next surviving episode she *again* brings Encolpius into this apartment, knocks him down on the bed, and belabours him with a broomstick (*harundo*; cf. 98.1, 135.8.10), which however breaks (as the narrative proceeds we shall see that everything in this house is rotten with age). Encolpius covers his head with his hands and bursts into tears; so does Proselenos, lamenting that she has lived to see this day. The priestess Oenothea enters and chides them for being so glum. Proselenos explains the reason, namely Encolpius' sexual failure, to which Oenothea responds that she, and nobody else, knows how to cure that problem; Encolpius has to sleep with her that night! In a poem she boasts of her magical powers (which nevertheless turn out to be ineffectual; e.g. 137.10); this poem has similarities both to a papyrus fragment which is classified either as a magical text or a novel fragment (see Courtney (1991) 38 and Stephens– Winkler 176–7) and to Ovid's poem (*Am.* 1.8) about the witch and procuress Dipsas, whose name, like that of Oenothea (cf. 136.11), indicates a fondness for the bottle.

In one of a sequence of brief excerpts (within which Proselenos seems to have departed in 135.2; she returns at 137.5) we find Oenothea lying down on the bed and kissing Encolpius, presumably with no response. In a longer passage she starts to prepare a meal; the emphasis throughout her preparation is on the decrepitude of all her equipment. First,

---

[14] Her words are (134.2) *ne a puero quidem te uindicasti*; Latinity permits this to mean:
(1) 'You didn't revenge yourself even on the boy'; so understood by *OLD uindico* 6b, but this seems to make no sense in this context.
(2) 'You didn't even rescue yourself from the boy'; this too seems perfectly irrelevant in the context.
(3) We expect the meaning to be something like that of the words of Proselenos in 134.8 *neque puero neque puellae bona sua uendere potest* ('He can't sell his goods to either boy or girl'), and to refer back to 128.7–129.1. How would Proselenos know about Encolpius' sexual failure with Giton? We shall have to assume that Encolpius has made the point in his defence between 132.1 and 2, when Proselenos is in the house (132.5). If this is right, we shall probably have to delete *a* and take *puero* as instrumental ablative ('You didn't prove yourself even with the boy'), as I suggested in *BICS* 17 (1970), 69.

she places an 'old' tray[15] on the altar, piles up live coals, and
melts pitch in order to repair a bowl which is also old and
cracked (*etiam uetustate ruptam*); we see that she is willing to
apply sacred utensils to profane purposes (her lack of respect
for the sacred will appear again in 137). Then she puts back on
the wall a peg which had fallen out when she had taken down
the bowl, lifts down from the larder a bag containing beans and
an 'ancient' and much-carved piece of pig's cheek, and sets
Encolpius to shelling the beans; he lazily just rejects those with
withered pods.

In a gap something occurred to stimulate Encolpius' admiration for how Oenothea coped with her poverty and the
resourcefulness shown in details; for 'poverty the mother of
invention' see Stöcker 32 n. 1, Otto 1358 and *Nachträge* 198.
This makes him burst into a verse description of the house
modelled on that of the house of Philemon and Baucis in Ovid,
Met. 8.637 sqq. and beyond that on Ovid's model in Callimachus' description of the house of Hecale, to which (according to
a likely emendation) Petronius refers (135.8.15–17), with two
specific verbal recalls of Callimachus (see Courtney (1991) 41);
compare how in 116 he referred to both Vergil and Theocritus.
So there is an implicit comparison between Encolpius on the
one hand and Theseus or the disguised gods on the other.
There is, however, a problem, because the idealization of the
house in this poem contrasts strongly with the decrepitude
insisted on in the prose both before and after the poem. Beck
(1973), 56 sees this as Encolpius' literary reconstruction of
what he himself expected from Oenothea at the time; to put it
another way, Encolpius is mocking his former naivety, induced
by the literary spectacles through which he then saw things,
and is signalling this naivety by the contrast with the prose
description. This explanation is too contrived and finds no
support in the text, nor is there anything to suggest that
something in the gap before 135.7 would have validated it. I

---

[15] *mensa* often, and certainly here, should be so translated; such a tray is
part of the apparatus for offerings to the gods (*OLD* s.v. 2, Wissowa 475, Latte
375–6, *RE, mensa* 946.68). Such trays, however, are not elsewhere used for
holding fire, so Stöcker 29 should probably be followed with *altariaque
[quam]*. It is perhaps a weaker argument that the singular *altare* is not
found until Apuleius.

think that we should rather consider the following approach. In
Ovid the emphasis is on the simplicity of the household, but
there are one or two hints that this simplicity verges on the
sordid. The very word *sordida* (here literally 'dirty') is applied
to the side of bacon hanging in the larder, and the beam from
which it hangs is black with soot (648; I think that this point
retains validity even if the bacon is being smoke-cured); the
coverlet of the couch is *uilisque uetusque*, cheap and old (658;
remember the emphasis on 'old' in Petronius); the table totters
because one leg is too short (660–1; it would not have been out
of place among Oenothea's furniture). I suggest that Petronius'
purpose here is not narratological, as Beck would have it, but
literary, as it was with his introduction of the 'Publilius' poem
in 55. Taking up Ovid's hints he is using the contrast between
verse and prose to stress the sordid realities which underly the
idealization of verse. In this particular case his relation to his
model is not just one of allusion but of parody in the sense of
putting the model in an absurd light; the poverty of Hecale and
of Philemon and Baucis, he implies, must have been not just
frugal and upright, but coarse and slovenly. The pretensions of
verse, in short, are being deflated with sardonic 'realism'; this is
consistent with the way in which throughout the novel he
brings theatrical attitudes up against reality (see Conte
116–17).

After the verse, the prose reverts to its former vein when
Oenothea puts back in the larder the pig's cheek 'as old as
herself' (this degrades Ovid's (649) *seruatoque diu resecat de
tergore partem*, 'She cuts a part from the flitch which had been
long kept'). To do so she stands on a stool, which, being as
decrepit as everything else, collapses, so that in falling she
breaks the kettle, which was originally (135.4) a 'huge' *cucuma*
but is now a diminutive *cucumula* in order to readjust Encolpius' reaction after the idyllic poetry (Stöcker 33–4). She also
falls on the fire and puts it out, so she has to go to a neighbour
to get some live kindling. Encolpius finds all this amusing.

While she is out three geese, which Encolpius the narrator
with hindsight calls *sacri*[16] and which, as he infers, were in the
habit of being fed by the priestess at that time of day, attack

[16] Against the deletion of this word because it is here premature in the
mouth of Encolpius the actor see above, p. 38.

Encolpius. He pulls a leg off the tray (which we know from
135.3 to have been old) and beats the most aggressive goose to
death. Encolpius looks back on this episode with self-mocking
pride as narrator (note that he does so with the verb *reor*, 'I
think', the tense of which shows the gap between event on the
one hand and on the other narration and subsequent interpretation of the event); he compares himself to the epic heroes
Hercules and the Boreads repelling the Stymphalian birds and
the Harpies. The other two geese, after picking up the beans
lying on the ground, return to the temple; Encolpius stuffs the
dead goose behind the bed and washes the bite on his leg with
vinegar (the specification of the bite as 'not deep' puts the
preceding heroics in the proper light); then, fearing reproach,
he decides to leave and gathers up his clothes. But at that very
moment Oenothea returns with fire in a vessel, so he throws
down his clothes and pretends to be waiting for her. She
explains that she has been delayed because she has had to
observe the social conventions and have three drinks with her
neighbour (her name suggests that not much compulsion
would have been needed to make her do this). 'What have
you been doing in my absence?' she asks; 'where are the beans?'
Encolpius proudly recounts the 'battle' to her and presents her
with the goose to compensate for the beans. Her reaction is
consternation; in reply to his puzzlement at this, she explains
that the goose was sacred to Priapus, at whose temple they are,
and that he is subject to crucifixion if this is found out, and she
herself to expulsion from her priesthood.[17] Encolpius, not yet
worried, says that he will replace the goose with an ostrich!
Proselenos returns and, when she is put in the picture, joins in
the wailing. Encolpius, worn out with boredom, now offers
monetary compensation. As soon as she sees the money,
Oenothea, whose hypocrisy towards her duties has been
remarked already, asserts that all her worry has been on his
behalf, an indication of affection, not of ill-will. So she will turn
her efforts to concealing the crime, and leave Encolpius to ask
pardon from the gods. All this evokes from Encolpius a
sardonic poem on the power of money.

By now we have become aware of two points. The first is

[17] Fr. 40 B = 37 M = *AL* 475 may belong in the gap after 137.3.

another recurring pattern, in that the scheme of the narrative
here is very like that of the Quartilla episode:

(1) Offence against the god Priapus.
(2) A priestess or devotary of Priapus, accompanied by another
    woman or other women, arrives on the scene, bursts into
    tears, sits on the bed (17.1, 137.5) professing to pity
    Encolpius (17.4, 137.5) and to be more concerned about
    him than the offence (17.6, 137.7).
(3) The women are appeased by an offer of compensation,
    which in each case involves sexual tribulation for Encolpius
    (here this comes in the next chapter).

The second point is that we have two literary recalls. One is
that in Ovid's Baucis and Philemon narrative the guests save
the goose from being killed; here we have another Petronian
reversal. The other is that in the Odyssean framework of the
plot the killing of the 'sacred' goose corresponds to that of the
cattle of Helios (*Od.* 12.260 sqq.), and Encolpius' attempt to
buy off the penalty recalls Eurylochus' promise of compensation in *Od.* 12.345–7.

When the narrative resumes Oenothea is apparently telling
Encolpius' fortune. He reacts sceptically to her first means;
then she cuts open the dead goose, pulls out its liver and uses it
to foretell the future (this is a parody of the Roman ritual of
extispicium, consultation of the liver of larger animals; Wissowa
419, *Der Neue Pauly* s.v. *Haruspices*). Next she economically
cooks the whole goose on a spit (we might recall how the widow
of Ephesus similarly does not let her husband's corpse go to
waste!); Encolpius points out the indifference now shown to the
sacred animal by remarking 'she prepared an elegant meal for
the man who, as she kept reminding him, shortly before had
been on the brink of incurring capital punishment'. Then she
embarks on erotic magic to cure his impotence, with unpleasant rituals that in part resemble Hipponax 92 West (this
was pointed out by Latte, *Hermes* 64 (1929), 385). The outcome of this has been lost, but Encolpius, evidently unable to
tolerate the lust of the drunken old women (fr. 21 perhaps came
here), which has been in the background since 134.11 and
135.2, runs off, with them following and shouting 'stop thief'.
At this point there seems to be a substantial gap in the

narrative, in which evidently it became known that Encolpius
was not a slave. How Circe felt about this we cannot tell; as for
Chrysis, misapprehension about his status had caused her
scorn in 126.9, but 138.5, which looks like a quotation from a
letter by Circe to Encolpius, reports that Chrysis now intends
to pursue him in his present status even at the risk of her life.
The next excerpt looks like a reply by Encolpius to this letter of
Circe, so that, as in 129–30, we have a matching pair of letters.
In this letter Encolpius praises Circe's beauty, expresses the
hope that if he could embrace her he would recover his virility,
and forgives her for his maltreament in 132.2–4.

The narrative now becomes so disjointed that reconstruction
is impossible. It looks as if Encolpius may have failed for a
third time; in a poem, discussed on pp. 48 and 154 above, he
complains of persecution by Priapus, characteristically comparing in the form of a Priamel his situation with those of epic
heroes persecuted by gods. We then find him talking with
Giton; here we may recall the scheme laid out above for
Encolpius' encounters, in which 139.2 would correspond to
stage (3) and this conversation with Giton to stage (4), though
the scheme is only partially reproduced here. He enquires of
Giton whether anyone has been looking for him; Giton replies
that a handsome woman (Chrysis presumably) had turned up
yesterday and, after beating around the bush, had said that
Encolpius had deserved punishment and would be punished
like a slave if the injured man persisted in his complaint.[18]
Perhaps at this point in the action (not in the narrative) Giton,
who has had no previous contact with Chrysis and Circe
(indeed he had avoided it at 129.2), revealed that Encolpius
is not a slave. Finally Chrysis herself arrives, embraces him,
and expresses her affection.

The outcome of all this has been lost; obviously the above
reconstruction is hazardous in detail.

(vi) 139.5–141.11, Legacy-Hunting Again

One of Eumolpus' newly-acquired slaves (who of course
regards Encolpius as another slave) now arrives and declares

---

[18] This last clause is particularly obscure, and it looks as if *perseuerasset*
should be *perseuerasses*, as implied in Sullivan's translation.

that their owner (i.e. Eumolpus) is angry with Encolpius for failing to perform his duties for two days now. Our natural assumption must be that this refers to the time which he has been devoting to Circe; let us construct a chronology:

(1) Day 1: 126.1–130.7, night 130.8. First failure and first exchange of letters.

(2) Day 2: 131.1–138.8 (mid-day 136.4). After Encolpius' second failure Chrysis visits his living-quarters, as reported by Giton on day 3 (139.3), and a second exchange of letters takes place.

(3) Day 3. Third failure by Encolpius and recall to duty 139.

After a gap we return to the motif of legacy-hunting. A highly respectable (!) woman called Philomela (for the name see Solin (1982) 557), now too old to gain legacies by self-prostitution as she had formerly done, was in the habit of prostituting her son and daughter instead, thus setting up a dynastic school of *captatio*. It has to be assumed that Encolpius and Eumolpus know this from gossip, since the latter is in tacit complicity with Philomela, just as the Pergamene boy had been with him (see above, p. 136). She came to Eumolpus to entrust the children to his wisdom and goodness (*bonitas*), saying that he was uniquely qualified to equip the young with sound 'precepts'; at this point we are forcibly reminded of the 'precepts' which Eumolpus gave the Pergamene boy (85.3), entrusted to him by the parents. So she wants to place the children in Eumolpus' house to imbibe his words, the only 'legacy' (a brilliantly shameless word in the context) she can leave them. Then she departs on the pious pretext of offering vows in a temple. To all this there is an analogy (I will not call it a parallel) in Xen. Eph. 3.1.7–8, when for money a father gives over his son προφάσει διδασκαλίας (on the pretext of education).

Eumolpus, says Encolpius, was so chaste (*frugi*; if the irony is removed, this prosaically means 'unchaste') that even Encolpius himself seemed to him to be a stripling suitable as an *eromenos* (of course to the eyes of anyone less lustful than Eumolpus he would appear to be too old for this). Eumolpus loses no time in inviting the girl to the 'ritual' of sodomy (at least this is the likeliest path of emendation of a corrupt word in the manuscripts, and it certainly fits the sexual tastes of Eumolpus; the point is further discussed in Ch. VIII (ii)); we may remark an episode of heterosexual sodomy in Apuleius, *Met.* 3.20. Note that Petronius makes Eumolpus choose the girl rather than the boy in order to underline his bisexuality, even if he has intercourse with her in homosexual fashion. However, Eumolpus had pretended to be gouty and suffering from lumbago (I do not know why translators are so determined to avoid this word), and had to keep up this pretence in order not to ruin the whole show (oddly designated by the word *tragoedia*, which is much less natural here than in 108.11; perhaps it means 'the tragic story of Eumolpus' loss of his son and his possessions'). So he persuades the girl to take the superior position, which is wittily expressed by 'sit' (cf. 126.10) 'above the good point (*bonitas*) to which she had been entrusted', taking up the mother's words (§2) *commendare liberos suos eius prudentiae bonitatique.* All here understand each other; Eumolpus and the girl both know what reality was hinted at behind the mother's fine words (Sullivan here, with wit matching that of Petronius, translates 'upright nature'; one may note with amusement that Columella 8.5.25 speaks of *mariti bonitas* in cocks). To produce the motions of intercourse he bids Corax get under the bed on his hands and knees and raise and lower the mattress by pushing. So Eumolpus achieves his ends, laughing heartily, as does everyone else.

The girl's brother has been watching her marionette-like performance through the keyhole. This presents Encolpius with an opportunity which he cannot let slip, so he tests whether the boy will submit to molestation; the boy is quite willing. All this is a replay in reverse of 26.4–5, where it is Quartilla who is playing the voyeur and simultaneously fondling Encolpius. This time, however, impotence yet again afflicts him.

After a gap we find that the impotence which had troubled him repeatedly since ch. 127–8 has been cured. *Dii maiores sunt qui me restituerunt in integrum*, he says to Eumolpus. In Latinity this could mean:
(1) 'It is the greater gods who have restored me', they being contrasted with the lesser gods such as Priapus (cf. e.g. *Priapea*

37.5, 53.5). This is a rather uncommon but well-attested (e.g. at 75.8) way of conferring emphasis in Latin; see B. Löfstedt, *Indog. Forsch.* 71 (1966), 253.

(2) 'The gods are greater' (sc. than witchcraft) 'and have restored me.'

(3) 'There are greater gods who have restored me'. Most translators adopt this, which, being compatible with the contrasts implied in either (1) or (2), is less committal.

Without the immediately preceding context choice between these can be based only on our individual understanding of the cause of Eumolpus' impotence (Priapus or not?) and how he himself sees this.

He continues 'Mercury, who as ψυχοπομπός escorts souls to and from the underworld, has restored to me what *manus irata* had taken away; you can see from this that I carry more influence than Protesilaus or anyone else of the ancients.' The first point to be established here is that Petronius' wording does not encourage us to see any reference to Hermes' gift of moly to Odysseus to protect him against Circe's attempt to make him ἀνήνωρ (unmanned), even if in *Priapea* 68.21–2 (an amusing distortion of the *Odyssey* into obscenity) moly is extemporarily equated with *mentula*. Rather we here again have the by now familiar equation of impotence and death, implying the converse erection and resurrection (this happy verbal rapprochement from Bowersock 113). Secondly, what does *manus irata*, wrathful hand, mean? Does it refer to witchcraft, like *mala manus* in 63.7 (also Plaut. *Amph.* 605, *CIL* 6.18817 = *ILS* 8006) or *saga manus* in *CIL* 6.19747 = *CLE* 987 = my *Musa Lapidaria* 165.3 (which however may mean 'a coven of witches')? It seems to me much more likely that it refers back to Encolpius' attempt at self-castration in 132.8.1 (and the verb *praecidere* used here by Petronius is applied quite often to literal castration). In that case we shall have to read ⟨*paene*⟩ *praeciderat*, had almost cut off. Thirdly, we should remember that as a ghost Protesilaus could not engage in sex (though some sources of his story do allow him to embrace Laodamia), whereas Encolpius has recovered sexual potency.

Encolpius now lifts his tunic and shows Eumolpus that he is indeed 'a whole man' (cf. 131.10). Eumolpus is thunderstruck at the size of his erection, then, to convince himself that he is not dreaming, handles Encolpius' genitals (as Proselenos had done in 131.5–6; Lichas had done the same for other reasons, 105.9); it is stressed that he needs both hands for this, and Proselenos too had applied 'hands' in the plural. This is the last we hear of the impotence theme, and it is followed by an excerpt the function of which in the narrative we cannot tell.

In the next two extracts Encolpius seems to be warning Eumolpus that so far he has not given the legacy-hunters anything concrete, so that their patience is running out and their generosity decreasing; their own ill fortune is about to take over again (thus fulfilling the apprehensions expressed by Encolpius in 125). Between 141.1 and 2 perhaps (though one could envisage other scenarios) Eumolpus pretended to have died and his will is published (compare the reading of Trimalchio's will at 71.4); all legacies will depend on the condition that the legatees, apart from his freedmen (i.e. Encolpius and Giton, whom he will have pretended to eman-cipate in his will), cut up Eumolpus' body and eat it in public (thus the carrion birds of 116.9 are turned into literal fact). He points out that in some countries the dead are regularly eaten by their relatives (he probably has in mind Herod. 3.38 and 4.26) and the ill are upbraided for the deterioration in quality of their flesh (this certainly derived from Herod. 3.99, with which cf. Pomponius Mela 3.64). So he urges his 'friends' to eat his flesh in the same spirit as they had cursed (why ever would anyone want to emend this word?) his continued life (*spiritus*), i.e. had wished for his death.

Bowersock 134, following an old idea (Studer, *Rh. Mus.* 2 (1843), 212, attributes it to Ignarra in 1770), sees in all of this a parody of the Last Supper, in which Christ according to the Synoptic Gospels says to the disciples 'Take, eat, this is my body . . . this is my blood of the new διαθήκη'; the Greek word can mean either 'testament, will' or 'covenant', the latter translation being nowadays generally preferred, though the former can be supported by the conception of the Christians as inheritors of the kingdom of God (e.g. James 2: 5).[19] Church

---

[19] Bowersock also draws attention to the contrast between 'body' and 'spirit', comparing it with Christ's remark 'the spirit is willing, but the flesh is weak' (Mark 14: 38, Matthew 26: 41); this, however, comes in a totally different context, and any resemblance is merely superficial.

tradition (Papias reported by Eusebius, Irenaeus) connects the Gospel of Mark (presumably identifying him as the Mark of 1 Peter 5: 13) with Rome and St Peter (cf. Ramelli 76), so that on that assumption it might be possible for Petronius to have read it, though many modern scholars see in ch. 13 a reference to the destruction of the Temple in AD 70. However, apart from oral tradition (no doubt flourishing at Rome in the aftermath of the great fire of 64 and the subsequent persecution), we have also to remember the document Q which modern scholarship postulates as a source for Matthew and Luke and sees as having contributed much to the Passion narrative. We cannot therefore reject Bowersock's theory out of hand, but we do not actually need it as a motivation for this episode; the metaphor of carrion birds and the irony of placing cannibalism in the Pythagorean, and hence vegetarian, foundation of Croton are quite sufficient. Other attempts to see parallels to the Gospel narratives have been rejected in Ch. IV n. 67.

A man called Gorgias (he owes his name to the famous Gorgias of Leontini, whose description of vultures (cf. 116.9) as 'living tombs' is intended to be recalled)[20] is ready to fulfil the conditions of the will, and exhorts a fellow-heir to do the same in a rhetorical *suasio* (here too we think of his namesake, the master rhetorician). In this he uses historical *exempla* (141.9) of cannibalism which had occurred in besieged cities, Numantia (also in Val. Max. 7.6. *ext.* 2; his book consists entirely of classified *exempla* for the use of orators), Saguntum (also in Juv. 15.114, a writer under strong rhetorical influence), Petelia (linked with Saguntum as a model of loyalty by Val. Max. 6.6 *ext.* 2); all three episodes are rhetorical inventions, not historical fact (Sil. It. 2.521 sqq. speaks of Saguntine

---

[20] This utterance (Diels–Kranz, *Fragmente der Vorsokratiker* 82 B 5a) is apparently recalled by Lucr. 5.993, despite the reservations of O. Skutsch, *Annals of Q. Ennius* (Oxford 1985) 277 (correct his reference to Soph. *El.* to 1488, but note his observation that the phrase of Gorgias did not actually include the word γῦπες, vultures). Though the metaphor of legacy-hunters as vultures is common, we can now see that 116.9 foreshadowed this passage. Consequently the introduction of the theme and its outcome are held together for the reader who appreciates the allusion, which as the text stands is not explicit but might have been made so in the gap between §5 and §6. One may note that those who quote the phrase of Gorgias make it plain that it was considered ridiculous.

cannibalism as a notion not put into effect). I will add that
Petronius is drawing directly on Valerius Maximus; compare
141.11 with Valerius' words about Numantia *complures inuenti
sunt artus et membra trucidatorum corporum sinu suo gestantes*
('Several people were found carrying in the folds of their dress
limbs and members of the slain corpses'), except that Gorgias
piles on the horror by turning the *complures* and *trucidati* into
mothers and their children.

This is where our text ends.

VIII

Overall Aspects

(i) *Mens ingenti flumine litterarum inundata*

In Ch. II (i) the novel and the *prosimetrum* form, taken into the Roman genre of satire, were called upon to account for the overall structure of the *Satyrica*; in Ch. VI (i) the *Odyssey* was added in relation to 100–39, and the Odyssean theme of persecution by the wrath of a god was accepted as a thread probably running through the whole novel. Many episodes in the novels have also been adduced when individual passages of Petronius were being considered, on the hypothesis that in at least some cases the topics had a common origin in now lost novels; the theoretical basis of this assumption is the fixity of incident within the generic framework of ancient literature (remarked on p. 105 above), and the fact that, if it is accepted that Petronius is writing a parody of the novel, he will also without a doubt parody specific incidents in novels. Plato's *Symposion* and Horace's *Cena Nasidieni* were found to be in the background of the *Cena Trimalchionis*. In a broad sense the discussions of literary theory in 1–5 and 118 and the theme of legacy-hunting at the end of our text relate to the tradition of Roman satire. Other authors whose writings have been found to lie behind passages of Petronius are Vergil, Horace, Ovid, Cicero, Sallust, Livy, Phaedrus, Seneca, Persius, Plautus, Valerius Maximus, and among the Greeks Herodotus, Aristophanes, Hipponax, Theocritus, Callimachus, Herodas, perhaps also the Old Testament (79–80). We must also note the parody of legal concepts by these lawless characters in 80–1 (also 83.5) and 132.8, on which see Courtney (1991) 34, and of religious ritual in 137.11.

This is a rich literary tapestry, and its exuberant versatility prevents explanation of the work by any single formula, despite the overall novelistic form. One can hardly avoid relating the literary texture to the words quoted at the head of this chapter from Eumolpus' discussion with reference to poetry in ch. 118. Ch. VII (ii) showed the many ambiguities which prevent, and were intended by Petronius to prevent, a straightforward interpretation of this, but the conclusion was reached that the theoretical points made by Eumolpus are ultimately to be taken seriously, even if his practical application of them is not. It was also remarked that the stress on absorption in literature revives points made by the rhetorician Agamemnon in 4–5, and that, although Agamemnon suffers from hypocrisy, he speaks much sense. In short, in both cases Petronius is putting on the reader the responsibility of discerning when these unreliable characters have nevertheless something worthwhile to say. It was noted above (p. 61) that Petronius had no impulse from the novel-tradition to set an episode in a rhetorical school; the fact that he chose to do so must surely indicate that he needed such an episode in order to say something that he wanted to say. In anticipation of points to be made below one may observe also that the novel-tradition gave him no motive to introduce a manic poet; the inspiration for this came from Horace and Ovid (above, p. 175). Eumolpus has been invented to underline the literary postures struck by the characters.

It will be apparent that this heterogeneity of themes and broad pattern of literary allusion are very alien to the Greek novel, in which the literary references rarely stray beyond the standard Homer, tragedy, and New Comedy, with Chariton adding Xenophon and Thucydides, and Longus bucolic and Sappho. How then does Petronius use all the literary background which he introduces?

In some cases he is employing previous writers just as a quarry to suggest to him ideas on which he can build. A very clear case was remarked above (p. 103) at 52.4, where Petronius makes actual an occurrence which Horace had envisaged. In such cases Petronius is not using his predecessors to convey any particular point either about themselves or about the action narrated by him. This is especially so in the case of authors who themselves write in a humorous or satiric vein, such as Seneca in the *Apocolocyntosis*, Horace in the *Cena Nasidieni*, Ovid frequently, Hipponax, Herodas, Aristophanes, Plautus. No doubt the same applied to his use of mime themes, which we can only rarely establish with security because of our lack of material. Somewhat similarly in 60.4 Sallust, and in 140 Herodotus and Valerius Maximus supply matter which can be heightened and turned to humorous use.

In the case of the novel overall and a few other instances his object is, at least in part, parody of the original; that is, to put the original in an absurd light. I have suggested on p. 203 that he treats the episode of Baucis and Philemon in Ovid *Met.* 8 in this deflating manner, and on p. 175 that he is poking fun at Ovid *Tristia* 1.11 and humorously bringing down Ovid himself to the level of a Eumolpus. Some of the allusions to Seneca also fit here, and I have argued that Trimalchio's quotation of 'Publilius' indirectly serves the same end.

At this point it is appropriate to say a little more about Petronius in relation to Seneca and Lucan. In Ch. I it was pointed out that Tacitus places Seneca and Petronius in pointed contrast, and that Seneca pens a criticism of the way of life of Petronius. It is frustrating that many of the works of Seneca cannot be firmly dated, but it is clear that those whose influence is apparent in Petronius range from an epigram no doubt written in Corsica (see Ch. III n. 9) and the *Apocolocyntosis* (AD 54) to productions of Seneca's last years (from AD 62 onwards), the *Epistulae Morales* (which supply more grist to Petronius' mill than any other work of Seneca), probably the *Phoenissae* (see above, p. 130), and the *Naturales Quaestiones* (in ch. 115, see Courtney (1962) 98; perhaps 88, see above p. 140; fr. 39 B = 35 M = *AL* 473, see Courtney (1991) 57). The last two of these were probably left respectively unfinished and not put into final form at Seneca's death (see Courtney (1991) loc. cit.), and therefore not available in published form to Petronius. We must accordingly assume that Petronius knew them from recitations or from drafts which were in circulation (like those of Ovid's *Metamorphoses* when his banishment was pronounced, *Tristia* 1.7.23–4). If the former, we should have to suppose that Petronius himself attended the recitations, since it is hardly likely that verbally accurate extracts were communicated to him by intermediaries. This might seem to run counter to the general assumption of hostility between the two, but that picture might well be over-simplified. Throughout history instances have not been lacking of courtiers by no means friendly to each other, willing to make indirect jabs, but observing the proprieties in social intercourse. We may note Quintilian's reference (8.3.31) to introductory remarks to a tragic recitation, though nothing implies that the actual recitation was delivered by Seneca himself.

However, as has been made plain, attendance by Petronius at recitations by Seneca is not an inevitable hypothesis. We have the same options available to us when we consider Petronius' knowledge of parts of Lucan's epic prohibited by Nero from publication; Lucan will have drafted and recited parts of his later books before the ban. Some chronological consequences can be drawn from all this. First, Petronius was composing the parts of the *Satyrica* which we have towards the end of his life, and very likely quite quickly; Lucan and Seneca too were fluent in composition. Second, we are freed from the chronological straight-jacket into which Rose bound himself (see above, p. 183).

How does Petronius use Seneca? Here one must start with the pastiche of Seneca's tragic style in 89, which, as argued on p. 142–3 above, surely betrays antipathy. Some of the other recalls fit into the category analysed above, that of providing phrases, ideas, and raw material in a neutral way; one instance not mentioned earlier is the description of Julius Proculus in 38.12 in relation to *De Ben.* 2.27.1 *diuitiarum maximum exemplum ante quam illum libertini pauperem facerent, hic qui quater miliens sestertium suum uidit* ('A great specimen of affluence before his freedmen made him poor, the man who saw his 400,000,000 sesterces'). In other cases characters in Petronius are intended to be implicitly set against what we read in parallel passages in Seneca (so 29.6, 46.8, 73.2, 78.5–6, 80.3–4, 125.4) without prejudice to Seneca; this technique will be more fully discussed below in relation to other literary reminiscences. Only seldom are clear allusions to Seneca couched in such a way as to parody or deflate the originals; so the allusions to the *Naturales Quaestiones* noted above, and 47.6, 71.1, to which one might add the parody of consolatory topics in 113, for though these are conventional, Seneca with three specimens was the most prominent practitioner of the genre at the time. There is also, if my understanding is correct, indirect parody of Seneca in 55. It should be added that different people will react differently to reminiscences of Seneca, and that my classifications will not necessarily be valid for everyone.

In most cases of literary allusion it is plain that the antics of Petronius' fictional characters are intended, in a spirit which may broadly be called mock-epic, to be set against the actions of grand prototypes, in much the same manner as the last-mentioned instances of Senecan recall. Attention is drawn to the posturing of these characters by the thematic recurrence of theatrical metaphors, discussed on p. 162 above. Conte puts it this way (116–17, after speaking of 'subversion of the hierarchy of literary genres'): 'the parody . . . is regularly generated by exposing the incongruity of the fantasies that guide the prot-agonist on his path through the world. These are nothing but melodramatic fancies, literary and declamatory poses which crumble under the parodic pressure of anticlimax.' One might, and perhaps should, stop there, setting the bounds of such literary allusion as a purely humorous device within the narra-tive. It is, however, hard to forget that Petronius lived within the circle of a stage-struck emperor, and that the sober record of events of the time often reads more like drama or declama-tion than reality. Consider the following passages:

Sen. *Contr.* 2.5.7 *caede uentrem, ne tyrannicidas pariat* ('Strike my belly, so that it may not give birth to slayers of tyrants').

Tac. *Ann.* 14.8.4 *(Agrippina) protendens uterum 'uentrem feri' exclamauit* ('Agrippina, pushing out her womb, cried "smite my belly"').

Dio Cass. 61.13.5 τὴν γαστέρα ἀπογυμνώσασα 'παῖε' ἔφη 'ταύτην, Ἀνίκητε, παῖε, ὅτι Νέρωνα ἔτεκεν' ('Baring her belly she said "smite this for giving birth to Nero"').

Octauia 368–72 *caedis moriens illa ministrum | rogat infelix | utero dirum condat ut ensem; | 'hic est, hic est fodiendus' ait | 'ferro, monstrum qui tale tulit'* ('As she was dying the poor woman asked the agent of murder to bury his sword in her womb; "this is what deserves to be pierced by the sword for bearing such a monster", she said').

Sen. *Oed.* 1038–9 *hunc, dextra, hunc pete | uterum capacem, qui uirum et natos tulit* ('Smite, hand, this capacious womb, which gave birth to a husband and sons').

[Sen. *Phoen.* 447 *hunc petite uentrem, qui dedit fratres uiro* ('Attack this belly, which gave brothers to my husband'). This line is deleted by Axelson, probably correctly; see O. Zwierlein, *Kritischer Kommentar zu den Tragodien Senecas* (Mainz 1986) 125).]

Where is the boundary between fantasy and reality here? Whatever the chronological relationship between the *Oedipus* of Seneca and the murder of Agrippina (the *Phoenissae* is probably later than the murder), it would appear, on the evidence of the elder Seneca, that Nero's own mother on the point of death struck a declamatory pose. When his own death was imminent Nero quoted a verse (Dio 63.28.5) which in the role of Oedipus he had recited on the stage (Suet. 46.3). Even the collapsible boat in which he intended to murder his mother was suggested by theatrical spectacle (Dio Cass. 61.12.2).

Things which we are told of Nero reveal similar attitudes. When acting he wore a mask depicting his own features (Suet. 21.3, Dio Cass. 63.9.5) or those of Poppaea (Dio) or whatever woman he was in love with (Suet.); when he was wearing the former a soldier, unable (one might say, like the characters in Petronius) to distinguish theatre from reality, tried to rescue him from his stage chains (Suet.). After his victories in the Greek games he entered Rome with a procession which blended theatrical pageant with a military triumph (Suet. 25.1–2, Dio 63.20). When preparing for a Gallic campaign he arranged to bring along stage equipment and his concubines attired as Amazons (Suet. 44.1). Even the Piso who conspired against him, and some of whose fellow-conspirators objected to Nero's acting, used to sing in tragic attire (*tragico ornatu canebat*; Tac. *Ann.* 15.65).

It is therefore tempting to see in Petronius' literary allusions not just a device for the purpose of characterization, but also a comment on the times. This matter will need to be considered further in (iii) below. For the moment let us return to the use of allusion for characterization. Such a purpose can be achieved in three ways:

(1) the characters themselves may interpret their actions at the time in a literary light.

(2) the narrator Encolpius looking back may impart such a hue.

(3) the author Petronius may set the characters in situations which recall literary precedents.

All these possibilities can be documented in Petronius.

(1) Instances of this are Encolpius' order to Giton to hide himself under the bed like Ulysses under the ram (97.4–5), Eumolpus' equation of their situation with being caught in the cave of the Cyclops (100.7), Giton's parallel with Alcibiades and Socrates (128.7), Encolpius' comparison of his situation with Ulysses and tragic heroes (132.13).

(2) It is rather harder to identify clear cases of this, but Encolpius' comparison of his killing of the goose with heroic exploits (136.6) must belong here (signalled by the present tense of *reor*). So too does his parallel between his tryst with Circe and the Deception of Zeus in 127.9, led up to by authorial preparation of type (3); likewise 105.9–10, the recognition of Encolpius paralleled by that of Odysseus, combines (2) and (3).

(3) This is so common that it hardly needs illustration. I will just mention the suggestion of Persius' moral austerity in ch. 5 by contrast with the hypocrisy of Agamemnon, and the hilarious recall of Vergil's underworld in 132.11 with other recalls in 72.7–73.1; this incorporates a hint of type (1) in the word *labyrintho* put in the mouth of the narrator Encolpius and related to the time of the action by the present tense, isolated in the context, *quid faciamus* ('What are we to do?'). Petronius was perhaps aware that such a deliberative question representing a thought of a character (as e.g. *Aen.* 9.399) was an innovation of Vergil, a facet of the 'empathy' between the poet and his characters emphasized by Brooks Otis. In Petronius this type (3) may be overtly combined with (1). In 9.2–6 Ascyltos is made to refer to the situational parallel with Lucretia and Tarquin which the author has set up; somewhat similar is Giton's evocation of a literary fratricidal situation at 80.3–4. In 126–7 first the author gives Encolpius an Odyssean pseudonym (admittedly it is possible that Encolpius chose it or Eumolpus chose it for him), which is type (3), then Circe takes this up

(type (1)), then the narrator (127.5) interprets her voice in an Odyssean light (2).

In 1962 I treated all this literary allusion, the range of which has no parallel in ancient literature for audacity and originality, mainly as a generic feature in relation to the *prosimetrum* tradition, which facilitates wide-ranging literary allusion and parody and the incorporation of themes and situations drawn from all sorts of literature. This is not wrong, but it is insufficient. We integrate the feature much better into the work if we link it more closely with the characterization. Petronius has given us a fully-rounded picture of vagabonds who at critical moments and in predicaments do not react in any way that is in touch with reality, but strike attitudes. Petronius' interest in the connection between reality and art, literature and life fits in well with his love of ambiguity and disguise both in his narrative and in his literary technique. All this results in frequent and abrupt changes of tone and level (e.g. between 79.8 and 9), and in a peculiar blend of fantasy and what is often called 'realism'. The last is not a word which I myself would rush to apply to Petronius; as it is commonly applied it generally means no more than the inclusion of sordid material. The one area in which the concept of 'realism' does have a validity is, as Auerbach used it (see above, pp. 87–8), in the concerns of Trimalchio's freedman guests in relation to their social setting, as revealed in their speeches.

The main characters, however, as just stated, are more interested in striking attitudes. When they verbalize these attitudes, they do so, like the protagonists of the Greek novel, in the forms of rhetoric; and rhetoric too, as Encolpius stresses in ch. 1, has to take its share of the blame for promoting such unreality in the themes invented for its *controversiae* (Encolpius of course is not the man to point this out; see above, p. 58). Note 1.3 'I believe that our hapless youngsters are turned into idiots in the schools of rhetoric because their ears and eyes are trained not on everyday issues' (Walsh). In theatrical and poetical terms similar points are made in the displaced poem in 80.9, the full reference of which is unfortunately lost with its context, and in 90.3 *saepius poetice quam humane locutus es* ('You have spoken more often like a poet than like a man'; cf. Ch. V n. 11). Note also 132.16, which unfortunately has lost its immediate context, coming after the poem in which Petronius momentarily, as I argued on pp. 199–201 above, steps out from behind his characters.

This is the feature in the characterization which Conte has christened 'mythomania', and this section may close with two quotations from his work which underline the point:

Whereas declamation gives the mythomaniac narrator his pretexts for mannered outbursts of eloquence, it is always the popular novel whose narrative model drives the protagonist into the snare of stereotyped situations. Once he has fallen into them he is impelled to dramatize them . . . The young *scholasticus*[1] becomes the unconscious victim of narrative schemata which eventuate in parodic reverses of the most typical scenarios of the idealized Greek romance (73) . . . It is enough to combine [situations like shipwrecks and trials] with weak characters always ready to lapse into the comic register, and all the advantages of parody can be extracted (75).

(ii) Sex in Petronius

Of the four main characters in the *Satyrica*, Encolpius, Giton, Ascyltos and Eumolpus, with one exception each has had sexual relations with each of the others. The exception is Eumolpus, who lusts after Giton until they board ship in 100 (and even then Encolpius is apprehensive about this lust), but does not actually achieve any consummation; his recorded sexual exploits are with the Pergamene boy and sodomy, as it appears, with the legacy-hunter's daughter (140). However, Encolpius also has attractions for him (140.5), so here we have an unrealized triangle. For his part Encolpius has relations with Giton and (9.10) Ascyltos, Ascyltos with Encolpius and Giton, Giton with Encolpius and Ascyltos; each is at the apex of a perfect love-triangle. In addition to that, Encolpius has heterosexual relations with Circe (so that in that episode there is another triangle Circe–Encolpius–Giton, though no line connects the first and third) and probably Quartilla, though the mutilation of that episode makes it hard to be sure, and Giton with Pannychis (26); Ascyltos is to be presumed to have gone to bed with the *eques* of 92.10. If the reconstructions of

[1] As I explain on pp. 39–40 above, I would not accept this word, which overplays the admittedly strong declamatory influence.

Ch. II (v) are correct, Encolpius had been involved both with Lichas and his wife Hedyle (another triangle), not to mention Tryphaena, who has also been involved with Giton (yet another triangle). Outside the main characters Trimalchio too was involved in a triangular relationship with his owner and his owner's wife (69.3, 75.11), though he hangs back from 'kissing and telling', and the story of the widow of Ephesus is so presented as to hint at such a relationship (see especially 112.7) between herself, her husband, and the soldier. Sex certainly plays a large role in this novel, and fidelity is not at a premium among its characters.

Both heterosexuality and homosexuality are here involved, which in the ancient outlook (discussed in Ch. II n. 56) is nothing particularly remarkable, but homosexuality certainly prevails, naturally so, since in opposition to the leading characters of the Greek novel Petronius has made all his protagonists male. It is more noteworthy that the sex often takes forms which the ancient world too regarded as deviant. We have voyeurism (which stimulates the voyeurs) in 26.4–5 and 141.11, heterosexual sodomy (140),[2] homosexual rape threatened or executed (8.3–4, 9.4–5 [cf. the equivocation at 133.2], 21.2, 23.5–24.4), castration threatened (108.10, 132.8), and contravention of the taboo[3] which frowned on willingness to perform both passive and active roles in homosexual intercourse (9.6[4] and 10, 81.4). There are no fewer than five instances of handling of the genitals for various reasons (20.2, 24.7, 105.9, 131.5, 140.13, this last of an exhibitionist nature). One may remark that, though it was pointed out above (p. 198) that Petronius had precedents for this, the penis is sometimes spoken of as if it had an existence independent of the man

[2] No doubt this was not non-existent in Roman life, particularly as a contraceptive measure (so already in the delicate reference at Herod. 1.61), but the jocular tone of most references to it shows how it was regarded.

[3] For this taboo see Cic. *In Catil.* 2.8, Dover 148–9. Nero himself took active and passive roles respectively with Sporus on the one hand and Pythagoras and Doryphorus on the other, and he and Otho interchanged roles (Suet. *Otho* 2.2); other emperors who flouted the taboo were Caligula (Suet. 36.1) and Vitellius (Suet. 12).

[4] Here *muliebris patientiae scortum* ('You whore, who submit to treatment as a woman') is based on the common phrase *muliebria pati*, to be treated as a woman (*OLD muliebris* 2c).

(130.4, 132.9–12); in 132.8.8 it is even *furcifera* (gallows-bird),
like a delinquent slave.

Sullivan attempted to relate all this to the psychology of
Petronius himself, because of what he perceived as lack of
literary antecedent. There is, however, one place where literary
precedent can be found, and that is in Priapea. Sullivan was
writing when everyone was under the influence of Buchheit's
contention that our extant collection (adduced by me in illustration of 92.9) was the work of one poet writing after Martial,
a contention now coming under attack; but in any case there
was a tradition of writing Priapea going back to the Hellenistic
Euphronius. It is admittedly true that the account of Tacitus
(see Ch. I) shows an interest in the orgies of Nero from which
Petronius himself was excluded, and, as remarked on p. 196
above, deep insight into sexual psychology is revealed by 130.5
(Encolpius' explanation for his impotence, 'Perhaps my body
was dilatory, and my desire outstripped it. Perhaps my longing
for complete fulfilment caused me to wait too long, and so
exhausted the pleasure' [Walsh]). But it is much more convincing to link such things with the characterization, and evidence
can be found for this view in the relationship, almost one of
identity, which the characters see between life and sex, death
and impotence. Identification is made by the size of Encolpius'
genitals (105.9); impotence is *mors* or *funus* of the penis (20.2,
129.1, implied also in the punning 130.1); Circe says that the
centre (cf. Adams 46–7) of Encolpius' body is dead (129.6) and
the coldness of death (cf. 20.2) may soon spread to his extrem-
ities; in a state of impotence one is in 'hell', as we would put it
(132.10–11, 140.12). This is not to say that Petronius invented
the equation; Ovid also has it, as remarked on p. 198 above, and
it is found in erotic epigrams by Scythinus (*AP* 12.232.4),
Philodemus (11.30.3–4 = Gow–Page, *Garland of Philip* 3331–
2 = D. Sider, *Epigrams of Philodemus* 19.3–4), and Automedon
(5.129.8 = GP 1516, 11.29.4 = 1520, the last quoted in Courtney (1991) 34).

At the same time we should bear in mind that certain forms
of sex often alluded to in humorous and satirical literature are
absent from Petronius: lesbianism (this is natural enough), all
forms of oral sex (though this is hinted at in insults in ch. 9; see
Ch. II n. 54), masturbation (it is very unlikely that *mascarpio* in

134.5 is a reference to this). Moreover the language applied to sex by the narrator[5] is notably decorous (cf. Ch. II n. 16); the word *sopio* in 22.1 is canonical in the context of the action there described (see Catull. 37.10). If a derivative of πυγή (rump), a word brought into Latin by Novius and Horace, is intended at 140.5, then it is deliberately chosen to make a paradoxical contrast of tone with the 'ritual' (for which see e.g. Ovid, *AA* 2.607, *Met.* 7.709) with which it is linked, and, if it is right to read e.g. *pygiaca sacra*, as I suggest, or the like, it is given a form coined for the occasion which will contrast with e.g. *Isiaca sacra*; in any case it constitutes a circumlocution for the downright *pedicatio*. A noteworthy instance in which sex seems to be referred to as 'dirty' is in 25.5, where Quartilla speaks of her sexual initiation as *inquinata sum* ('I was defiled'), but it is clear that the word is drained of all unfavourable undertones. Otherwise Petronius operates mainly with euphemisms, ellipses, and circumlocutions. The reason for this is, I suggest, that Petronius did not wish to take us too far from the object of his parody, the Greek novel, in which sex is generally underplayed, referred to in forms of language like those employed by Petronius, and kept within conventional bounds.

Nevertheless in Petronius we are in a world far more earthy than that of the Greek novel, which cannot compare with him either in quality or quantity of sex. Here we may also remind ourselves of the reversals of the sexual situations from those in the Greek novel, which were fundamental to his mode of parody; these have been briefly mentioned on pp. 28–9 and in Ch. II n. 56, and particular instances have been remarked in the detailed elucidation. We also have to recall the suggestions, in the tale of the Pergamene boy, of the perversion of the true love-relationship as it existed between Alcibiades and Socrates; this clearly does introduce an implicit note of moral judgement. Yet generally Petronius' attitude to sex is humorous and not meant to arouse disgust. His characters live largely for sex, but it is often unsatisfying and unsuccessful sex, with Encolpius particularly prone to sexual inadequacy and envy. V. Rudich, *Dissidence and Literature under Nero* (London 1997) 208–10,

---

[5] Trimalchio's coarse *debattuere*, 'grind', 69.3 is a different matter; so is the metaphorical *laecasin* ('go fuck itself') of Seleucus 42.4.

argues that in Petronius sexuality and power blend to produce sado-masochism, which however results in no sexual arousal, but failure and impotence. The word 'power' here derives from his general thesis, which links Petronius more closely to the ethos of Nero's court than I think can be verified in detail, but it is true that Encolpius is continually beaten and twice (20, 138) sexually tortured; the words *extorqueo* (9.4, 87.3 twice; 21.2 is different) and *iniuria* (140.11; this casual use is on a different plane from the legal metaphors discussed on p. 128 above) are applied to sex. Yet in the end the casual use of words like *iniuria* and *inquinare* by the narrator Encolpius shows that he at any rate was not worried by all this; the author Petronius in large degree leaves it to us, the readers, how we react.

(iii) Symbolism in Petronius

Symbolism means that vocabulary or visual images used to convey their ordinary signification may also convey a second implication, whereas allegory is sustained metaphor in which vocabulary and images do not convey their normal significance but another veiled meaning. The two were not distinguished by ancient literary criticism, but apparently first by Goethe; however, as often happens, practising writers were ahead of theorists, and no one can deny that Vergil employed symbolism, though different views may be held about the extent to which he did so. To take a visual example, the blindfold, scales, and sword of the figure of personified Justice are concrete things, but symbolically represent the impartiality and strictness of abstract justice. To take a simple literary instance, the twelve swans pointed out by Venus to Aeneas (*Aen.* 1.393 sqq.) represent, as Venus herself says, the twelve ships which have survived the tempest.

How do we recognize symbolism? 'Primarily, we think, in the recurrence and persistence of the "symbol". An "image" may be invoked once as a metaphor, but if it persistently recurs, both as presentation and representation, it becomes a symbol, may even become part of a symbolic (or mythic) system' (R. Welleck and A. Warren, *Theory of Literature* (ed. 3, New York 1963) 189).

This last remark precisely fits what we find in Petronius, who had a particular motive for adopting this literary technique. If the writer of a first-person narrative put into the mouth of a strongly-characterized narrator wishes personally to convey something, he has to do so by indirect means. If we find recurring themes, symbols, and narrative patterns, we have to look carefully at these as potential vehicles for things which the author wishes to convey to us, since it is he who has chosen to introduce them, not the narrator, who only reacts to them. In fact we find that Petronius makes a sustained use of subtle symbolism to a degree which in Latin literature can be matched only by Vergil. In Ch. IV (v) and (vii) attention was drawn to some such features in relation to the *Cena*, and it was pointed out that on one level Petronius wrote so that his work could be read simply as hilarious comedy; one symptom of this is the frequence of reference in the text to laughter (see the concordances under *rideo* and *risus*). However, on a deeper level various recurrent themes and symbols were indicated. One such was the underlying implication, conveyed in many passages, that the meal and all its circumstances represent a living death.

Another such theme was that of trickery and deceit, often resulting in a sense of unreality because things are not what they seem; and this sense of unreality is often heightened by the introduction of terminology of the theatre (more fully discussed on p. 162 above) and other spectacles. One may remark that Tacitus portrays Petronius himself as playing a role for most of his own life (note especially the phrase 'imitation of vices'), though it is hard to know how much weight to give to this. Ch. IV (ii) and (v) remark examples of this deceptiveness in the *Cena*, where the foods in particular are often fake; other instances are the 'long-haired Ethiopians' (34.4), and the painted dog which Encolpius takes for real (29.1–2). Trickery of course is everywhere in the novel, and this chimes in with the characters of the protagonists, who have to live off their wits (*extra legem uiuentibus*, 'living outside the law', 125.4); the victims see themselves as having been mocked (*deridere*; 16.3, 100.3, 106.1).

Yet another extremely important symbol is conveyed by the manner in which the characters repeatedly lose their way and seem to go round in circles, coming back to their starting-point and making little progress towards any goal, whereas in the novels the actors do have and move towards a goal; a subset of this category lies in the recurrence of situations already experienced. Thus in 6.3–4 Encolpius loses his way and keeps coming back to the same point; in 8.2 Ascyltos loses his way; in 79.1–4 both of them and Giton too lose the way, but the 'Ariadne's thread' previously devised by Giton directs them to their destination (it seems clear also that in the gap after 9.1 he guided Encolpius and Ascyltos). The image of the labyrinth was evoked in 73.1 (after another indirect allusion to Giton as Ariadne), and the significance which that could have in this context is shown by Sen. *Ep.* 44.7, where it is said that people seeking a good life go astray, *quod euenit in labyrintho properantibus; ipsa illos uelocitas implicat* ('A thing which happens to those who hurry in a labyrinth; their very speed entangles them'). The labyrinth, which (as indicated on pp. 117–18 above in relation to 73.1) also links with the funereal imagery that permeates the *Cena*, of course implies Daedalus, who has a prominent place in the previous category of deceit and who is linked by Trimalchio (52.2) in muddled fashion with yet another symbol of deceit, the Trojan horse, it too implicit in ch. 49 in relation to the cook Daedalus; for all this see Ch. IV (ii). In these cases Petronius is operating with mythological archetypes. One should not forget that the supreme trickster is Odysseus; the false name assumed by Encolpius at Croton is related to him, and after the Odyssean allusion at 101.7 Encolpius and Giton disguise themselves.

To return to recurrent situations, we have the quarrels, 'divorces', and division of property between Encolpius on the one hand and on the other Ascyltos (10, 79) and Eumolpus (94.5–6), with many parallels in detail; the men who gravitate to Ascyltos for immoral purposes (8, 92.10); the role of Giton as attendant slave in the baths (26.10, 91.1) and preparer of meals (9.2, 16.1); voyeurism and its stimulation of lust (26.4–5, 140.11); the parallels between Psyche and Quartilla on the one hand and on the other Chrysis and Circe, in each case involving a transgression by Encolpius against Priapus and an 'atonement' (see above, pp. 205–6); the restarting of a meal after a bath (21.4, 73.5); the appearances of the *cinaedus* on, as it appears, successive days (21.2, 23.2) and the amusement of

Giton at the proceedings (20.8, 24.5); and, on a rather different level, repeated and parallel sexual failures of Encolpius with Circe. Note too the pattern of recurrence in reverse order remarked by Bodel (see above, pp. 91 and 119) in the *Cena*.

These thematic recurrences, emphasized as a feature of the work by Hubbard (with considerable forced imposition of a pattern), are so many that one cannot but infer that Petronius introduced them with deliberate intent to convey something by them, for nobody could accuse him of lack of invention. The point surely is to underline the futility of the aimlessness of his characters, whose life, as remarked above, makes no progress in the portion of the text remaining to us, but keeps lapsing into déjà vu. This is a 'moralistic' point in the sense indicated in Ch. IV (vii), and it very well fits the sense of world-weariness which comes across in Tacitus' account of Petronius. Of course it is notoriously perilous to link an author's biography with his work, but the case of Dickens alone may encourage us to take some tentative steps into this minefield.

In any case, quite independently of that, as we close the novel of Petronius we must surely do so with profound admiration of his mastery of the subtle techniques by means of which he has created a work rich in multi-layered meaning, one which can arouse a response in different facets of widely diverse temperaments. What a feast we would have had if a complete text had survived!

Addenda

p. 109. I should have remarked that both Alcibiades and Habinnas come from other parties.

p. 111. The weighing of the ear-rings has a counterpart in the inscription on the silver dishes at 31.10 of their weight.

p. 121 n. 67. The account of Matthew 26: 7 agrees with Mark, on whom Ramelli's discussion is focused, in specifying the head of Christ, but John l. c. and Luke 7: 37 specify the feet, which might suggest a link with Petron. 70.8 (cf. p. 8 n. 4). Though Petronius does not say so explicitly, the nard will have been to anoint the corpse.

pp. 115, 122. Grottanelli in O. Murray–M. Tecusan (eds.), *In Vino Veritas* (London 1995) 70–1 illustrates a relief from Amiternum which shows a funeral procession, trumpeters and all, with the corpse reclining on the bier in the dress and posture of a banqueter.

p. 170. For another widow who starved herself see Appian *BC* 4.23.

p. 178, l. 4 of text. In view of what follows in Petronius, I should have pointed out that Aeaea is the island of Circe.

I did not have the opportunity to read M. A. Doody, *The True Story of the Novel* (New Brunswick, 1996), until my book was with the Press. My readers will in particular wish to note what she has to say on pp. 60–1 about novel trials, on pp. 136–41 and 387 sqq. about ecphrasis of paintings, on pp. 144–7 about literary allusion and on pp. 152–4 about the role of epistles, in relation to my pp. 163, 139, 214, 194 and 207.

Index

Entries for the main characters in general would be too voluminous to be useful; in some other cases incidental references are omitted.